Formal Software Development

UNIVERSITY OF
GLOUCESTERSHIRE
at Cheltenham and Gloucester

FORMAL SOFTWARE DEVELOPMENT

From VDM to Java

Quentin Charatan and Aaron Kans

First published 2004 by
PALGRAVE MACMILLAN
Houndmills, Basingstoke, Hampshire RG21 6XS and
175 Fifth Avenue, New York, N.Y. 10010
Companies and representatives throughout the world

PALGRAVE MACMILLAN is the global academic imprint of the Palgrave Macmillan division of St. Martin's Press, LLC and of Palgrave Macmillan Ltd. Macmillan® is a registered trademark in the United States, United Kingdom and other countries. Palgrave is a registered trademark in the European Union and other countries.

ISBN 0–333–99281–4 paperback

This book is printed on paper suitable for recycling and made from fully managed and sustained forest sources.

A catalogue record for this book is available from the British Library.

10 9 8 7 6 5 4 3 2 1

01 12 11 10 09 08 07 06 05 04

Printed in China

To my sister, Madhu (A.K.)
To my brother, Ivan (Q.C.)

Contents

Preface

This book is intended for final-year undergraduate and postgraduate computing students specializing in the field of software engineering. The text concentrates on the challenges that high integrity software development poses, and how formal methods can help meet these challenges.

Formal methods have long been advocated for the development of high integrity software. However, these methods are often perceived as being difficult to learn and apply. In particular, the step from formal specification to code is often left uncovered in text books. Without this, however, it is the authors' experience that students tend to view such methods as purely academic tasks, divorced from the realities of the software development process. So, as well as providing a thorough introduction to the use of a formal method, we motivate the student by demonstrating the development of programs from formal specifications.

When formal program development is covered in many other text books, it tends to be in the context of proof obligations. We have found that students have greatest difficulty with this area – and in addition it is hard, in a text book, to demonstrate the complete formal development of a working application. In recent years, however, a lightweight approach to formal methods has been put forward. This approach places far less emphasis on the discharge of proof obligations and instead advocates the use of run-time assertions to ensure the integrity of final code. It is the lightweight approach we adopt in this book.

The formal method we have chosen is VDM (the Vienna Development Method). This is one of the most mature and widely used formal methods, with an internationally recognized standard. The implementation language we have chosen is Java – one of the most common programming languages taught at universities. While we assume no previous knowledge of VDM, we do assume that the reader is familiar with the basics of programming in Java. The UML notation is also used to informally specify classes. Most readers should be familiar with this notation, but a brief overview is provided.

The book is organized into 14 chapters. The last two of these constitute an extended case study and need not necessarily form part of any taught course. The remaining 12 chapters make the text highly suitable for a 12-week (one semester) course. Tutorial questions are provided at the end of each chapter and examples are used extensively throughout.

The book is organized so that, after the introductory chapters on high integrity software and logic (Chapters 1 and 2), a chapter is dedicated to an aspect of VDM-SL and the following chapter to the subsequent Java implementation. Instructors might prefer to present the entire material on VDM-SL first (Chapters 3, 5, 7, 9 and 11), followed by the material on Java implementation (Chapters 4, 6, 8, 10 and 12).

All the Java classes discussed in the text, plus additional supporting material for tutors, are available on the accompanying website (see http://www.palgrave.com/resources).

There is also an appendix on the website that describes some of the more advanced aspects of the Java programming language that we have utilized in the text.

We would like to thank Dave Hatter, our publisher, and John Fitzgerald for his insightful and helpful comments on the text. We would also like to thank our friends and families for their patience and support, and the students of the University of East London for their comments and feedback.

CHAPTER **1**

High Integrity Software Development

1.1 Introduction

Today, software is pervasive. It is used not only to provide applications on our desktop PC, or distributed business applications across a network of machines, but also to control many systems all around us. Often the software is integrated into a mechanical or electronic system. The growth in such **embedded software**, as it is known, is one of the reasons for the huge rise in the demand for software in recent years.

Ideally all software products, be they traditional off-the-shelf desktop products such as word processors, or specialist embedded software dedicated to monitoring temperatures in a chemical reactor, should be released without errors. In reality this is not feasible and residual errors in applications are to be expected. For example, when it comes to off-the-shelf software products, it is common for software companies developing such products to release 'patches' for them. Essentially, these patches are fixes for mistakes in the application's original source code. Manufacturers of operating systems, for example, often find the need to release patches for their products soon after release, as errors are uncovered. Consumers tolerate a certain level of residual errors in such applications, as the consequence of software failure is not disastrous. Sometimes a system reboot may solve the problem; other times the product might not be usable until a patch is available. While this may be annoying it does not pose any danger. For these kinds of products, delivering the product quickly to market, and at an affordable price, is more important than reducing defects to an absolute minimum.

Think of the alarm that would be raised, however, if similar patches were suddenly released for software controlling the brakes on your car or the signalling system on a railway network! For these kinds of systems (compared to off-the-shelf desktop applications) the costs of software failure are dangerously high and therefore a much higher degree of confidence in the correctness of the software is required.

1.2 High Integrity Software

We refer to software that has a higher than normal expectation of correctness as **high integrity software**. This expectation of correctness is closely linked to the *risks* inherent in software failure. As risks increase so too does the need to ensure that there are as few software errors as possible. However, the resources (cost, time and so on) required to help ensure correctness also rise. Therefore, the development of high integrity software demands greater resources than the development of a 'regular' software product.

1

A concept closely related to that of *high integrity software* is that of **critical software**. The term *critical software* applies to software that poses dangers should it fail. Critical software can further be categorized depending upon the *types* of danger imposed by failure. For example, failure of **business critical software** could adversely affect the economic success of an enterprise; examples include the software used to control a bank's ATM transactions and software aimed at providing security for sensitive information. Failure in **mission critical software**, on the other hand, could impair the goal of the given mission. Examples here include such applications as satellite and rocket launch systems. Finally, failure of **safety critical software** could result in harm to people, property or the environment. Examples include medical control software and air traffic control software.

There can be *degrees* of danger posed by software failure, so that some software is of higher integrity than other software; that is, a higher degree of confidence is required in its correctness than is the case for other software. For example, consider the software used to monitor air traffic flow around an airport and software used to monitor the temperature in a fridge freezer. Although both are examples of critical software, failure in the former could have far more catastrophic consequences than failure in the latter. Amongst other things, software failure in a fridge freezer is likely to be protected against by some form of hardware lock, whereas hardware locks cannot protect against errors in air traffic software. We refer to these degrees of integrity as **integrity levels**.

Often, a legal framework or an industry standard stipulates what is to be considered as a dangerously high level of failure. Industry-specific standards may also stipulate how many integrity levels are to be considered and which bands of failure are associated with each integrity level. The higher the integrity level of the software, the greater the resources that can be justified in reducing software errors.

Since the failure of high integrity, critical software can lead to such high costs (be they financial or physical) it is not surprising that such failures receive much more media attention than failures of other types of software. Table 1.1 describes some high

Table 1.1   Some high profile examples of high integrity software failures

The loss of NASA's Mars Climate Orbitor in November 1999.	The Mars Climate Orbitor was lost because of a type mismatch error in the software. The assumption was that metric measurements would be used but the software was developed to use imperial measurements. This resulted in the Orbitor attempting to orbit Mars at an altitude of just 37 miles instead of the planned 93 miles. It was believed the minimum altitude at which the orbitor could survive would have been 53 miles.
The crash of the European space agencies' Ariane5 rocket in July 1996.	An error in the specification, design and testing procedures of the fault protection software incorrectly shut down two processors within the first minute of launch. This resulted in the crash of the rocket which took 10 years and 7 billion dollars to develop.
Radiation overdoses administered by the Therac-25 machine in the USA during the 1980s.	Software errors that could have resulted in radiation overdose were undetected for a long period due to the presence of hardware locks. Eventually it was decided, for safety reasons, to replace these hardware locks with software locks. These software locks failed to detect the error in the original software resulting in the radiation overdose and death of several patients.

profile examples of such failures. More examples can be found at the RISK forum website (**http://catless.ncl.ac.uk/Risks**).

As the demands placed upon computer systems have grown over the years (owing to advances in microchip technology, the growth of the internet and so on) so too has the complexity of the software associated with such systems. During this time, several software development methods (such as structured development, object-oriented development and rapid application development) and associated modelling tools (such as Jackson Structured Design and the Unified Modelling Language) have evolved to deal with this issue of complexity. While these advances in methodologies and tools have helped to deal with the issue of software complexity, all these approaches share common weaknesses that make them less than ideal, on their own, for the development of high integrity software. The weaknesses stem from the nature of the specification document.

1.3   The Importance of the Specification

When we say that a piece of software contains an 'error' we mean it does not behave as expected. There could be two reasons for this: either the software does not conform to its specification or there are errors or omissions in the original specification.

For the software development methods mentioned above, it is the process of **testing** that aims to locate these software errors. Testing involves running a program with a set of inputs and comparing the actual outputs from the program against the expected outputs (as defined in the specification). There are several limitations to using testing as the sole approach to software error detection:

1. Testing cannot take place until some implementation is available, so correcting errors uncovered by testing could involve retracing many steps and undoing work previously done. The earlier the error occurred the more work this involves. If testing is the only approach to error detection then errors in the specification involve the greatest amount of work to rectify.
2. Testing can only help to uncover errors – it cannot guarantee the absence of them. Since, for any application, it is impossible to test every set of input values, residual errors will always have to be accepted.
3. Testing is always carried out with respect to requirements as laid down in the specification. If the specification document is in any way ambiguous it is open to interpretation, and hence misinterpretation, making testing a rather inexact science.

Clearly the specification plays a vital role in the reliability of the software produced. The design, and subsequent implementation, is based upon the information in the specification, and the testing process relies upon the developers' understanding of the specification to determine whether or not the software is behaving correctly. Misunderstandings in the specification can lead to the delivery of final applications that do not match user requirements (see Figure 1.1).

For the vast majority of software applications in use today, the specification is captured in a mix of natural language and diagrams. For example, the Unified Modelling Language (UML) notation is used to specify and design systems according to the principles of **object-oriented** development, whereby a system is thought of as being composed of a number of fundamental units called **objects**. There are two important aspects to an object: the information that it holds (referred to as its **attributes**) and the things it can do (referred to as its **methods** or **operations**). Central to this is the notion of a **class**, which is the template (or blueprint) for all the objects belonging to that class. In UML a class can be specified using a **class diagram**. Figure 1.2 depicts a typical UML class diagram specifying a *BankAccount* class.

The name of the class, *BankAccount*, is given in the top compartment of the UML diagram, the attributes are listed in the second compartment and the methods in the final compartment. Types are allocated to attributes and methods. In Figure 1.2, the account number and name are both given string types whereas a real number is the appropriate type to model the balance. Methods require types for input parameters and any output result. In UML, the types allocated to any input parameters are listed in round brackets following the method name (with an empty pair of brackets

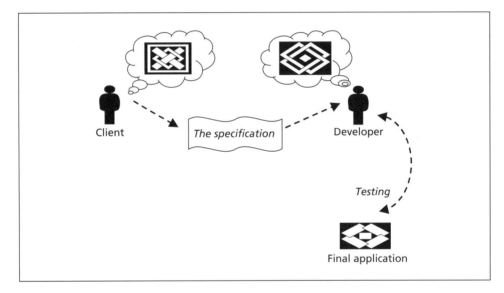

Figure 1.1   Ambiguities in the specification and the limitations of testing can result in errors in the final application

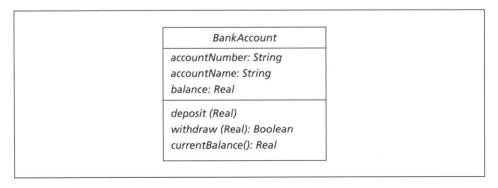

Figure 1.2   A typical UML diagram for the *BankAccount* class

indicating that no input parameter is required for the method). If the method outputs a result, the type of that result is listed *after* the brackets (if no type is listed this indicates that no result is returned from the method). Figure 1.2 indicates that the *withdraw* method, for example, takes a single real number as a parameter and returns a boolean value.

Often, a diagram such as this is supplemented by a natural language description for each method. For example, the *withdraw* method of the *BankAccount* class might have its UML specification supplemented with the following natural language description:

> **withdraw**: *receives a requested amount to withdraw from the bank account and, if there are sufficient funds in the account, meets the request. Returns a boolean value indicating success or failure of the attempt to withdraw money from the account.*

Diagrams and natural language descriptions, such as this, have the advantage that they are easy to follow by non-computing experts and so provide a good medium for discussions with clients. Unfortunately, natural language and diagrams do not have a fixed meaning from one person to the next and so are open to many different interpretations. We say these notations do not have a fixed **semantics**.

To illustrate, examine the natural language specification of the *withdraw* method given above. On first reading the meaning of this method might be clear. It is, however (like all natural language statements), ambiguous and open to interpretation. Consider the restrictions placed on the method that the requested amount should be withdrawn only '... *if there are sufficient funds* ...'. What is meant by the term 'sufficient'? Is it that the bank account must contain *at least* the amount of money that is requested for withdrawal? Or is there a minimum balance that must be maintained? Or is there an agreed overdraft limit?

A boolean value is returned from this method to indicate success or failure: does a value of *false* indicate that an error has occurred or that there was no error? Also, the amount to be withdrawn is specified to be a real number; is this to be a positive or a negative real number? All of the issues highlighted will obviously be crucial to the correct functioning of this method.

Not only is the original specification of this method **ambiguous**, it is also *incomplete* and could be *inconsistent* with the specification of the rest of the class. A specification can be considered **incomplete** when the behaviour is not completely defined. In this case the specification of the *withdraw* method describes what should happen when there are 'sufficient' funds in the account, but does not make clear what should happen when there are *insufficient* funds. Should the method withdraw as much money as is allowed or withdraw no money at all? The danger here is that the incompleteness is overlooked and that assumptions are made during design and programming, leading to the delivery of a faulty system.

Finally, a specification is **inconsistent** when it contains contradictions. For example, an overdraft facility might be specified elsewhere. One interpretation of the *withdraw* method is that without funds in the bank account a given amount cannot be withdrawn. Both behaviours cannot be satisfied in an implementation.

With misinterpretations of a few lines like this, think how many different ways a specification running to many dozens of pages could be interpreted. Such misinterpretations might be even greater if the development team crosses national and cultural boundaries. Clearly, to use these notations alone to describe critical software is unwise. To overcome these difficulties it is desirable to use a specification notation with a fixed, unambiguous semantics.

Notations that have a fixed semantics are known as **formal notations**, or **formal languages**. A fixed semantics is achieved by defining a language in a completely unambiguous way using a mathematical framework. Ideally a specification should describe *what* the system is to do without saying *how* to do it. That is, a specification should be as **abstract** (not cluttered by implementation details) as possible. The language of mathematics is perfectly suited for this task as it allows a far more abstract description of the system to be captured using simple mathematical concepts such as sets, relations and functions.

In all other branches of engineering (such as civil, mechanical and electrical), the use of mathematics to help build reliable products is the normal approach. The idea that an aircraft or a bridge would be constructed without the aid of mathematical models, or the idea that the only way to identify defects would be to observe the behaviour of test scenarios after the construction of the final system, would be unthinkable. Yet this is how the large majority of software applications are developed!

1.4 Formal Methods

Formal methods constitute a branch of software engineering that incorporates the use of mathematics for software development. A formal method provides a formal language in which to express the initial specification *and* all future design steps towards the final program. These design steps are often referred to as transformations (see Figure 1.3).

A formal method is more than just a specification language for recording these transformations. It also includes a **proof system** for demonstrating that each transformation preserves the formal meaning captured in the previous step. A proof system is a means of guaranteeing the correctness of a statement and relies upon

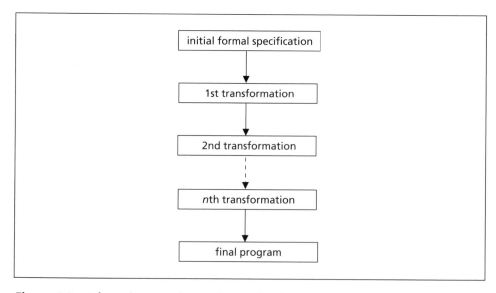

Figure 1.3 A formal approach to software development

mathematical logic. In theory, if every transformation can be shown to describe a system whose behaviour is consistent with the previous step then, by the time the last step is reached, the final program will have been shown to be consistent with the original specification. This is a much more robust approach to checking for program correctness than testing alone, as proofs demonstrate correctness for *all* possible test cases, whereas testing demonstrates correctness only for the test cases investigated.

In reality the skill (and tools) required to carry out such a proof means that the proofs could themselves contain errors. Also, there is no guarantee that the initial formal specification captures the original user requirements accurately, and there is always the risk of introducing erroneous behaviour when replacing the abstract data structures in the specification (such as sets and mappings) with their more concrete code-level counterparts (such as arrays and linked lists). For this reason, testing still plays an important role in a formal approach to software development. However, the use of formal methods offers many advantages:

- Formal specifications can help considerably in generating suitable test cases.
- The discipline required in producing a formal specification of user requirements and the ability to *analyse* a specification (which only arises if the specification language has a well-defined semantics) allows for feedback on system specifications at early development stages, increasing confidence that the specification accurately captures the real system requirements.
- Important properties (such as internal consistency) of the initial specification can be checked mathematically and incorporated as run-time checks in the final program.
- Proofs can help uncover design errors as soon as they are made, rather than having to wait for testing of the final implementation.
- A proof of program correctness can be constructed that is a much more robust method of achieving program correctness than is testing alone.

Despite these gains, the perceived difficulty of applying formal methods and the shortage of software developers trained in their use means that their application has tended to be restricted to the development of high integrity software, where correctness is essential. For the development of some high integrity software, their use may be mandatory. For example, the UK's Ministry of Defence (as stipulated in defence standard 00-55) requires that safety critical software produced for it be formally developed.

1.5   Classifying Formal Methods

Many formal methods have been established over the years. A common way of classifying these formal methods is by the approach taken in the method of specification. The two principal approaches are **algebraic** and **model-based** approaches.

Using an algebraic approach, once a list of operations has been identified, their behaviour is captured indirectly by describing the relationship between these operations as a set of properties (or axioms as they are sometimes known). All software developed from these specifications has to show that it obeys the same properties as those specified.

Table 1.2   Classifying some leading formal methods

	Algebraic	Model-based
Sequential systems	Larch	Vienna Development Method (VDM) Z B
Concurrent systems	Calculus of Communicating Systems (CCS) OBJ	Prototype Verification System (PVS) Communicating Sequential Processes (CSP)

In a model-based approach an abstract mathematical model is built of the data, using abstract mathematical types such as sets. The behaviour of the operations is then specified directly with respect to this model. Often this leads to much more concise specifications than those arrived at using an algebraic approach.

Finally, some formal methods are more suited for the specification of sequential systems, while others are designed for the specification of concurrent systems. Table 1.2 classifies some of the leading formal methods according to these distinctions.

The most common and well-established formal methods are those that are model-based and developed to specify sequential systems. Part of the reason for this is that model-based approaches are considered easier to use as they map better on to our intuitive understanding of systems as a store of data and a set of operations. Also, specifying concurrent systems involves subtle timing considerations that are not always easy to capture formally.

Of those model-based methods used to develop the sequential systems listed, **VDM** (the Vienna Development Method) is the most mature, having been developed in the late 1970s. It has a recognized international standard (**www.ifad.dk/vdm/bnf.html**) that gives the formal semantics of the language. The method also has a comprehensive set of tools supporting it. Since it is one of the longest established formal methods it also has the longest history of use in industry. Of the others, both Z (pronounced Zed) and B are now well established with well-documented industrial experience. All share a strong similarity with VDM. Because of its relative maturity, VDM is the method we shall be following in this text.

1.6   Lightweight Formal Methods

Informal methods of software development (such as the Structured System Analysis and Design Methodology) often prescribe strict rules for progressing from one stage of software development to the next. The majority of formal methods, on the other hand, provide a selection of tools for the development of reliable software systems rather than prescribe their use at every stage of development. Thus, for software of high integrity, all the tools provided by a formal method (such as a modelling language for specification and a formal proof system for software design and implementation) could be utilized. Proofs themselves may be carried out (discharged) totally formally (that is, where every step is justified using the method's proof system) or proofs may just be *rigorous* (in which case they can be discharged by means of a sound argument rather than a complete proof). Again, the integrity level of the software will inform this decision.

Where software is of lower integrity the modelling tools available in the language might be adopted for software specification, but development may then proceed using more traditional approaches with integrity checks being argued informally or by means of run-time assertions (checks) embedded into code. Using a formal method in this way, with less reliance upon the discharge of proof obligations, is often referred to as a **lightweight** approach to the use of formal methods. It is a lightweight approach that we shall adopt in this text (Figure 1.4).

As you will come to see, a VDM specification corresponds closely to the notion of a class in an object-oriented methodology. The approach we will take in this text is to record the informal specification of software using the UML class notation. We will then provide a formal specification for a UML class in the form of a VDM specification.

Following each chapter that deals with an aspect of the modelling (specification) language of VDM (known as VDM-SL), we demonstrate the development of Java programs from the VDM specifications. The correctness of any design decisions we make will be argued rigorously rather than formally, and backed up by assertions embedded in the final Java code.

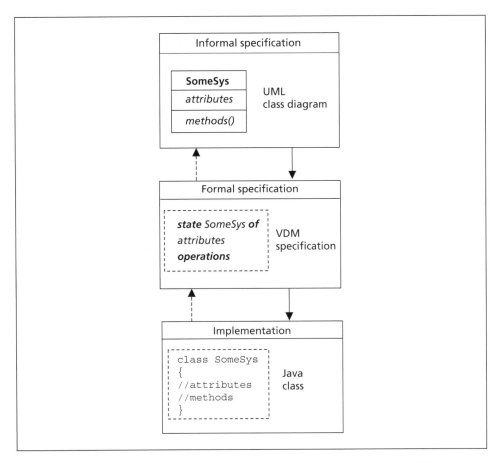

Figure 1.4   A lightweight approach to formal program development in VDM

Over the course of this text we will examine the data types (such as natural numbers, sets and sequences) available in VDM-SL, and demonstrate their use through example specifications. Before we embark upon these topics, however, the next chapter covers the topic of mathematical logic that forms the backbone of all formal methods.

EXERCISES

1. Identify five examples of *safety critical software* and try and rank them in terms of their levels of integrity.
2. Give an example of software that is both *mission* and *safety* critical.
3. Explain why testing cannot guarantee that a program is correct.
4. Why is natural language a poor choice for expressing specifications?
5. Identify any weaknesses in the following requirements definition:

'Software is required to monitor a collection of documents kept in a library. There may be multiple copies of each document. Some of the documents are deemed to be of high importance. Documents can be borrowed from the library by certain members of staff. There must always be at least one copy of any document deemed to be of high importance left in the library. All other documents may be removed. The software needs to record each document's identity code (consisting of letters and numbers), and whether or not it is of high importance, as well as the number of copies. Documents can be removed from the library only by providing the correct document code.'

CHAPTER 2

Propositional and Predicate Logic

2.1 Introduction

In this chapter we present the aspects of classical logic that are necessary for the understanding of formal development methods. Mathematical logic was developed in order to give a precise and agreed meaning to statements made in a natural language such as English. Providing such a rigorous framework makes it possible to reason precisely about statements made in the natural language, and allows us to develop a set of laws that are internally consistent.

We begin by presenting the propositional logic, which deals with simple truth-valued statements that can be combined according to a set of rules. We then go on to present the even more powerful predicate logic, which is an essential tool needed in the formal specification of systems.

2.2 Propositions

In classical logic, propositions are statements that are either TRUE or FALSE.
The following are examples of propositions that evaluate to TRUE:

There are seven days in a week
Accra is the capital of Ghana
2 + 4 = 6

The following propositions evaluate to FALSE:

The angles of a triangle add up to 360°
London is the capital of France
2 − 4 = 7

In mathematics we often represent a proposition symbolically by a variable name such as P or Q.
For example:

P: I go shopping on Wednesdays
Q: 102.001 > 101.31

In the worlds of computing and mathematics, occasions arise when it is not possible to evaluate expressions precisely – maybe a program terminated incorrectly, or perhaps somebody tried to evaluate the square root of a negative integer. As you will find out later in this chapter, it is possible to account for such situations by defining a three-valued logic, which allows a proposition to take the value UNDEFINED as well as TRUE or FALSE.

2.2.1 LOGICAL CONNECTIVES

Simple propositions can be combined into compound statements by operators called **logical connectives**. The purpose of defining these connectives is to provide a rigorous framework that gives precise meaning to such words as 'and' and 'or' that occur in the natural language. The way we give semantic meaning to these connectives is to provide tables known as **truth tables**, which give a value for every possible combination of the values of the individual statements that make up the compound proposition. This is made clear below as we explain the meaning of the various connectives.

The *and* operator

The operator known as **and** is represented by the symbol $\land$. The statement *P and Q* is therefore represented by:

$P \land Q$

Thus if P represented the statement *I like shopping* and Q represented the statement *The sun is shining* then $P \land Q$ would represent the statement *I like shopping and the sun is shining*.

The precise meaning of this operator is given in the following truth table, where TRUE and FALSE are represented by T and F, respectively. You can see that the first two columns of the truth table provide all the possible combinations of the values of P and Q – and for each row, the final column shows the corresponding value of the combined statement $P \land Q$.

P	Q	P∧Q
T	T	T
T	F	F
F	T	F
F	F	F

It can be seen from the table that for the compound statement $P \land Q$ to be TRUE requires that both individual statements P and Q are TRUE; if either P or Q is FALSE, then $P \land Q$ is FALSE.

Combining two propositions with the *and* operator is known as **conjunction**; each individual proposition in the compound statement is known as a **conjunct**.

The *or* operator

The operator known as **or** is represented by the symbol $\lor$. The statement *P or Q* is therefore represented by:

$P \lor Q$

Thus if *P* represented the statement *It is raining* and *Q* represented the statement *Today is Tuesday* then $P \vee Q$ would represent the statement *It is raining or today is Tuesday*.

The precise meaning of this operator is given in the following truth table.

P	*Q*	*P*∨*Q*
T	T	T
T	F	T
F	T	T
F	F	F

It can be seen from the table that the compound statement $P \vee Q$ is FALSE only when both individual statements *P* and *Q* are FALSE; if either *P* or *Q* is TRUE, then $P \vee Q$ is TRUE. Using the above example, if the statement *It is raining or today is Tuesday* were FALSE, then we could conclude both that it is not raining *and* that today is not Tuesday.

Combining two propositions with the *or* operator is known as **disjunction**; each individual proposition in the compound statement is known as a **disjunct**.

The *implication* operator

In defining an **implication** operator we attempt to give meaning to the expression *P implies Q*. The implication operator is represented by the symbol $\Rightarrow$. The statement *P implies Q* is therefore represented by:

$$P \Rightarrow Q$$

An alternative way of expressing implication is *if P then Q*. Thus if *P* represented the statement *It is Wednesday* and *Q* represented the statement *I do the ironing* then $P \Rightarrow Q$ would represent the statement *If it is Wednesday I do the ironing*.

The truth table for implication appears next, and requires some explanation.

P	*Q*	*P*⇒*Q*
T	T	T
T	F	F
F	T	T
F	F	T

The first two rows of the table capture the central idea of implication: if the first and second statements are both TRUE, then the statement that the first implies the second is also TRUE, whereas if the first is TRUE but the second is not, then the statement that the first implies the second is FALSE.

The meaning of the third and fourth rows is not so apparent, however. This is because the statement *P implies Q* in fact says nothing about the case when *P* is FALSE. In other words, it does not deal with the concept of 'otherwise'. In order to understand this, it is useful to think about the way we deal with selection in programming languages. The implication operator is analogous to an IF ... THEN statement. When making use of such a statement in a program, we do not define any alternative behaviour – if the condition is met then we perform a set of statements; if not, we do nothing and carry on with the program. To define alternative behaviour – in other words to deal with the 'otherwise' clause, we would have to use an IF ... THEN ... ELSE statement, which is a more powerful statement than the one suggested by the implication connective; as we shall see in a moment, there is another connective that deals with the concept of 'otherwise'.

In capturing the meaning of implication, the value of the compound statement when the first proposition is FALSE could really be chosen arbitrarily. In fact, as can be seen from the truth table, we choose to define the value as TRUE in both cases. Making this choice helps to make the mathematics more complete, so that when we combine the implication connective with other connectives we arrive at results that more truly follow our logical way of thinking. For example, with implication defined as above, the value of the compound statement $P \wedge Q \Rightarrow P$ evaluates to TRUE for all possible values of P and Q.

Looking at the truth table, you can see that there is a further way of expressing the meaning of $P \Rightarrow Q$ in words, namely as *P only if Q*. This is because in the case where the compound statement is TRUE, then P is TRUE only when Q is TRUE.

The *equivalence* operator

The idea of **equivalence** deals with the 'otherwise' part of implication, and is analogous to an IF ... THEN ... ELSE statement in a programming language; it is represented by the symbol ⇔. Effectively it states: *if P is TRUE then Q is TRUE, otherwise Q is FALSE*; in other words, *P is equivalent to Q*, which is represented by:

$$P \Leftrightarrow Q$$

The truth table for equivalence is as follows.

P	Q	P ⇔ Q
T	T	T
T	F	F
F	T	F
F	F	T

It can be seen from the table that equivalence represents two-way implication: *P implies Q and Q implies P*. Another way of expressing equivalence is *P if and only if Q*, which is sometimes written:

P iff *Q*

The *exclusive or* operator

When we presented the *or* operator above, we noted that the compound statement *P or Q* was TRUE as long as either or both of the disjuncts were TRUE. In fact, this does not represent the most common use of the word 'or' as used in natural language, where the assumption is usually made that one or other of the disjuncts is TRUE, but not both. For example, if somebody were to say *I will go to the theatre or I will go to the cinema*, it is likely that what is meant is that the person will go to either the theatre or the cinema, but not to both. The natural language 'or' usually implies that only one or other of the statements is TRUE but not both. This corresponds to the logical operator known as **exclusive or** (sometimes referred to as **xor**), which is represented by the symbol $\oplus$. Thus, the statement represented by *P or Q but not both* is represented by:

$P \oplus Q$

The truth table for *exclusive or* is as follows.

P	Q	$P \oplus Q$
T	T	F
T	F	T
F	T	T
F	F	F

2.2.2 NEGATION

The operation known as **negation** yields a proposition with a value opposite to that of the original one. The operator in question is called the **not** operator and is represented by the symbol $\neg$ (or sometimes by $\sim$). Thus if P is a proposition, then *not P* is represented by:

$\neg P$

By definition, if P is TRUE, then $\neg P$ is FALSE; if P is FALSE then $\neg P$ is TRUE. For example if P represented the statement *I like dogs*, then $\neg P$ represents the statement *I do not like dogs*. This is summarized in the truth table for the **not** operator, as follows:

P	$\neg P$
T	F
F	T

2.2.3 COMPOUND STATEMENTS AND THE ORDER OF PRECEDENCE OF OPERATORS

Ambiguity can easily arise in compound statements that contain more than one proposition. Consider, for example, the statement:

$P \wedge Q \vee R$

This could be evaluated in two ways: we could evaluate $P \wedge Q$, and then evaluate the disjunction of this value with R; alternatively, we could evaluate $Q \vee R$, and then evaluate the conjunction of this value with P.

It is necessary to agree an order of precedence on the operators, and in VDM the agreed order of precedence is (starting with the highest) as follows:

$$\neg, \wedge, \vee, \Rightarrow, \Leftrightarrow$$

As with any branch of mathematics, brackets are used to indicate the highest precedence of all, and any expression in brackets must therefore be evaluated first.

Thus, as an example, the expression:

$$\neg P \wedge Q$$

means *the conjunction of $\neg P$ with Q*, whereas the expression

$$\neg (P \wedge Q)$$

means *the negation of the conjunction of P with Q*.

To illustrate this, assume that P represented the statement *Physics is easy* and Q represented the statement *Chemistry is interesting*, then:

$\neg P \wedge Q$ would mean *Physics is not easy and chemistry is interesting*.
$\neg (P \wedge Q)$ would mean *It is not true both that physics is easy and that chemistry is interesting*.

2.2.4 LOGICAL EQUIVALENCE

Two compound propositions are said to be logically equivalent if identical results are obtained from constructing their truth tables. This is denoted by the symbol $\equiv$. We shall demonstrate this by proving the following identity (which is known as De Morgan's law):

$$\neg (P \wedge Q) \equiv \neg P \vee \neg Q$$

Firstly we construct the truth table for the left-hand side of the identity:

P	Q	$P \wedge Q$	$\neg(P \wedge Q)$
T	T	T	F
T	F	F	T
F	T	F	T
F	F	F	T

Now we do the same for the right-hand side:

P	Q	$\neg P$	$\neg Q$	$\neg P \vee \neg Q$
T	T	F	F	F
T	F	F	T	T
F	T	T	F	T
F	F	T	T	T

We can see that the results in the final column of each truth table are the same, thus demonstrating the truth of the identity.

As a further example we will return to the discussion of the previous section, and demonstrate that:

$$(P \land Q) \lor R \not\equiv P \land (Q \lor R)$$

The left-hand side of the expression:

P	Q	R	$P \land Q$	$(P \land Q) \lor R$
T	T	T	T	T
T	T	F	T	T
T	F	T	F	T
T	F	F	F	F
F	T	T	F	T
F	T	F	F	F
F	F	T	F	T
F	F	F	F	F

The right-hand side of the expression:

P	Q	R	$Q \lor R$	$P \land (Q \lor R)$
T	T	T	T	T
T	T	F	T	T
T	F	T	T	T
T	F	F	F	F
F	T	T	T	F
F	T	F	T	F
F	F	T	T	F
F	F	F	F	F

Clearly the last columns of the truth tables are not the same, showing that the two expressions are not logically equivalent.

2.2.5 TAUTOLOGIES AND CONTRADICTIONS

A statement which is always TRUE (that is, all the rows of the truth table evaluate to TRUE) is called a **tautology**.

For example, the following statement is a tautology:

$P \lor \neg P$

This can be seen from the truth table:

P	$\neg P$	$P \lor \neg P$
T	F	**T**
T	F	**T**
F	T	**T**
F	T	**T**

A statement which is always FALSE (i.e. all rows of the truth table evaluate to FALSE) is called a **contradiction**.

For example, the following statement is a contradiction:

$P \land \neg P$

Again, this can be seen from the truth table:

P	$\neg P$	$P \land \neg P$
T	F	**F**
T	F	**F**
F	T	**F**
F	T	**F**

In both the above cases, this is entirely what we would expect from the semantic meaning of the $\lor$, $\land$ and $\neg$ operators.

2.2.6 THREE-VALUED LOGIC

Classical logic assumes that all expressions evaluate to TRUE or FALSE. In reality, this is not always the case when evaluating an expression, because sometimes an expression can be undefined – for example, the expression 0/0. Undefined terms are very common in programming situations – for example, when a variable is first declared and has not yet been assigned a value.

It is therefore important to provide results from expressions that contain undefined terms, and for this purpose a three-valued logic has been developed; in this system of logic a proposition could have the value TRUE, FALSE or UNDEFINED. The truth tables for the connectives in our three-valued system are presented next.

P	Q	P ∧ Q
T	T	**T**
T	F	**F**
T	UNDEFINED	**UNDEFINED**
F	T	**F**
F	F	**F**
F	UNDEFINED	**F**
UNDEFINED	T	**UNDEFINED**
UNDEFINED	F	**F**
UNDEFINED	UNDEFINED	**UNDEFINED**

P	Q	P ∨ Q
T	T	**T**
T	F	**T**
T	UNDEFINED	**T**
F	T	**T**
F	F	**F**
F	UNDEFINED	**UNDEFINED**
UNDEFINED	T	**T**
UNDEFINED	F	**UNDEFINED**
UNDEFINED	UNDEFINED	**UNDEFINED**

P	Q	P ⇒ Q
T	T	**T**
T	F	**F**
T	UNDEFINED	**UNDEFINED**
F	T	**T**
F	F	**T**
F	UNDEFINED	**T**
UNDEFINED	T	**T**
UNDEFINED	F	**UNDEFINED**
UNDEFINED	UNDEFINED	**UNDEFINED**

P	Q	$P \Leftrightarrow Q$
T	T	**T**
T	F	**F**
T	UNDEFINED	**UNDEFINED**
F	T	**F**
F	F	**T**
F	UNDEFINED	**UNDEFINED**
UNDEFINED	T	**UNDEFINED**
UNDEFINED	F	**UNDEFINED**
UNDEFINED	UNDEFINED	**UNDEFINED**

P	Q	$P \oplus Q$
T	T	**F**
T	F	**T**
T	UNDEFINED	**UNDEFINED**
F	T	**T**
F	F	**F**
F	UNDEFINED	**UNDEFINED**
UNDEFINED	T	**UNDEFINED**
UNDEFINED	F	**UNDEFINED**
UNDEFINED	UNDEFINED	**UNDEFINED**

P	$\neg P$
T	**F**
F	**T**
UNDEFINED	**UNDEFINED**

2.3   Predicate Logic

One of the limitations with the propositional logic is that, while it allows us to argue about individual values, it does not give us the ability to argue about *sets of values*. As we shall see in Chapter 5, a **set** is any well-defined, unordered, collection of objects. For example we could refer to the set containing all the people who work in a particular office; the set of whole numbers from 1 to 10; the set of the days of the week; the set of all the breeds of cat in the world. In mathematics, we often represent a set in a generalized format, denoting the name of the set by an upper-case letter and the elements by lower-case letters. For example:

$A = \{s, d, f, h, k\}$
$B = \{a, b, c, d, e, f\}$

The symbol $\in$ means 'is an element of'. Therefore the statement 'd is an element of A' is written:

$d \in A$

The statement 'p is not an element of A' is written:

$p \notin A$

For the purpose of reasoning about sets of values, a more powerful tool than the propositional logic has been devised, namely the **predicate logic**.

A **predicate** is a truth-valued expression containing *free variables*. These allow the expression to be evaluated by giving different values to the variables. Once the variables are evaluated they are said to be **bound**.

2.3.1 EXAMPLES OF PREDICATES

Predicates can be named with either a single letter, or with a word that expresses the meaning of the predicate; the variables are placed in brackets after the name. This is made clear in the following examples:

$C(x)$:   *x is a cat*
Studies(x,y):   *x studies y*
Prime(n):   *n is a prime number*

A statement such as $C(x)$ can be read *C of x*.

2.3.2 BINDING VARIABLES

Predicates such as those above do not yet have a value – they only have a value when the variables themselves are given a value. There are two ways in which this can be done.

1. By substitution (giving a value to the variable)
For example, using the above three predicates:

$C(Simba)$:   *Simba is a cat*
Studies$(Olawale, physics)$:   *Olawale studies physics*
Prime(3):   *3 is a prime number*

The above expressions now have a value of TRUE or FALSE.

2. By quantification

A **quantifier** is a mechanism for specifying an expression about a *set* of values. There are three quantifiers that we can use, each with its own symbol:

–The universal quantifier ∀

This quantifier enables a predicate to make a statement about all the elements in a particular set. For example, if $M(x)$ is the predicate *x chases mice*, we could write:

$$\forall x \in Cats \bullet M(x)$$

This reads *For all the x which are members of the set Cats, x chases mice*, or, more simply, *All cats chase mice*.

– The existential quantifier ∃

In this case, a statement is made about whether or not *at least one* element of a set meets a particular criterion. For example, if, as above, $P(n)$ is the predicate *n is a prime number*, then we could write:

$$\exists n \in \mathbb{N} \bullet P(n)$$

This reads *There exists an n in the set of natural numbers such that n is a prime number*, or, put another way, *There exists at least one prime number in the set of natural numbers*.

–The unique existential quantifier ∃!

This quantifier modifies a predicate to make a statement about whether or not *precisely one* element of a set meets a particular criterion. For example, if $G(x)$ is the predicate *x is green*, we could write

$$\exists! x \in Cats \bullet G(x)$$

This would mean *There is one and only one cat that is green*.

If the set over which the predicate is defined is clearly stated in advance, it can be omitted from the expression (as in Exercise 6 below).

EXERCISES

1. Let P be 'It is cold' and Q be 'It is raining'. Give simple sentences which represent the following statements:

   (a) $\neg P$
   (b) $P \wedge Q$
   (c) $P \vee Q$
   (d) $Q \vee \neg P$
   (e) $\neg P \wedge \neg Q$
   (f) $\neg\neg Q$

2. Let P be 'She is tall' and Q be 'She is intelligent'. Express each of the following statements symbolically:

   (a) She is tall and intelligent.
   (b) She is tall, but not intelligent.
   (c) It is false that she is tall or intelligent.

(d) She is neither tall nor intelligent.
(e) She is tall, or she is short and intelligent.
(f) It is not true that she is short or unintelligent.

3. Show that 2(f) above is equivalent to 2(a).

4. Construct truth tables for the following:

(a) $\neg P \wedge Q$
(b) $(P \Rightarrow Q) \Rightarrow (P \wedge Q)$

5. Use truth tables to show that:

(a) $P \vee \neg(P \wedge Q)$ is a tautology
(b) $(P \wedge Q) \wedge \neg(p \vee Q)$ is a contradiction

6. Consider the following predicates defined over the domain of people:

S(x) : x is a student
W(x): x works hard

Now express the following expressions in English:

(a) *S(Natalie)*
(b) $\forall x \bullet (S(x) \Rightarrow W(x))$
(c) $\exists x \bullet W(x) \Rightarrow \neg S(David)$
(d) $\exists! x \bullet (S(x) \wedge W(x))$

7. Consider the following predicates defined over the domain of vegetables:

R(x): x is a root vegetable
T(x): x tastes nice

Additionally the proposition *P* is defined as:

P: Peas are blue

Now express the following statements symbolically:

(a) If peas are blue then cabbage tastes nice.
(b) There exists a root vegetable that tastes nice.
(c) Lettuce is a root vegetable and peas are blue.
(d) All root vegetables taste nice.
(e) Peas are blue or there is a vegetable which is a root vegetable and which does not taste nice.

CHAPTER 3

An Introduction to Specification in VDM-SL

3.1 Introduction

In Chapter 1 you were introduced to the idea of using formal mathematical methods for the purpose of developing high integrity software. As we explained in that chapter, the methodology that we will be using in this book is VDM, and now that we have covered the fundamental mathematical concepts that you need for an understanding of formal methods, we are in a position to begin our study of VDM-SL, the *Specification Language* component of VDM.

We begin by analysing the requirements for a very simple system, and using the notation of the Unified Modelling Language (UML) to specify the software informally; from there we develop our first formal specification in VDM-SL.

Once we have familiarized you with the basic concepts, we go on to make our case study more realistic by adding greater complexity, and from there we derive a complete specification for the new software, and produce a standard template for VDM specifications.

3.2 The Case Study: Requirements Analysis

The example we will use throughout this chapter will be that of an incubator, the temperature of which needs to be carefully controlled and monitored in order to provide the correct conditions for a particular biological experiment to be undertaken. We will specify the software needed to monitor and control the incubator temperature.

In developing any software system the first stage in the process involves an analysis of the system and an initial statement of the requirements. As we said in the introduction, in the first instance we are going to develop an extremely simple version of the system; later in the chapter we will add to the complexity of the system, and therefore produce a new specification.

It is very important, in any requirements definition, to be clear about the system boundaries, and we should make it clear here that in this initial version, *control* of the hardware lies outside of our system. In other words, for the time being we will be specifying a system that simply *monitors* the temperature of the incubator. Later in the chapter we will modify the software requirements by adding a mechanism that actually *controls* the hardware as well as monitoring the temperature of the incubator.

The hardware increments or decrements the temperature of the incubator in response to instructions (from someone or something outside of our system), and each time a change of one degree has been achieved, the software is informed of the

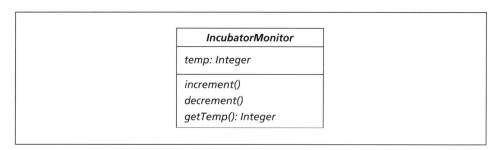

Figure 3.1   The specification of the *IncubatorMonitor* class

change, which it duly records. However, safety requirements dictate that the temperature of the incubator must never be allowed to rise above 10° celsius, nor fall below −10° celsius.

3.3 The UML Specification

In the simple system described in the previous section, we can identify a single class, *IncubatorMonitor*. Figure 3.1 shows the UML specification for the *IncubatorMonitor* class.

    You can see that we have identified one attribute and three methods. The single attribute records the temperature of the system and will be of type integer. The system is, of course, rather a crude one, dealing as it does with whole numbers only, but there will be plenty of time for developing more sophisticated and realistic systems once we have more tools at our disposal. With regard to the methods, the first two do not involve any input or output (since they merely record an increase or decrease of one degree). The final method reads the value of the temperature, and therefore will output an integer.

3.4 Specifying the State

The first thing we will consider for our formal specification is what is known as the **state** of the system. In VDM-SL the state refers to the permanent data that must be stored by the system, and which can be accessed by means of operations. It corresponds to the attributes in the class diagram. The state is specified by declaring variables, in a very similar manner to the way that this is done in a programming language; the notation is not dissimilar from that used in the UML diagram. We specify one or more **variables**, giving each a name, and stating the *type* of data that the variable represents – in other words, the allowable values that the variable could take.

    Throughout this text we will be making use of the intrinsic types available in VDM-SL – these are also common to the world of mathematics. They are:

$\mathbb{N}$:   natural numbers (positive whole numbers)
$\mathbb{N}_1$:   natural numbers excluding zero
$\mathbb{Z}$:   integers (positive and negative whole numbers)
$\mathbb{R}$:   real numbers (positive and negative numbers that can include a fractional part)
$\mathbb{B}$:   boolean values (TRUE or FALSE)
Char: the set of alphanumeric characters

To illustrate how we specify the state in VDM-SL, we can consider our incubator monitor system. We have seen in the previous section that for our simple system, the only data item that we need is the current temperature of the incubator; this will be of type integer, and we shall call it *temp*.

So now we are in a position to specify the state of the *IncubatorMonitor* system, which we do in the following way:

---

state *IncubatorMonitor* **of**

$\quad$ *temp* : $\mathbb{Z}$

end

You can see from the above how this is done; the declaration of the state is introduced with the line:

state <Name> **of**

where <Name> is the chosen name for our system. The state definition is terminated with the keyword **end**. By convention the system name usually begins with an upper-case letter (as it does in UML).

The variables are then listed with the chosen name separated from its type by a colon. By convention, variable names usually begin with a lower-case letter (again this is also the convention in UML).

In the above specification the variable *temp* (to hold the temperature) is an integer and is therefore declared to be of type $\mathbb{Z}$. As this is the only item of data to record here, our state definition is now complete.

3.5 Specifying the Operations

We will now consider the very important matter of the behaviour of the system. We will need to specify a number of **operations** that the system should be able to perform and by which means the data (that is the *state*) can be accessed. In VDM we tend to use the word *operation*, whereas in most object-oriented texts you will tend to see the word *method*. In VDM, operations by definition access the state in some way, either by reading or writing the data, or both.

We saw in section 3.3 that in our system there are three operations that we need to consider: an operation that records an increment in the temperature; an operation that records a decrement; and one that simply reads the value of the temperature. In VDM-SL an operation consists of four sections, which we explain below. The four sections are:

- the operation header
- the **external** clause
- the **precondition**
- the **postcondition**.

We will consider the *increment* operation first. We present the complete operation specification below, and analyse it afterwards:

---

increment()

ext wr   *temp*:$\mathbb{Z}$

pre   *temp* < 10

post   *temp* = $\overline{temp}$ + 1

As we have said, there are four parts to consider here. The first line comprises the operation name – in this case *increment* – followed by a pair of brackets. By convention, operation names are usually written in upper case in VDM texts; however, here we will use lower case so that the operation names will correspond to the UML diagrams, and later to the Java code, where the convention is also to use lower case. The UML diagram (Figure 3.1) indicates that for this operation we do not require the input of any parameters; were there to be any, however, they would be placed inside these brackets – each name followed by its type (separated by a colon) and each item in the list separated from the next by a comma. You will see examples of this later in the chapter. Similarly, if there were an output from the operation, this would be placed, along with its type, after the brackets.

The next line is called the **external clause**, introduced by the VDM keyword **ext**. Keywords are written in lower case, and you will find in most texts (including this one) that they are bold and non-italic, whereas variable and type names are plain but italicized. The purpose of the external clause is to restrict the access of the operation to only those components of the state that are specified, and to specify the mode of access, either read-only (indicated by the keyword **rd**) or read-write (indicated by the keyword **wr**). In our example, there is only one component to the state (*temp*) and in this operation it is necessary to have read-write access to that component, since the operation needs actually to change the temperature. Thus the line is written:

ext wr *temp* : $\mathbb{Z}$

Notice that we have to state the type (in this case $\mathbb{Z}$) along with the component of the state to which we are providing access.

The third and fourth lines of the operation are known as the **precondition** and **postcondition**, respectively. We will deal with the postcondition first, as it is easier to understand the purpose of the precondition once the postcondition has been explained.

The postcondition – which is introduced by the keyword **post** – is perhaps the most important part of the whole operation, for it is here that the essence of the operation is captured. The postcondition states the conditions that must be met after the operation has been performed; it is a predicate, containing one or more variables, the values of which must be such as to make the whole statement true. It is important to note that the only state variables that can be included in the postcondition are those that are referred to in the **ext** clause.

Before considering this in regard to the *increment* operation, it is necessary to introduce some new notation. Any operation that has write access to a component of the state can change the value of that component. It is therefore necessary to find a way of distinguishing between the value of the state component *before* the operation takes place and the value *after* it has taken place – in other words the *old* value and the *new* value. In VDM-SL we do this by placing an overscore over the old value, to distinguish it from the new value.[1] Thus the postcondition for our *increment* operation is:

$$\textbf{post } temp = \overline{temp} + 1$$

We are saying that after the operation has terminated the new value of *temp* should be equal to the old value plus 1.

It is very important to stress that here we are describing *what* should happen, and not *how* it should happen. There is no question of our suggesting any particular algorithm that should be used to bring about the postcondition (like assignment, for example) – all we are saying is that any eventual implementation of a particular operation must guarantee the truth of the postcondition. Thus the postcondition above could equally well be stated as:

$$\textbf{post } \overline{temp} + 1 = temp$$

or as:

$$\textbf{post } temp - \overline{temp} = 1$$

Now we can consider the precondition, which is introduced by the VDM keyword **pre**. The purpose of the precondition is to place any necessary constraints on an operation. In our incubator system, for example, we know that the temperature must be allowed to vary only within the range -10 to $+10$ degrees. If we did not specify a precondition here, we would be allowing the system to record a temperature that was outside of the allowed range – we would be allowing abnormal behaviour of the system. Effectively, by including a precondition, we are specifying the outcome of the operation (that is the postcondition) only if certain conditions are met prior to the operation being invoked. If our precondition is not met we are saying nothing about what should happen.

Another way of thinking about the purpose of the precondition and the postcondition is this: anybody implementing an operation is obliged to guarantee the truth of the postcondition – but only if the precondition is met. The responsibility of ensuring that the precondition is met therefore rests with the *caller* of the operation.

You can see, then, that the precondition for the *increment* operation is as follows:

$$\textbf{pre } temp < 10$$

We are saying that, prior to calling the operation, the temperature must be below 10 degrees. If this is the case, invoking this operation should bring about the state of

---

1 There are a number of different ways of indicating the old value of the state, and in other texts you might see $\overline{temp}$, $temp^-$, or $temp\sim$.

affairs specified in the postcondition. However, if the precondition is not met – that is to say that the temperature is not less than 10 degrees – we are making no statement about what should happen.

We can now go on to specify the other operations. The *decrement* operation is structurally the same as the *increment* operation and does not require any further discussion:

---

decrement()

ext wr $temp : \mathbb{Z}$

pre $temp > -10$

post $temp = \overline{temp} - 1$

Finally we come to the operation that reads the temperature, and which we shall call *getTemp*. Here is the complete operation:

---

getTemp() *currentTemp*: $\mathbb{Z}$

ext rd $temp : \mathbb{Z}$

pre TRUE

post $currentTemp = temp$

There are a few things here that need some explanation. Figure 3.1 shows that this operation requires there to be an output; as we indicated earlier, the output variable is placed after the brackets that follow the operation name, together with its type. In our case we have called this variable *currentTemp* – as recorded in the UML diagram in Figure 3.1 it is an integer, and therefore of type $\mathbb{Z}$ in our VDM specification.

This operation does not require write access to *temp*, since it is not going to change this value, but simply read it – hence the use of the keyword **rd** in the external clause.

Now we come to the precondition, which you might at first find strange, since it consists simply of the word TRUE. In fact, what we are effectivelty saying is that this operation needs no precondition – it is a simple read operation and there is no set of circumstances under which the operation should not take place. A precondition with a value of TRUE is the weakest possible precondition that we can have. In fact, it is perfectly acceptable in such a case to leave the precondition out altogether, rather than to specify it as TRUE.

Finally we come to the postcondition, which is very straightforward – we just declare the output value, *currentTemp*, to be equal to that of the temperature of the incubator, *temp*:

post $currentTemp = temp$

It must be emphasized once again that in this and other postconditions, there is no notion of *assignment*, and you should resist any temptation to think of the above statement as assigning the value of *temp* to that of *currentTemp*. We are working entirely at the specification level, and our postconditions are simply predicates that we say must be true once any implementation that meets our specification is executed. So, once again, the postcondition could have been stated like this:

post $temp = currentTemp$

3.6 Declaring Constants

As with many programming languages, it is possible in VDM-SL to specify constants. This is something that is not essential to any specification, but can greatly enhance its readability. It is done by using the keyword **values**, and the declaration would come immediately before the state definition. In the case of the *IncubatorMonitor* it would look like this:

---

values

$MAX : \mathbb{Z} = 10$

$MIN : \mathbb{Z} = -10$

Here the convention is to use upper case for constant values.

These values could then be used in our functions and operations, so, for example, the precondition of the *decrement* operation would now look like this:

pre $temp > MIN$

3.7 Specifying Functions

In the previous section, we described one way in which the readability of the specification could be enhanced, namely by specifying constant values. Here we introduce another tool that is indispensable when specifying more complex systems, namely the specification of **functions** that we can utilize later in our operations.

A function is a set of *assignments* from one set to another. Thus, the function receives an input value (or values) and maps this to an output value according to some rule – for example it could accept an integer and output the square of that integer, or it could accept the name of a person and output that person's telephone number.

There are two ways in which we can specify a function in VDM-SL. The first way is to specify the function **explicitly**. The style of this specification is algorithmic, and we explicitly define the method of transforming the inputs to the output. This is illustrated in the following very simple function that adds two numbers together:

$add: \mathbb{R} \times \mathbb{R} \to \mathbb{R}$
$add(x, y) \triangleq x + y$

The first line is called the function **signature**. Its purpose is to state the input types that the function accepts (to the left of the arrow), together with the type of the output (to the right of the arrow). In the above example, the function takes two inputs, both of type $\mathbb{R}$ (real numbers), and outputs a value that is also of type $\mathbb{R}$.

The second part is the definition, and describes the algorithm that is used for transforming the inputs to the output; this definition is placed on the right of the $\underline{\Delta}$ symbol, which is read 'is defined as'.

The second method is to specify the function **implicitly**. Here we use a pre- and postcondition in the same way as we described for operations – a function, of course, does not access the state variables. Here is the *add* function defined implicitly.

$add(x : \mathbb{R}, y : \mathbb{R})\ z : \mathbb{R}$

pre   TRUE

post $z = x + y$

As a further example we will specify implicitly and explicitly an *abs* function, which calculates the absolute value of an integer. Firstly the implicit specification:

$abs(z : \mathbb{Z})\ r : \mathbb{N}$

pre   TRUE

post $z < 0 \wedge r = -z \vee z \geq 0 \wedge r = z$

You can see that the postcondition that must be satisfied is a predicate consisting of two disjuncts; for the predicate to be true, then one of these disjuncts must be true. The first disjunct, $z < 0 \wedge r = -z$, ensures that if the input, z, is negative, then the output, r, will be equal to $-z$. The second disjunct, $z \geq 0 \wedge r = z$, ensures that if z is positive (or zero), the output, r, will be equal to z. Both disjuncts cannot, of course, be true at the same time.

And now the explicit definition, which introduces the use of the keywords **if, then** and **else**:

$abs : \mathbb{Z} \rightarrow \mathbb{N}$

$abs(z)\ \underline{\Delta}$ **if** $z < 0$

     then $-z$

     else z

If a function requires a precondition, then, in the explicit definition, this is placed after the definition.

Some functions can be neatly specified by a **recursive** definition, whereby the function calls itself. An example is given below, where a *factorial* function is defined:

$factorial : \mathbb{N} \rightarrow \mathbb{N}$

$factorial(n)\ \underline{\Delta}$ **if** $n = 0$

     then 1

     else $n \times factorial(n - 1)$

While it is acceptable to use either an implicit or an explicit function specification in VDM-SL, the implicit specification has the advantage of being more abstract – in other words it does not suggest any particular algorithm. Additionally, implicit function definitions often lead to more concise specifications. In this text we will tend to specify functions implicitly.

3.8   Specifying a State Invariant

You have seen that our requirements definition states that the temperature of the incubator must stay within the range -10 to $+10°$ celsius. In VDM-SL there is a mechanism by which we can incorporate such a restriction into the specification of the state. This mechanism involves specifying a function known as a **state invariant**. By specifying such a function, we are creating a *global* constraint, rather than just a local constraint as we did with our preconditions.

The invariant definition uses the keyword **inv**. In section 3.7 we introduced the idea of function signatures. In the case of an invariant function, *inv*, its signature will be:

inv: *State* $\rightarrow \mathbb{B}$

The function maps a value of the state onto a boolean – either TRUE or FALSE; and by specifying such a function we are saying that the state variables must be such that the result of the function is TRUE. For the *IncubatorMonitor* system the invariant is specified as:

inv mk-*IncubatorMonitor*(*t*) $\underline{\Delta}$ *MIN* $\leq t \leq$ *MAX*

After the keyword **inv**, we have the expression **mk**-*IncubatorMonitor*(*t*), which effectively is the input to the *inv* function. This expression is itself a function, and is known as a **make function** (the *mk* is pronounced 'make'). You will find out more about make functions in Chapter 9, but for now you just need to know that their purpose is to construct an object – in this case an *IncubatorMonitor* – from the values in the parameter list in the brackets. The parameter names are arbitrary; they are matched, in order, to the components of the state. In our case there is only one component, *temp*. As you have seen, the symbol $\underline{\Delta}$ is read 'is defined as', and on the right of this symbol we place the predicate that the input parameters must satisfy. In this case it is that the temperature lies between -10 and $+10°$ celsius (*MIN* and *MAX* as we have defined them), hence the expression *MIN* $\leq t \leq$ *MAX*, on the right-hand side of the 'is defined as' symbol.

This discussion of the invariant gives us our first opportunity to think about the idea of mathematical proof and integrity checking in connection with software development. One of the integrity checks that we should undertake is to show that none of our operations violates the invariant; in our example this means that none of our operations ever raises the temperature above $10°$ celsius or decreases it below $-10°$ celsius. In a simple system such as this it would not be worth the effort of writing a formal proof for each operation – it is good enough to provide a rigorous argument. In the *increment* operation, for example, we can argue that because the precondition states that the temperature must be below 10 degrees before the operation can take place, this means that the temperature will never rise above 10 degrees as a result of this operation. A similar argument can be provided for the *decrement* operation. Of course, we have to take account of the possibility of violating the invariant only in the case of operations that have write access to the state – an operation such as *getTemp*, which has read-only access, cannot change the values of the state variables, and therefore cannot violate the invariant.

In the next chapter you will see how these integrity checks can be incorporated into a program.

3.9   Specifying an Initialization Function

You may already have identified one of the shortcomings of the above specification, namely that we have not yet made any statement about what the value of the temperature should be when the system is first brought into being. It is all very well having operations that increment and decrement the temperature, but if we do not know what the initial value of the temperature was, then they are not very meaningful. We can solve this problem by specifying an **initialization** function, which is given the name **init**. This function is specified after the declaration of the invariant, and prescribes the conditions that the system must satisfy when it is first brought into being.

Let us illustrate this with our *IncubatorMonitor* example. We will assume that the system works in the following way: when the incubator is turned on, its temperature is adjusted until a steady 5° celsius is obtained. At this point the software system is activated. Thus, our initialization function should state that when the system is first invoked, the temperature should be set to 5.

We write the initialization function like this:

$$\textbf{init } \textbf{mk-}\textit{IncubatorMonitor}(t) \; \underline{\Delta} \; t = 5$$

This is similar in style to the invariant function, and has the same signature; the interpretation in this case is that the expression on the right-hand side of the $\underline{\Delta}$ symbol defines the conditions that must be true after the system is first brought into being.

It is very important to note that the initialization function – as with the operations – must preserve the invariant. Once again, in our example, we are able to argue that since this function sets the temperature to 5 degrees, which is within the constraints allowed, the invariant is not violated.

3.10   User-defined Types

So far we have seen four components of a complete VDM-SL specification – the declaration of constants, the state definition (along with an invariant and initialization function), functions and operations. At the end of this chapter we present the complete template for a VDM-SL specification, and you will see there that the above components are presented in that order. There is one more component to the specification, which must come at the beginning. This is the declaration of any user-defined types that we are going to use in the remainder of the specification. You will see how this is done in section 3.12.

3.11 The *nil* Value

In the next section we are going to look at a more complex – and more useful – version of our incubator system. Before we do that, there is one more concept that we need to introduce to you, namely the idea of a **nil** value.

In Chapter 2 we noted that it was common in the programming world for a value to be undefined. VDM-SL allows for this concept by including the possibility of a term or expression having the value **nil**, meaning that it is undefined. Of course, if we want to allow for this possibility, then we need to slightly modify the type of the variable. We do that by placing square brackets around the type name – for example [$\mathbb{N}$] or [$\mathbb{Z}$] – meaning that a variable of that type can take the value of **nil**. Effectively we are extending the type to include the **nil** value.

3.12 Improving the Incubator System

In order to introduce these new concepts to you, we made our first system very simple indeed – the software simply recorded information about the temperature of an incubator. Let us now make the software more realistic.

In our enhanced system, the software will not only record the current temperature of the system, but will also control the hardware. The system will be able to respond to a request from the user to change the temperature, and subsequently to signal the hardware to increase or decrease the temperature accordingly. The hardware itself will still operate in such a way as to either increment or decrement the temperature of the incubator, and to signal the software each time that a change of one degree has been effected. When the software receives such a signal it must, in addition to recording the new temperature, send back a response, telling the hardware whether or not further changes are required to achieve the temperature that has been requested.

Our new system will also behave a bit more realistically in regard to the initial temperature of the incubator. In this new system, the temperature of the incubator will not be recorded until a message is received from the hardware; other operations on the system will not be able to go ahead until the initial temperature is set.

You will probably already have worked out that it will be necessary for the software to record both the actual temperature of the system and the requested temperature; we will also need some additional operations. Figure 3.2 shows the UML diagram for our new software.

You will notice that three of the operations (*requestChange, increment* and *decrement*) have an output of type *Signal*. This is not a standard UML type such as *Integer*. The internal details of this *Signal* class are relevant to the specification of the *IncubatorMonitor* class so it needs to be analysed further before proceeding to the formal specification.

The signal that must be sent to the hardware could be one of three possible values: either instructing the hardware to increase the temperature, decrease the temperature or do nothing. A type that consists of a small number of named values is often referred to as an *enumerated type*. A standard method of marking a UML class as an enumerated type is to add <<enumeration>> above the type name. The possible

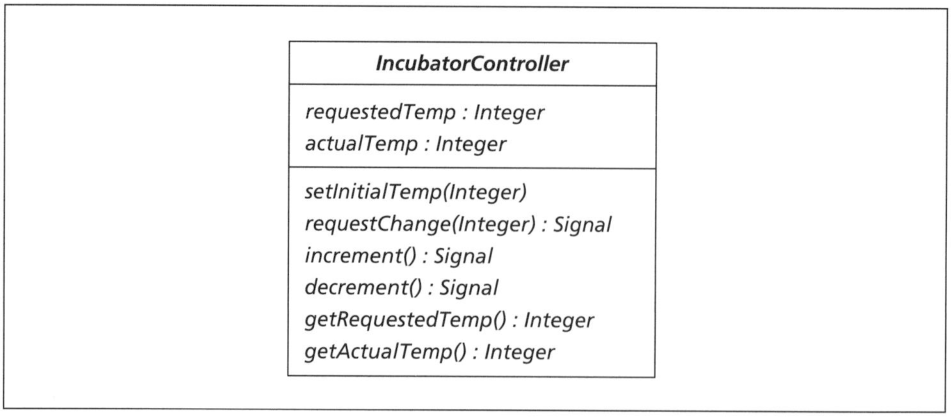

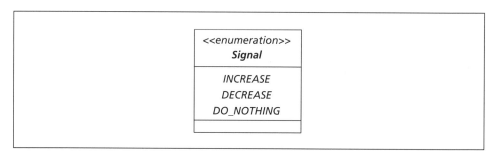

Figure 3.2   The specification of the *IncubatorController*

Figure 3.3   UML specification of the *Signal* type

values of the type are then listed below the type name and the method compartment is left blank. The UML specification of the *Signal* type is given in Figure 3.3.

  We turn now to the formal VDM specification of the *IncubatorController* class. As we mentioned in section 3.10, user-defined types such as *Signal* can also be defined in a VDM specification. The **types** clause is the appropriate place to define new types. The *Signal* type is defined as follows:

types

  $Signal = $ <INCREASE> | <DECREASE> | <DO_NOTHING>

  Here we are defining a type by **type construction**. This form of type construction allows enumerated types to be specified formally in VDM-SL. Values such as <INCREASE>, <DECREASE> and <DO_NOTHING> are called **quote types**, and a type such as *Signal* is **a union of quote types** in VDM. A quote type defines a single value, and at the same time defines a type containing just that value. These quote types correspond to the values specified in the UML diagram of Figure 3.3. Note that, by convention, type names begin with an upper-case letter.

We can now proceed with the re-specification of our new *IncubatorController* system in VDM-SL.

3.13 Specifying the State of the *IncubatorController* System

As we have indicated in the previous section, there now need to be two components of the state – one to hold the actual temperature, and one to hold the temperature that has been requested. Now, as we stated above, when the system first comes into being these values will be undefined, and must therefore be set to **nil**. As we explained in section 3.11 this means that the type of these values will be written as $[\mathbb{Z}]$ rather than $\mathbb{Z}$. So our new state definition now becomes:

> **state** *IncubatorController* **of**
>
> $\quad$ *requestedTemp* : $[\mathbb{Z}]$
>
> $\quad$ *actualTemp* : $[\mathbb{Z}]$

Now for the invariant. As before, the actual temperature must not be allowed to go outside the range of -10 to $+10$ degrees; however we need to allow for the possibility that it could be equal to the **nil** value. Exactly the same is true for the requested temperature. This gives us an invariant comprising two conjuncts:

> **inv mk-***IncubatorController* (r, a) $\underline{\Delta}$
>
> $\quad (MIN \leq r \leq MAX \vee r = \textbf{nil}) \wedge (MIN \leq a \leq MAX \vee a = \textbf{nil})$

Notice that now there are two inputs to the *make* function.

In section 3.7, we discussed the use of functions in VDM. The above invariant provides us with an opportunity to illustrate this point. Let us define a function *inRange* as follows:

> *inRange*(*val*: $\mathbb{Z}$) *result* : $\mathbb{B}$
>
> **pre** $\quad$ TRUE
>
> **post** $\quad$ *result* $\Leftrightarrow MIN \leq val \leq MAX$

The purpose of this function is to check whether an integer value, *val*, is within the range *MIN* and *MAX* as defined earlier. You can see that the use of the equivalence connective ensures that the output is true if the input is in range, but is otherwise false.

Now we can use this function in the invariant, which we can rewrite as:

> **inv mk-***IncubatorController* (r, a) $\underline{\Delta}$ $(inRange(r) \vee r = \textbf{nil}) \wedge (inRange(a) \vee a = \textbf{nil})$

This makes the invariant much more readable, and also has the advantage that we can re-use our function throughout the specification, as we shall see in a moment.

Next we need to think about our initialization function. Since both the requested temperature and the actual temperature will be undefined at the point when the system is created, these should both be set to **nil**. Hence the initialization function is:

$$\textbf{init } \textbf{mk-}\textit{IncubatorController} \; (r, a) \; \underline{\Delta} \; r = \textbf{nil} \wedge a = \textbf{nil}$$

3.14   Specifying the Operations for the *IncubatorController* System

As we explained in section 3.12, it is going to be necessary to provide an operation that can be used to set the initial temperature of the system – this will be invoked by the hardware when the incubator has established a steady initial temperature. It is very important not to confuse this with the initialization clause. The initialization clause is simply a function that states the conditions that must exist when the system first comes into being – it is not an operation that can be invoked during the system's life time, whereas the *setInitialTemp* operation that we are now specifying can, of course, be invoked once the system has been created.

The operation is specified below:

$$\textit{setInitialTemp}(\textit{tempIn} : \mathbb{Z})$$

$$\textbf{ext wr}\quad \textit{actualTemp} : \; [\mathbb{Z}]$$

$$\textbf{pre}\quad\quad \textit{inRange}(\textit{tempIn}) \wedge \textit{actualTemp} = \textbf{nil}$$

$$\textbf{post}\quad\quad \textit{actualTemp} = \textit{tempIn}$$

This time we have an operation that requires an input parameter, which, as you can see, is placed in the brackets after the operation name. Notice that we need read-write access to the *actualTemp* component of the state, but do not need access to *requestedTemp*.

The precondition is interesting. You can see that there are two parts to it. The first of the two conjuncts is effectively validating the input – if the input value is out of range, then the behaviour of the system for this operation is not defined; notice the use of our *inRange* function here. The second part ensures the actual temperature of the incubator has a value of **nil**, which will be the case immediately after the system has come into being. Once the temperature has been set, the temperature has an actual value, and this operation could not take place again unless some other operation set the temperature back to **nil**; and since no such operation is provided, this means that the operation can be performed only once.

The postcondition is straightforward: the value of the output should be equal to that of the current temperature.

Now let us consider the *requestChange* operation. Remember that its purpose is to record the value of the temperature that has been requested by the user of the system, and to signal the hardware to take the appropriate action in order to bring about the change.

It will therefore require an input of an integer, and will result in an output of type *Signal* (refer again to Figure 3.2).

The operation is specified as follows:

$requestChange(tempIn : \mathbb{Z})$ $signalOut : Signal$

ext wr $requestedTemp : [\mathbb{Z}]$

    rd $actualTemp : [\mathbb{Z}]$

pre $inRange(tempIn) \wedge actualTemp \neq$ **nil**

post $requestedTemp = tempIn \wedge$

        $(tempIn > actualTemp \wedge signalOut = <\text{INCREASE}>$

        $\vee\ tempIn < actualTemp \wedge signalOut = <\text{DECREASE}>$

        $\vee\ tempIn = actualTemp \wedge signalOut = <\text{DO\_NOTHING}>)$

The first item to which we draw your attention is the external clause. We need access to both components of the state, but the mode of access is different in each case. In the case of *requestedTemp*, it will be necessary to have write access to this component because we must record the temperature that has been requested. In the case of *actualTemp*, the operation is not going to change this value, but needs read access in order to compare it to the requested temperature and thence determine the action that must be taken by the hardware.

The precondition is similar to that of the previous operation:

---

pre $inRange(tempIn) \wedge actualTemp \neq$ **nil**

However, in this case we are checking that the actual temperature is *not* undefined, thus ensuring that the initial temperature had been properly set.

The postcondition might at first glance appear rather more complex, but in fact it is very simple to unravel. It consists of two conjuncts, the first of which simply states that the requested temperature must be equal to the value that was input into the operation. The second conjunct looks like this:

$(tempIn > actualTemp \wedge signalOut = <\text{INCREASE}>$

    $\vee\ tempIn < actualTemp \wedge signalOut = <\text{DECREASE}>$

    $\vee\ tempIn = actualTemp \wedge signalOut = <\text{DO\_NOTHING}>)$

It deals with the value of the signal that is sent out. You can see that it consists of three disjuncts, each of which deals with a different case – the first when the input temperature is greater than the actual temperature, the second when it is less than the actual temperature, and the third when it is equal to the actual temperature. The fact that they are 'OR-ed' means that only one has to be true to make the compound statement true – and indeed, logically, only one of these *can* be true at any one time. So if, for example, the input temperature were greater than the actual temperature, then for the whole statement to be true, the output signal must be equal to INCREASE – and similarly for the other two disjuncts. Once again the nature of this postcondition should bring home the fact that postconditions are predicates, *not* assignment statements!

Now for the new version of the *increment* operation:

---

increment () *signalOut* : *Signal*

ext rd *requestedTemp* : $[\mathbb{Z}]$

   wr *actualTemp* : $[\mathbb{Z}]$

pre $actualTemp < requestedTemp \wedge actualTemp \neq \mathbf{nil} \wedge requestedTemp \neq \mathbf{nil}$

post $actualTemp = \overline{actualTemp} + 1 \wedge$

        $(actualTemp < requestedTemp \wedge signalOut = <\text{INCREASE}>$

           $\vee\ actualTemp = requestedTemp \wedge signalOut = <\text{DO\_NOTHING}>)$

The operation header and the external clause should not require further explanation.

The precondition consists of three conjuncts. The first of these checks that the actual temperature is less than the requested temperature (otherwise we should not increment it). Since all operations must preserve the invariant we can assume that the requested temperature will not be greater than *MAX*, so this conjunct automatically checks that the actual temperature is less that the maximum allowed temperature. The second and third conjuncts check that an initial and requested temperature have been set.

Here again the postcondition has to deal with the value of the signal output as well as dealing with the need to increment the actual temperature. In this operation, however, there are only two alternatives, as the possibility of the actual temperature being greater than the requested temperature has been eliminated by the precondition.

The *decrement* operation is similar and does not require further explanation.

Finally we need to provide read operations for the requested temperature and the actual temperature:

---

getRequestedTemp() *currentRequested* : $[\mathbb{Z}]$

ext rd   *requestedTemp* : $[\mathbb{Z}]$

pre   TRUE

post $currentRequested = requestedTemp$

$getActualTemp()\ currentActual : [\mathbb{Z}]$

ext rd $actualTemp : [\mathbb{Z}]$

pre   TRUE

post $currentActual = actualTemp$

---

types
   $SomeType = ...$

values
   $constantName : ConstantType = someValue$

state *SystemName* **of**
   $attribute_1 : Type$
             $:$
             $:$
   $attribute_n : Type$

   inv mk-$SystemName(i_1{:}Type, ..., i_n{:}Type)\ \underline{\Delta}\ Expression(i_1, ..., i_n)$
   init mk-$SystemName(i_1{:}Type, ..., i_n{:}Type)\ \underline{\Delta}\ Expression(i_1, ..., i_n)$

end

functions
   specification of functions .....

operations
   specification of operations .....

Figure 3.4   The standard template for VDM-SL specifications

3.15   A Standard Template for VDM-SL Specifications

We are now in a position to provide a generalized template for a VDM-SL specification; any specification that we now present will conform to this template, which is shown in Figure 3.4. You should note that not every clause would necessarily appear in every specification.

3.16   Including Comments

As with program code, the readability of a VDM-SL specification is greatly enhanced by the inclusion of comments. This is done by introducing the comment with the symbol – –. A new line ends the comment. Examples are provided in the next section.

3.17   The complete specification of the
IncubatorController system

We conclude this chapter by presenting the complete specification of the *Incubator* system, which you can see conforms to the standard template that we provided in the previous section:

---

types
$Signal$ = <INCREASE> | <DECREASE> | <DO_NOTHING>

values
   $MAX : \mathbb{Z} = 10$
   $MIN : \mathbb{Z} = -10$

state *IncubatorController* **of**
   requestedTemp : $[\mathbb{Z}]$
   actualTemp : $[\mathbb{Z}]$

   –– both requested and actual temperatures must be in range or equal to **nil**
   inv mk-*IncubatorController* $(r, a) \; \underline{\Delta} \; (inRange(r) \; \vee \; r = \textbf{nil}) \; \wedge \; (inRange(a) \; \vee$
$$a = \textbf{nil})$$

   –– both requested and actual temperatures are undefined when the system is initialized
   init mk-*IncubatorController* $(r, a) \; \underline{\Delta} \; r = \textbf{nil} \wedge a = \textbf{nil}$

end

functions
$inRange(val : \mathbb{Z})$ *result* : $\mathbb{B}$
pre TRUE
post *result* $\Leftrightarrow MIN \leq val \leq MAX$

operations
–– an operation that records the intitial temperature of the system
setInitialTemp$(tempIn : \mathbb{Z})$
ext wr *actualTemp* : $[\mathbb{Z}]$
pre $inRange(tempIn) \wedge actualTemp = \textbf{nil}$
post $actualTemp = tempIn$

–– an operation that records the requested temperature and signals the hardware to increase
–– or decrease the temperature as appropriate
requestChange$(tempIn : \mathbb{Z})$ *signalOut* : *Signal*
ext wr *requestedTemp* : $[\mathbb{Z}]$
    rd *actualTemp* : $[\mathbb{Z}]$
pre $inRange(tempIn) \wedge actualTemp \neq \textbf{nil}$
post $requestedTemp = tempIn \wedge$
          $(tempIn > actualTemp \wedge signalOut = $ <INCREASE>
          $\vee \; tempIn < actualTemp \wedge signalOut = $ <DECREASE>
          $\vee \; tempIn = actualTemp \wedge signalOut = $ <DO_NOTHING>)

––an operation that records a one degree increase and instructs the hardware
  ––either to continue increasing the temperature or to stop

---

increment () *signalOut* : *Signal*

ext rd *requestedTemp* : $[\mathbb{Z}]$

   wr *actualTemp* : $[\mathbb{Z}]$

pre   *actualTemp* $<$ *requestedTemp* $\wedge$ *actualTemp* $\neq$ **nil** $\wedge$ *requestedTemp* $\neq$ **nil**

post   *actualTemp* $=$ $\overline{actualTemp} + 1 \wedge$
         (*actualTemp* $<$ *requestedTemp* $\wedge$ *signalOut* $=$ $<$INCREASE$>$
         $\vee$ *actualTemp* $=$ *requestedTemp* $\wedge$ *signalOut* $=$ $<$DO_NOTHING$>$)

–– an operation that records a one degree decrease and instructs the hardware
  –– either to continue decreasing the temperature or to stop

decrement () *signalOut* : *Signal*

ext rd *requestedTemp* : $[\mathbb{Z}]$

wr   *actualTemp* : $[\mathbb{Z}]$

pre *actualTemp* $>$ *requestedTemp* $\wedge$ *actualTemp* $\neq$ **nil** $\wedge$ *requestedTemp* $\neq$ **nil**

post *actualTemp* $=$ $\overline{actualTemp} < 1 \wedge$
      (*actualTemp* $>$ $\overline{requestedTemp}$ $\wedge$ *signalOut* $=$ $<$DECREASE$>$
      $\vee$ *actualTemp* $=$ *requestedTemp* $\wedge$ *signalOut* $=$ $<$DO_NOTHING$>$)

getRequestedTemp() *currentRequested* : $[\mathbb{Z}]$

ext rd   *requestedTemp* : $[\mathbb{Z}]$

pre   TRUE

post   *currentRequested* $=$ *requestedTemp*

getActualTemp() *currentActual* : $[\mathbb{Z}]$

ext rd   *actualTemp* : $[\mathbb{Z}]$

pre   TRUE

post   *currentActual* $=$ *actualTemp*

EXERCISES

1. Consider the *IncubatorController* system from this chapter. Specify an operation, *isEqual*, which reports on whether or not the actual temperature is equal to the requested temperature.
2. (a) Provide both an explicit and an implicit definition for a VDM function that accepts two integers as input and outputs the greater of the two; if both integers are of equal value, the function should output this value.
   (b) Adapt the function so that it accepts only numbers that are unequal.
3. Consider a system that records the current mode of an industrial robot, which can either be working, idle or broken.
   (a) Declare a type, *Mode*, for use in the specification.
   (b) Write the specification of the state of the system, including an initialization function that ensures that the robot is set to idle when the system first comes into existence.
   (c) Write specifications for the following operations:
      (i) An operation called *setMode* that accepts and records a value for the mode of the robot.
      (ii) An operation called *get*Mode that outputs the current mode of the robot.
      (iii) An operation called *isIdle* that checks whether or not the robot is idle.
   (d) Modify the *setMode* operation so that the mode of a robot cannot be changed directly from broken to working.

4. Software is required to monitor the position of a land-craft that is undertaking investigative work on a distant planet by scanning the surface for the existence of a particular mineral. The particular section of the planet surface under investigation is thought of as being divided into a two-dimensional grid consisting of 10 rows and 10 columns. The scanning system of the craft can be on or off at any time, but must not be on when the craft is anywhere in the first row of the grid. When the application comes into being, the craft will always be located in the cell corresponding to row 1, column 1.

The software should be capable of recording the position of the module, recording and reporting on the status of the scanner, and reporting on the row currently occupied and the column currently occupied. The UML diagrams for the *LandCraft* class, and the *Status* type are shown below:

LandCraft
row: Integer
column: Integer
status: Status
recordPosition(Integer, Integer)
recordStatus(Status)
showStatus(): Status
showRow(): Integer
showColumn(): Integer

<<enumeration>> **Status**
ON
OFF

Specify the software in VDM-SL.

From VDM Specifications to Java Implementations

4.1 Introduction

In this chapter we will explore ways in which to implement a VDM specification in Java. We begin by looking at some key features of the Java programming language that make it suitable for the implementation of VDM specifications. We then go on to look at some general guidelines for translating a VDM specification into Java while developing implementations of the *Incubator* specifications of the previous chapter.

4.2 Java

Formal methods are used to help ensure the reliability of a software product. The programming language can also have a bearing on the reliability of the final program. For example, languages with strong type checking help identify and remove many errors before run-time. We have chosen Java as our language for the following reasons:

- **Java is object-oriented**   This allows programs to be developed by defining classes that have encapsulated attributes, and public methods. This encapsulation of data allows secure systems to be built with less chance of data corruption. As you have already seen, a VDM specification corresponds very closely to the idea of a class, so an object-oriented programming language is an obvious choice for implementing VDM specifications.
- **Java is portable**   Because Java classes are compiled down to *byte code* rather than platform-specific machine code, final applications can run successfully on any platform that incorporates a *Java Virtual Machine*. In particular, calculations and evaluation of expressions return identical results regardless of platform. For example, the range of an integer variable in C will differ depending upon whether or not the language is compiled on a 16 or 32 bit platform, whereas the range for an integer variable in Java is common across all platforms. This is obviously important for the development of any high integrity software.
- **Java is robust**   Certain programming features that are commonly associated with software errors in other languages are not part of the Java programming language. In particular Java does not support *pointers* and *multiple inheritance*. These features can result in software failure because their use requires considerable skill and they have a complex semantics. In particular, they make it harder to analyse a program for correctness, whether by inspection, proof or testing. In addition to this, Java's *garbage collection* removes the memory management burden on programmers

(another common source of programming errors) and a comprehensive *exception handling* mechanism allows programs to deal safely with unexpected behaviour. While features such as pointers and manual memory management are sometimes necessary when resources are limited, program reliability is greatly improved by removing such error-prone constructs and incorporating such additional features.

- **Java is high level** When developing applications from VDM specifications, it helps considerably if the types available in the specification language are also available in the implementation language. So far we have only shown you the simple types available in VDM-SL but over the coming chapters we shall look at the abstract collection types (such as sets and maps) available in VDM-SL. These abstract types are much higher level than traditional low-level programming collection types such as arrays and linked lists. This allows for very concise specifications. In addition to low-level collection types such as arrays, Java also offers its own high-level collection classes such as vectors and hash tables. These collection classes very closely resemble the abstract collection types of VDM-SL and allow for relatively concise implementations from VDM specifications.

For these reasons Java is a good choice for implementing VDM specifications. Of course, the language was not designed with this purpose in mind, so there are times when the translation process needs to be smoothed by providing additional utility classes. These classes, which we have developed, can be downloaded from the accompanying website. We will discuss them as and when we need to use them.

4.2.1 FORMAL DEVELOPMENT OF JAVA PROGRAMS: A LIGHTWEIGHT APPROACH

As we described in Chapter 1, the approach we will be taking to formal program development is one that is often referred to as a *lightweight* approach. Here, formality is applied with a light rather than rigorous touch. Important consistency checks, which can be derived from the formal specification, will be checked at run-time once an implementation has been derived, rather than by means of a formal proof before an implementation is developed. This reduces the formal obligations on the developer while maintaining important consistency checks on the final running system.

Throughout this chapter, and the rest of this book, we provide you with a lightweight method of developing Java programs from VDM specifications. While the final Java programs produced can be used to help validate the original specification, this should not be viewed as the primary role of the translation. Indeed, if this is the sole aim then VDM interpreters (such as the IFAD VDM-SL Toolbox[1]) are commercially available where VDM specifications can be executed directly for testing purposes without the need to translate into an intermediate programming language such as Java first. While these interpreters are useful for specification validation, however, a final system will still need to be developed in a programming language and it is this stage that we address in the method presented. We do not consider issues such as program efficiency or the user interface here – these are aspects you might wish to improve when developing a final implementation. We assume that you are already familiar with programming in Java. A coverage of some of the more advanced features that we utilize (such as exceptions and anonymous classes) can also be found in the appendix on the accompanying website.

---

1 For more information on this tool visit **http://www.ifad.dk/**.

4.3 From VDM-SL Types to Java Types

Up to this point we have presented you with the basic types of VDM-SL: integers, natural numbers, real numbers, booleans and characters. Java has several *primitive* (non-class) types that can be used to provide a concrete representation of these abstract types. Table 4.1 provides suitable primitive Java types for these VDM-SL types.

Table 4.1 From VDM-SL base types to Java primitive types

VDM-SL type	Java type
$\mathbb{N}$	int
$\mathbb{N}_1$	int
$\mathbb{Z}$	int
$\mathbb{R}$	double
$\mathbb{B}$	boolean
Char	char

As you can see from Table 4.1, Java does not provide distinct types for natural numbers and integers. The int type provides for both negative and positive whole numbers so can be used whenever variables are declared in VDM-SL to be of type $\mathbb{N}$, $\mathbb{N}_1$ or $\mathbb{Z}$. Care needs to be taken, however, when the int type is being used to model the natural number types, since negative numbers are not allowed.[2] We will see examples of this later in the book.

It is also important to bear in mind that, while VDM-SL number types have no upper or lower limits to their size, upper and lower limits are placed on the primitive number types of Java ($-2\,147\,483\,648$ to $2\,147\,483\,647$ for the int type and $+/-4.9 \times 10^{-324}$ to 1.8×10^{308} for the double type). For the purposes of most applications these number ranges will be sufficient.[3] Let us now take a look at the implementation of a VDM specification into Java.

4.4 Implementing the *IncubatorMonitor* Specification

In Chapter 3 we considered a system that monitored the temperature of an incubator. The system was specified formally in VDM-SL as follows:

values

$$MAX : \mathbb{Z} = 10$$
$$MIN : \mathbb{Z} = -10$$

---

2 In addition, care needs to be taken that a zero value is not allowed for variables declared to be of type $\mathbb{N}_1$ in VDM-SL.
3 If these number ranges are not sufficient then the Java classes BigInt and BigDouble can be used for integers and real numbers with no upper or lower limit.

state *IncubatorMonitor* **of**

$temp : \mathbb{Z}$

inv mk-*IncubatorMonitor*(t) $\underline{\Delta}$ $MIN \le t \le MAX$

init mk-*IncubatorMonitor*(t) $\underline{\Delta}$ $t = 5$

end

operations

increment( )

ext wr $temp : \mathbb{Z}$

pre $temp < MAX$

post $temp = \overline{temp} + 1$

decrement( )

ext wr $temp : \mathbb{Z}$

pre $temp > MIN$

post $temp = \overline{temp} - 1$

getTemp( ) *currentTemp* : $\mathbb{Z}$

ext rd $temp : \mathbb{Z}$

pre   TRUE

post $currentTemp = temp$

A VDM specification will be implemented in Java as a class. So a class called `IncubatorMonitor` is to be developed in Java:

```
class IncubatorMonitor
{

    // code goes here

}
```

The VDM specification consists of a **values** clause, a **state** clause, **invariant** and **initialization** functions and **operation** specifications. We will look at these in turn.

4.4.1 TRANSLATING A VALUES CLAUSE INTO JAVA

Constants defined in the **values** clause of the VDM specification can be implemented as constant attributes of the Java class. It is useful to declare constant class values as `public` – allowing access to them outside of the class.

VDM-SL	Java

values
 	
    MAX : $\mathbb{Z} = 10$
    MIN : $\mathbb{Z} = -10$
	`public static final int` MAX = 10;
	`public static final int` MIN = -10;

Notice how the Java `int` type was used to provide a concrete representation of the VDM-SL integer type ($\mathbb{Z}$). The VDM-SL convention of naming constants in upper case is also common to Java programs.

4.4.2 TRANSLATING A STATE CLAUSE INTO JAVA

The state attributes of the VDM specification constitute the hidden data members of the specified software. As such they correspond to the `private` attributes of a Java class:

VDM-SL	Java
state *IncubatorMonitor* **of** *temp* : $\mathbb{Z}$	`private int` temp;

Again, the convention of starting attribute names with a lower-case letter is common to both VDM-SL and Java.

4.4.3 TRANSLATING AN INVARIANT INTO JAVA

The invariant is a record of a global constraint on the software being specified. It can be implemented in Java as a (`public`) method that returns a `boolean` result. A result of TRUE would indicate that the invariant has been met and a result of FALSE would indicate that it has not been met. Here is the translation:

VDM-SL	Java

inv mk-Incubator*Monitor*(*t*) $\underline{\Delta}$ MIN $\leq t \leq$ MAX	`public boolean inv ()`
	
	`{`
	
	`return (MIN <= temp && temp <= MAX);`
	
	`}`

As you can see, the Java method returns the result of the `boolean` expression specified in VDM-SL. It is important to remember to always refer to the full attribute name (`temp`) in the Java code.

The implementation of an invariant method in the Java class is not essential, but it allows important run-time consistency checks to be carried out. It is useful to mark a class as having such a check available. To allow for this, we have defined an `InvariantCheck` interface as follows:

The *InvariantCheck* interface

```
interface InvariantCheck

{

  public boolean inv();

}
```

Classes, such as `IncubatorMonitor`, that contain an invariant method can then claim to implement this interface:

```
class IncubatorMonitor implements InvariantCheck

{

    public boolean inv()

    {

      return (MIN <= temp && temp <= MAX);

    }

// more code here

}
```

We will demonstrate how this invariant can be checked later in this chapter. As can be seen in the `IncubatorMonitor` invariant, VDM-SL tests may consist of comparison and logical operators. Table 4.2 gives the Java equivalent to the comparison operators.[4]

---

4 At the moment we are only comparing primitive values. When we compare objects we will have to use object methods such as `equals` for comparisons.

Table 4.2 Comparison operators

VDM-SL	Java
$a = b$	$a == b$
$a \neq b$	$a\ != b$
$a < b$	$a < b$
$a > b$	$a > b$
$a \geq b$	$a >= b$
$a \leq b$	$a <= b$

Table 4.3 Logical operators

VDM-SL	Java
$a \wedge b$	$a \&\& b$
$a \vee b$	$a\ \|\| b$
$\neg a$	$!a$
$a \Leftrightarrow b$	$a == b$
$a \Rightarrow b$	$(!a)\ \|\| b$

Table 4.3 gives the Java equivalent to the basic logical operators.

Care has to be taken when using the conjunction and disjunction operators in Java. Unlike their VDM-SL counterparts, the order in which they appear can be significant when using these operators in Java. This is the case when one of the operands may possibly be undefined.

We discussed, in Chapter 2, how classical logic can be extended to deal with undefined terms. Consider the following VDM-SL expression involving a conjunction:

$$x \div y > 1 \wedge y \neq 0$$

Since zero divided by zero is undefined, the expression would resolve to the following if both x and y were equal to zero:

UNDEFINED $\wedge$ FALSE

This in turn would resolve to FALSE. An undefined term used in a programming expression, however, can cause that program to fail. It would be unwise to implement this test as follows:

```
x/y > 1 && y!= 0
```

An attempt would be made to evaluate the first conjunct. If y and x were both zero, this would be an undefined expression[5] causing a *division-by-zero exception*[6] and possible program termination!

---

5   In fact, only the value of y need be zero for the expression to be undefined in Java.
6   An exception is an object that is generated when an error occurs. If left undealt with such an exception object can cause program termination.

Fortunately, Java has what is known as *lazy evaluation*. This means that once the first operand is evaluated, if the outcome of the expression can be determined the second operand is not evaluated. In the case of disjuncts, if the first operand evaluates to TRUE the whole expression evaluates to TRUE without having to evaluate the second operand. In the case of conjuncts, if the first operand evaluates to FALSE the whole expression evaluates to FALSE without having to evaluate the second operand. For this reason it is wiser to place the potentially undefined conjunct second in the expression as follows:

```
y! = 0 && x/y > 1
```

Now, if the value of y is equal to zero the first conjunct will resolve to FALSE, which in turn will resolve the whole expression to FALSE without the need to evaluate the second potentially undefined expression. Essentially all this means is that potentially undefined operands should always be placed second in an expression.

4.4.4 THE VDM CLASS

If you look back at Table 4.3, you can see that the implication operator ($\Rightarrow$) has no direct counterpart in Java. Instead, the implication can be translated into an equivalent expression involving NOT and OR operators.[7] However, in order to smooth the translation process and avoid having to translate implications in this way, we have provided a utility class (called VDM) that contains, in addition to several other methods, an `implies` method (see Table 4.4). This class can be downloaded from the website.

Table 4.4 Methods of the VDM class

Method	Description
implies	Implementation of the implication ($\Rightarrow$) operator
forall	Implementation of the universal quantifier ($\forall$)
exists	Implementation of the existential quantifier ($\exists$)
uniqueExists	Implementation of the unique existential quantifier ($\exists!$)
preTest	Checks a precondition and throws an exception if the precondition is broken
postTest	Checks a postcondition and throws an exception if the postcondition is broken
invTest	Checks the invariant of an object and throws an exception if the invariant is broken

The methods listed in Table 4.4 are all class methods, so they are invoked with the class name. Here is an example of how the `implies` method might be used:

VDM-SL	Java
$x > y \Rightarrow y + x > 1$	`VDM.implies(x > y, y +x > 1)`

---

7 The following equivalence holds: $A \Rightarrow B \equiv \neg A \lor B$.

The `implies` method behaves in exactly the same was as the implies operator ($\Rightarrow$). It receives two `boolean` expressions and returns TRUE if the first implies the second and FALSE otherwise. The obvious code for the *implies* method in our utility class is given as follows:

```
public static boolean implies (boolean a, boolean b)

{

    return ((!a)||b);

}
```

We will demonstrate the use of this and the other methods in the VDM class throughout this text.

4.4.5 TRANSLATING THE INITIALIZATION CLAUSE INTO JAVA

The initialization clause of the VDM specification defines valid initial values for attributes of the corresponding class. A constructor is the mechanism used to initialize class attributes in Java. The initialization clause in VDM receives no outside parameters so we need to develop a parameterless constructor in our Java class:

```
public IncubatorMonitor()

{

    // initialization code goes here

}
```

Of course, the initialization clause of the VDM specification indicates *what* condition must hold after the initialization is complete – it does not indicate *how* to achieve this. We are asked to ensure that the temperature is equal to 5 upon initialization.

init mk-*IncubatorMonitor* (*t*) $\underline{\Delta}$ *t* = 5

Once again, it is important to be careful that the attribute name (*temp*) is used in the code for the Java constructor, not the name that is pattern matched to this attribute in the VDM specification (*t*). The obvious way to satisfy the initialization equality is with an assignment to the attribute *temp*.

```
temp = 5;
```

After this assignment, *temp* will be equal to 5 and the initialization predicate will be satisfied. Throughout this text we will treat this as an assignment **axiom** (a rule that does not have to be proven). That is, after an assignment in Java of the following form:

```
x = y;
```

(where y is any expression) the following equality will hold:

$x = y$

Note that if the assignment expression, y, makes reference to the assigned variable x, then the equality that holds will be with respect to the old value of x. So, for example, after the following assignment in Java:

```
x = 2 X x;
```

The following equality will hold

$x = 2 \times \overline{x};$

This assignment axiom is the only formal proof rule that we will use to argue program correctness. As we are using a lightweight approach to program development, we will just argue the correctness of other aspects of the final program and rely upon run-time integrity checks to trap any errors that might have been made.

One very important integrity check in VDM is that the initial state respects the state invariant (we know this class has an invariant because we have marked the class as implementing the `InvariantCheck` interface). It is useful to incorporate this check into the constructor. As noted in Table 4.4, we have included an `invTest` method in our VDM class to check whether or not the invariant holds on a given object. The parameter of this method must be an object that implements the `InvariantCheck` interface. Since objects of this `IncubatorMonitor` class implement the `InvariantCheck` interface we can send in **this** object to the method.

```
VDM.invTest(this);
```

The `invTest` method checks the invariant method defined for the given object. If the invariant holds, no action is taken by the method, but if the invariant has been broken this method throws an exception. We have created our own exception class (`VDMException`) for this purpose so that exceptions generated by VDM implementations can be distinguished from exceptions that arise from other sources in your final program. We have made `VDMException` an *unchecked* exception class (meaning that callers of this method are not obliged to acknowledge that the method might throw an exception). When we discuss program testing later in this chapter we will show you one way of dealing with such exceptions. Here then is the complete translation of the initialization function:

VDM-SL	Java

init mk-*IncubatorMonitor* (t) $\underline{\Delta}\, t = 5$	```
	public IncubatorMonitor()
	{
	    temp = 5;
	    VDM.invTest(this);
	}
	``

This completes the translation of the state specification. Now we turn to the operation specifications.

4.4.6 TRANSLATING OPERATION SPECIFICATIONS INTO JAVA

VDM operations amount to the public interface of the system. The public interface of a class consists of its `public` methods, so each VDM-SL operation will correspond to a `public` Java method within the class. Consider the following translation of the *increment* operation and then we will discuss it:

VDM-SL	Java
| *increment*( ) <br><br> **ext wr**  *temp* : $\mathbb{Z}$ <br><br> **pre**    *temp* $<$ *MAX* <br><br> **post**    *temp* $=$ $\overline{temp}$ $+$ 1 | ```java
public void increment()

{

    VDM.preTest(temp < MAX);

    temp = temp + 1;

    VDM.invTest(this);

}
``` |

The inputs and outputs

It is clear that the inputs and outputs of the Java method are determined directly from those of the VDM operation – in this case there are none:

VDM-SL	Java
increment( )	`public void increment()`

The ext clause

Java methods have write and read access to *all* state attributes and this access cannot be restricted as in the VDM-SL **ext** clause. Consequently there is no corresponding part to the **ext** clause in the Java method. However, the **ext** clause does have an influence on the way we implement the method. Earlier we discussed an important integrity check in VDM – that the initial state satisfies the invariant. Another important integrity check is that all operations also respect the invariant. If an operation has write access to the state, the invariant could potentially be broken. The *increment* method has write access to the *temp* attribute, so we have included an invariant check
```

at the end of this method to help ensure that the method preserves the invariant:

VDM-SL	Java

ext wr *temp* : $\mathbb{Z}$	`// rest of method here`
	
	`VDM.invTest(this);`

The precondition

You will recall that the responsibility for ensuring that the precondition is met lies with the caller of the method. If it has been met then the operation can go ahead. If the precondition is not met the behaviour of this operation is not specified. We have decided that, in this circumstance, it is safest to throw an exception to alert the caller of this method that something has gone wrong. This provides the caller of the method with the opportunity of checking if the precondition is met by trapping the exception within a **try ... catch** block (as we will demonstrate in the next section). As listed in Table 4.4, we have provided a method (`preTest`) in our utility class for testing the precondition.

VDM-SL	Java
pre *temp* < *MAX*	`VDM.preTest(temp < MAX);`

If the precondition does not hold the method throws a VDMException. If the precondition does hold, no exception is thrown and the operation can proceed to implement the postcondition.[8]

The postcondition

The main body of the method is concerned with implementing the equality in the postcondition. This has been implemented by the single assignment statement:

VDM-SL	Java
post *temp* = $\overline{temp}$ + 1	`temp = temp + 1;`

---

8   At time of writing, a version of Java has been released that includes an **assert** statement. This statement behaves in a very similar way to our `preTest` and `invTest` (and `postTest`) methods. Like the methods provided in our VDM class, the **assert** statement throws an exception when a test fails. You might wish to use this statement in place of the methods in our VDM class.

Again, remember the postcondition states *what* must be satisfied upon successful completion of the operation, not *how*. The assignment axiom ensures that, after this assignment, *temp* is one greater than the old value of *temp* required by the postcondition.

The decrement operation

Using the guidelines given above, the *decrement* operation can be translated in a similar way:

VDM-SL	Java

decrement()
 	
 ext wr *temp* : $\mathbb{Z}$
 	
 pre *temp* > *MIN*
 	
 post *temp* = $\overline{temp}$ − 1
	```public void decrement()```
	
	 ```{```
	
	 ``` VDM.preTest(temp > MIN);```
	
	 ``` temp = temp − 1;```
	
	 ``` VDM.invTest(this);```
	
	 ```}```

The getTemp operation

The *getTemp* operation has been implemented as follows:

VDM-SL	Java

getTemp() *currentTemp* : $\mathbb{Z}$
 	
 ext rd *temp* : $\mathbb{Z}$
 	
 pre TRUE
 	
 post *currentTemp* = *temp*
	```public int getTemp()```
	
	 ```{```
	
	 ``` return currentTemp;```
	
	 ```}```

The Java method returns an integer as determined by the VDM-SL operation header. Notice that, while a name is given to the output in the VDM-SL header, no name is associated with the Java return type.

You should be aware that the exception object returned by the assert statement will not, unlike our VDM methods, reveal whether a precondition or an invariant (or a postcondition) has been broken. This must be determined by program inspection.

You can see that, since the precondition is TRUE, there is no need to run a precondition test in the Java method. The postcondition indicates that the value returned by this method must be equal to the temp attribute. When an operation is to send back an output, a **return** statement must be used for this purpose in the associated Java method:

```
return    temp;
```

There is no need to test the invariant here as this method does not write to the state.

In addition to the methods specified in the VDM specification, it is often useful (for testing purposes) to include a method that returns a string representation of the class attributes. A standard way of doing this in Java is to redefine (override) the toString method that all classes inherit from the Object class. The Object class is a *super superclass* from which all Java classes are derived. In this class, such a method will not be that useful as there is only a single attribute (*temp*) and we have already provided read access to this attribute. If we were to define such a method, however, we could do so as follows:

```
public String toString() // this is the standard interface for the toString method
{
    return "temp = " + temp;
}
```

When implementing a VDM specification as a Java class we will always provide a toString method.

4.5   Testing the Java Class

Eventually this class will need to interact with the hardware components of the incubator. Before then the class needs to be tested to ensure the implementation behaves in the way specified (verification), and that the original specification meets the user requirements (validation).

We will provide a tester class with a user interface to allow us to interrogate the system. We do not concern ourselves with the details of this interface. It may be anything from an elaborate graphical user interface to a simple text-based interface. We have provided a simple utility class (EasyIn.class) to simplify text-based input (which can otherwise be cumbersome in Java). A list of all the methods provided in our EasyIn class is given in Table 4.5 and the class itself can be downloaded from the accompanying website.

Table 4.5   The methods of the EasyIn class

`EasyIn` method	Description	Example
`getByte()`	returns a value of type **byte** entered at the keyboard	`byte x = EasyIn.getByte();`
`getShort()`	returns a value of type **short** entered at the keyboard	`short x = EasyIn.getShort();`
`getInt()`	returns a value of type **int** entered at the keyboard	`int x = EasyIn.getInt();`
`getLong()`	returns a value of type **long** entered at the keyboard	`long x = EasyIn.getLong();`
`getFloat()`	returns a value of type **float** entered at the keyboard	`float x = EasyIn.getFloat();`
`getDouble()`	returns a value of type **double** entered at the keyboard	`double x = EasyIn.getDouble();`
`getChar()`	returns a value of type **char** entered at the keyboard	`char x = EasyIn.getChar();`
`getString()`	returns the string entered at the keyboard	`String x = EasyIn.getString();`
`pause(String)`	displays a message on the screen and pauses the program until the <Enter> key is pressed	`EasyIn.pause` `   ("press <Enter>to quit");`

Here is the code for a simple menu-driven tester. Take a look at it and then we will discuss it.

The IncubatorMonitorTester class

```
public class IncubatorMonitorTester
{
public static void main(String[] args)
{
   char choice;
   try // to monitor for invariant violation of initial object
   {
   // generate a new IncubatorMonitor object
   IncubatorMonitor inc = new IncubatorMonitor();
    do
    {
       System.out.println("\n\t\tIncubatorMonitor Tester\n");
       System.out.println("1. Display temperature");
       System.out.println("2. Increment temperature");
       System.out.println("3. Decrement temperature");
       System.out.println("4. Quit");
       System.out.println("Enter choice 1 -4");
       choice = EasyIn.getChar(); // accepts a character entered at the keyboard
```

```
      System.out.println(); // blank line
      try // to monitor for VDMExceptions from menu options
      {
        switch(choice) // process choice
        {
        case '1' : option1(inc); break;
        case '2' : option2(inc); break;
        case '3' : option3(inc); break;
        default : break;
        }
    }
  catch (VDMException e) // to catch invariant and precondition violations
  {
    e.printStackTrace();
  }
 }while(choice !='4');
}
 catch (VDMException e) // if initial object breaks invariant
 {
    System.out.println("Initial object breaks invariant"); // error message
    EasyIn.pause("\nPress <Enter> to quit"); // pause method of EasyIn
 }
}
// test VDM operation implementations
public static void option1(IncubatorMonitor incubatorIn)
{
   System.out.println("Current temperature is: " + incubatorIn.getTemp());
}
public static void option2(IncubatorMonitor incubatorIn)
{
   incubatorIn.increment(); //this method could throw a VDMException
}
public static void option3(IncubatorMonitor incubatorIn)
{
   incubatorIn.decrement(); //this method could throw a VDMException
}
}
```

Most of the above program should be self-explanatory. We draw your attention to only a few points here. First, an object of the class being tested (IncubatorMonitor in this case) needs to be generated by calling the parameterless constructor of the given class:

```
IncubatorMonitor inc = new IncubatorMonitor();
```

This constructor checks the invariant method that has been defined in the IncubatorMonitor class. If the invariant has been broken this constructor does not create an initial object and instead throws a VDMException. We have monitored for this situation in the tester by including the call to the constructor in a **try** block and providing an error handler in a **catch** block:

```
try // to monitor for invariant violation of initial object
{
        IncubatorMonitor inc = new IncubatorMonitor();
        // rest of testing code here
}
catch (VDMException e) // if initial object breaks invariant
{
        System.out.println("Initial object breaks invariant"); // error message
        EasyIn.pause("\nPress <Enter> to quit"); // pause method of EasyIn
}
```

If no exception is thrown then the initial state satisfies the invariant and testing can proceed, otherwise testing cannot really proceed and the error handler displays an appropriate error message

If testing can proceed, the menu processing code calls worker methods that test the various IncubatorMonitor methods. Two of these IncubatorMonitor methods, increment and decrement, may themselves throw a VDMException if their preconditions are violated, or if they break the invariant. Rather than catching these exceptions in the worker methods, we have allowed them to be thrown back up to the main method for handling. Within the main method, the menu processing has been enclosed within another **try ... catch** block, so that all exceptions thrown from these methods are caught in a single **catch** block. We have used the standard printStackTrace method of the exception object to display the cause of the exception on the console:

```
try
{
    switch(choice) // process menu
    {
      case '1' : option1(inc); break;
      case '2' : option2(inc); break;
      case '3' : option3(inc); break;
      default : break;
    }
}
catch(VDMException e) // thrown if the invariant or a precondition is violated
{
    e.printStackTrace(); // built-in exception method
}
```

The entire menu processing code is placed within a loop and testing can continue even after exceptions are thrown from the IncubatorMonitor methods:

```
do
{
    // menu display and processing here
}while(choice != '4');
```

The following output example shows the effect of attempting to increase the temperature beyond the maximum of 10 degrees Celsius:

```
                    Incubator Tester
1. Display temperature
2. Increment temperature
3. Decrement temperature
4. Quit
Enter choice 1-4
2

VDMException: Pre-condition violation
at VDM.preTest(Compiled Code)
at IncubatorMonitor.increment(Compiled Code)
at IncubatorMonitorTester.option2(Compiled Code)
at IncubatorMonitorTester.main(IncubatorMonitorTester.java:24)
```

In this case, an attempt to increase the temperature beyond 10 degrees breaks the precondition of the `increment` method. The `printStackTrace` method in the exception handler provides detailed information about the cause of the error. The first line will provide an error message:

```
VDMException: Pre-condition violation
```

This is the message we have coded into our `preTest` method. The second line will confirm the source of the error:

```
at VDM.preTest(Compiled Code)
```

An attempt to check a precondition failed, in other words a precondition did not hold. The method in which the precondition was tested is listed in the third line:

```
at IncubatorMonitor.increment(Compiled Code)
```

So, the precondition of the increment method was violated. This is as expected as the temperature is already at its maximum, attempting to increase it again will break the precondition. The remaining lines indicate the route the exception object took before being caught.

```
at IncubatorMonitorTester.option2(Compiled Code)
at IncubatorMonitorTester.main(IncubatorMonitorTester.java:24)
```

In a more sophisticated tester we might choose to catch the exceptions in each method as they are thrown, rather than allow them all to be sent up to the main method and caught in a single **catch** block. This would allow us to respond differently to each individual exception rather than have a general approach to handling all exceptions.

Writing specifications is not always as smooth as we have presented in the last chapter. Often, mistakes will creep into the initial specification and the final specification will be arrived at after several iterations. Implementing the specification and testing it in the way we have shown you in this chapter is one way of identifying any mistakes. For example, assume we had specified the precondition of the *increment* operation not as we did originally

pre   *temp* < MAX

but as follows:

pre   *temp* ≤ MAX

This is a very common error to make – you can see that it would in fact allow the temperature to be increased past the maximum allowed and so break the invariant. When implementing this version we used the tester to increment the temperature six times (remember it starts at 5° celsius) and got the following result:

```
VDMException: Invariant violation
   at VDM.invTest(Compiled Code)
   at IncubatorMonitor.increment(Compiled Code)
   at IncubatorMonitorTester.option2(Compiled Code)
   at IncubatorMonitorTester.main(IncubatorMonitorTester.java:24)
```

The stack trace makes clear that the increment method has broken the invariant. A violation of the invariant means either the code or the original specification has an error in it. Inspection of both can help identify the original problem and allows the problem to be fixed.

Since testing can never guarantee the absence of errors, final programs should always monitor for exceptions. This is known as a **defensive programming** strategy. A defensive programming strategy assumes faults may still be left in the final program and tries to manage them should they arise. In this case we have simply displayed a message should the invariant be broken (or the precondition violated). In the final system we may take other forms of action and use defensive programming strategies of **forward** or **backward** recovery. With forward recovery we may move the system into some safe state (such as resetting the temperature back to the initial temperature). With **backward** error recovery we try to undo the damage caused (by dropping the temperature back to the old value for example).

That completes the implementation and testing of the *IncubatorMonitor* specification. Now we turn to the more complex *IncubatorController* specification.

4.6   Implementing the *IncubatorController* Specification

A system that not only monitored but also controlled the temperature of the incubator was specified in Chapter 3. Leaving the operations for a while, here again is the specification:

---

types
Signal = <INCREASE> | <DECREASE> | <DO_NOTHING>
values
      $MAX : \mathbb{Z} = 10$
      $MIN : \mathbb{Z} = -10$
state *IncubatorController* **of**
      requestedTemp : [$\mathbb{Z}$]
      actualTemp : [$\mathbb{Z}$]
inv mk-*IncubatorController* (*r, a*) $\underline{\Delta}$ (*inRange*(*r*) $\vee$ *r* = **nil**) $\wedge$ (*inRange*(*a*) $\vee$ *a* = **nil**)
init mk-*IncubatorController* (*r, a*) $\underline{\Delta}$ *r* = **nil** $\wedge$ *a* = **nil**
end

functions
inRange(*val* : $\mathbb{Z}$) *result* : $\mathbb{B}$
pre   TRUE
post   *result* $\Leftrightarrow$ *MIN* $\leq$ *val* $\leq$ *MAX*

4.6.1   TRANSLATING THE *SIGNAL* TYPE INTO JAVA

This state specification involves a user-defined *Signal* type:

      Signal = <INCREASE> | <DECREASE> | <DO_NOTHING>

As you know, this is an example of a union of three quote types. The union of quote types in VDM-SL corresponds closely to an *enumerated* type in programming languages. Java does not provide a direct mechanism for defining enumerated types. Instead, a class with class constants and a **private** integer value can be declared. Here is an appropriate `Signal` class in Java. Take a look at it and then we will discuss it:

Implementing the *Signal* type in Java

```
class Signal
{
  private int value; // a single private attribute is all that is required
  // class constants representing the named quote values
  public static final Signal INCREASE = new Signal (0);
  public static final Signal DECREASE = new Signal (1);
  public static final Signal DO_NOTHING = new Signal (2);
  // this constructor is declared private and is used by the class constants
  private Signal(int x)
```

```
{
  value = x;
}
// see the discussion below
public boolean equals(Object objectIn)
{
  Signal s = (Signal) objectIn;
  return value == s.value;
}
// a toString method is useful for testing purposes
public String toString()
{
    switch (value)
    {
     case 0: return "INCREASE";
     case 1: return "DECREASE";
     default: return "DO-NOTHING";
    }
  }
}
```

We wish to allow for only three possible values for the Signal type, and these values will represent the three quote values (INCREASE, DECREASE and DO-NOTHING). The way we do this is to have a constructor that sets the value of a private integer attribute. This constructor is declared **private**:

```
class Signal
  {
   private int value; // this value can be set only by the private constructor
   private Signal(int x)
   {
    value = x;
   }
  }
```

Since this constructor is **private**, it can be called only from within this class. We call it when giving values to three class constants:

```
public static final Signal INCREASE = new Signal (0);
public static final Signal DECREASE = new Signal (1);
public static final Signal DO_NOTHING = new Signal (2);
```

The class constants are given names that correspond to the names used in the VDM-SL quote types. Now, wherever these values are needed in that Java program, class constants may be used in their place. When a class constant is to be used it must be preceded with the class name. For example:

VDM-SL	Java
...... $<$INCREASE$>$......	...... Signal.INCREASE ......

When checking one `Signal` object against another, we cannot use the comparison operator (==) from Table 4.3 as this is meant for the comparison of primitive values, not objects. Instead, an `equals` method is often used when comparing two objects in Java. For example, here is how we might translate a precondition that compares two signal objects:

VDM-SL	Java
pre *signalIn* = $<$DECREASE$>$	VDM.preTest(signalIn.equals(Signal.DECREASE));

There is a standard `equals` method that is inherited from the `Object` class. Often, this inherited `equals` method does not behave as would be expected for objects of the class being defined and so should be overridden. Here is the overridden `equals` method in the `Signal` class:

```
public boolean equals(Object objectIn)
{
    Signal s = (Signal) objectIn;
    return value == s.value;
}
```

Notice that the interface for the `equals` method requires that the input parameter be of type `Object`:

```
public boolean equals(Object objectIn)
```

This needs to be type cast back to a `Signal` object:

```
Signal s = (Signal) objectIn;
```

The integer attribute of the `Signal` object is then examined against the hidden integer attribute to determine whether or not the two signals are equal:

```
return value == s.value;
```

As with all classes it is useful to have a meaningful string representation of the `Signal` object, so we have also provided a `toString` method for this class that returns the signal name.

```
public String toString()
{
    switch (value)
    {
        case 0: return "INCREASE";
        case 1: return "DECREASE";
        default: return "DO-NOTHING";
    }
}
```

This will be the standard approach we use to implement types defined as a union of quote types.

4.6.2 TRANSLATING NIL VALUES INTO JAVA

This VDM specification also makes use of the generic **nil** value to represent the notion of an undefined value. In future chapters we will have state attributes that are objects in Java and not values of the primitive types (**int, double** and **char**). The **null** value of Java is one approach to representing the generic **nil** value of VDM-SL in these cases.

When it comes to the primitive types there is no one single value that can be used to represent the **nil** value for all possible variables. Instead, a different value may be required for each variable to represent the **nil** (undefined) value for that variable. The value chosen must not be one that could be an appropriate value for the given variable when defined. In this example, two variables may have **nil** values associated with them, the actual temperature and the requested temperature.

state *IncubatorController* **of**

    requestedTemp : [$\mathbb{Z}$]

    actualTemp : [$\mathbb{Z}$]

Both of these values have maximum and minimum temperatures associated with them, and zero is one of the defined values within this range. So we must choose another value to represent **nil** – the undefined temperature. For example, one possible value could be -999.

Rather than use this value throughout the code, it is useful to name it as a constant. This will be suitable as a **nil** value for both variables so only a single constant need be declared:

```
class IncubatorController implements InvariantCheck

{

    public static final int NIL = -999; // declare a NIL constant

    // more code here

}
```

Here is the complete translation of the state specification. As usual, you should inspect it first and then read the discussion that follows.

```
class IncubatorController implements InvariantCheck
{
    public static final int NIL = -999;
    // declare constants as before
    public static final int MAX = 10;
    public static final int MIN = -10;
    // declare state attributes
    private int requestedTemp;
    private int actualTemp;
    // initialisation satisfied by constructor
    public IncubatorController()
    {
        requestedTemp = NIL;
        actualTemp = NIL;
        VDM.invTest(this); // remember to check invariant
    }
    // invariant
    public boolean inv()
    {
        return (inRange(requestedTemp) || requestedTemp == NIL)
                && (inRange(actualTemp) || actualTemp == NIL);
    }
```

```
// inRange function coded as a private method
private boolean inRange(int val)
{
    return (MIN <= val && val <= MAX);
}
// VDM operations coded here as Java methods
}
```

As you can see, the attributes of the class follow directly from the VDM specification. The constructor is used to deliver an initial system that satisfies the initialization clause. Here the initialization clause has two conjuncts to satisfy, this can be achieved by two assignments:

VDM-SL	Java
$r = \text{nil} \wedge a = \text{nil}$	`requestedTemp = NIL;` `actualTemp = NIL;`

After this pair of assignments both conjuncts of the initialization predicate will be true. Notice how we use the `NIL` constant in the Java code to represent the **nil** value of our VDM specification. Following these instructions the invariant is checked as before.

The invariant itself is translated using the same strategy as before. This time, however, it makes use of an *inRange* function. Functions do not form part of the public interface of the software so we can code this as a **private** Java method.

VDM-SL	Java

inRange (*val* : $\mathbb{Z}$) *result* : $\mathbb{B}$
 	
 pre   TRUE
 	
 post   *result* $\Leftrightarrow$ *MIN* $\leq$ *val* $\leq$ *MAX*
	`private boolean` *inRange*(`int` *val*)
	
	 `{`
	
	   `return` (*MIN* `<=` *val* `&&` *val* `<=` *MAX*)`;`
	
	 `}`

The VDM postcondition indicates the condition (*MIN* $\leq$ *val* $\leq$ *MAX*) that should be logically equivalent to the output (*result*). We can ensure that this is the case by returning the value of this condition.

Turning to the translation of the operation specifications, we look only at the *requestChange* operation. The translation of the remaining operations we leave as an exercise. Here, once again, is the specification of *requestChange*.

$$requestChange(tempIn : \mathbb{Z}) \; signalOut : Signal$$

ext wr $requestedTemp: [\mathbb{Z}]$

  rd $actualTemp : [\mathbb{Z}]$

pre $inRange(tempIn) \wedge actualTemp \neq \textbf{nil}$

post $requestedTemp = tempIn \wedge$

  $(tempIn > actualTemp \wedge signalOut = <\text{INCREASE}>$

  $\vee tempIn < actualTemp \wedge signalOut = <\text{DECREASE}>$

  $\vee tempIn = actualTemp \wedge signalOut = <\text{DO\_NOTHING}>)$

Here is the translation of this operation into Java:

```java
public Signal requestChange(int tempIn)
{
    // check precondition
    VDM.preTest(inRange(tempIn) && actualTemp != NIL);
    // implement the postcondition
    // satisfy first conjunct
    requestedTemp = tempIn;
    // satisfy second conjunct
    // declare and initialize output variable
    Signal signalOut = Signal.DO_NOTHING;
    // set appropriate value for output variable
    if (tempIn > actualTemp)
    {
        signalOut = Signal.INCREASE;
    }
    if (tempIn < actualTemp)
    {
        signalOut = Signal.DECREASE;
    }
    if (tempIn == actualTemp)
    {
        signalOut = Signal.DO_NOTHING;
    }
    VDM.invTest(this); // check invariant before method ends
    // send back output value
    return signalOut;
}
```

The VDM operation has both an input and an output parameter. Notice how use is made of the `Signal` type in the Java method header:

VDM-SL	Java
requestChange(tempIn:ℤ)signalOut:Signal	`public Signal requestChange(int tempIn)`

The precondition of the operation is tested as before by calling our `preTest` method.

VDM-SL	Java
pre *inRange(tempIn)* ∧ *actualTemp* ≠ **nil**	`VDM.preTest(inRange(tempIn)&& actualTemp != NIL);`

The postcondition of this operation is more complex than those we have translated before. There are two parts to this postcondition that we have to satisfy, separated by an AND. The first part is satisfied by a simple assignment.

VDM-SL	Java
requestedTemp = temp	`requestedTemp = tempIn;`

The second part involves a series of disjuncts (ORs) that define valid values of the `Signal` output. An appropriate output variable is declared and initialized:

```
Signal signalOut = Signal.DO_NOTHING; // signal initialised to DO_NOTHING
```

A series of disjuncts can usually be satisfied by a series of **if** statements in the final implementation. Each disjunct will normally have a part that corresponds to the test of the **if** statement and a part that corresponds to the action of the **if** statement. The test will involve old values of variables and/or inputs, and the action will involve new values of variables and/or outputs. In this case the tests relate to the value of the input parameter (*tempIn*) and the action to the value of the output variable (*signalOut*). For example:

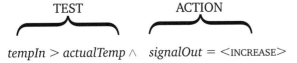

TEST   ACTION

tempIn > actualTemp ∧ *signalOut* = <INCREASE>

This can be satisfied by the following **if** statement in Java

```
if (tempIn > actualTemp)

{

    signalOut = Signal.INCREASE;

}
```

When the test of this **if** statement (tempIn > actualTemp) is TRUE the first conjunct of the VDM-SL expression (*tempIn* > *actualTemp*) is also TRUE. The assignment axiom ensures that when the assignment within the **if** statement (signalOut = Signal.INCREASE;) is executed the second conjunct is also satisfied (*signalOut* = <INCREASE>).

Here is the Java translation of the series of disjuncts as a series of **if** statements:

VDM-SL	Java

(*tempIn* > *actualTemp* ∧
 	
    signalOut = <INCREASE>
	`if (tempIn > actualTemp)`
	`{`
	    `signalOut = Signal.INCREASE;`
	`}`

∨ *tempIn* < *actualTemp* ∧
 	
    signalOut = <DECREASE>
	`if (tempIn < actualTemp)`
	`{`
	    `signalOut = Signal.DECREASE;`
	`}`

∨ *tempIn* = *actualTemp* ∧
 	
    signalOut = <DO_NOTHING>)
	`if (tempIn == actualTemp)`
	`{`
	    `signalOut = Signal.DO_NOTHING;`
	`}`

Notice how we made use of the constants in the Signal class to represent a quote type. For example:

VDM-SL	Java
signalOut = <INCREASE>	`signalOut = Signal.INCREASE`

As this method has write access to the state, it is useful to check that the invariant still holds before returning the output signal with a **return** statement:

```
VDM.invTest(this); // check invariant
return signalOut; // return output
```

That completes the implementation of the *requestChange* operation. One of the exercises you have been set is to proceed with the implementation of the remaining *IncubatorController* operations.

EXERCISES

1. Why is Java a good choice for implementing VDM specifications?
2. What is meant by *lazy evaluation* in Java and why is it important when translating tests from VDM-SL to Java?
3. Explain the invariant preservation integrity check and how this check can be incorporated into Java classes.
4. How would the following union of quote types, specified in VDM-SL, be implemented in Java?

   WeekDay = <MON>|<TUE>|<WED>|<THUR>|<FRI>

5. Complete the implementation of the remaining operations of the *IncubatorController* specification.
6. Test the `IncubatorController` class by developing an appropriate tester program.
7. In Exercise 1 of the previous chapter, you were asked to specify an *isEqual* method for the *IncubatorController* specification. Now add the implementation of this method into your `IncubatorController` class. Then amend the tester you developed, in question 6 above, to test this method.
8. Implement the *land-craft* specification you developed in Exercise 4 of the previous chapter.
9. Test the class of question 8 above by developing an appropriate tester program.

CHAPTER 5

Sets

5.1 Introduction

The data used in the formal specifications that we have considered so far have been modelled by simple types such as numbers and booleans and by enumerated values. However, many systems deal with data *collections*, not just elementary values. To model such data collections, VDM-SL provides a number of collection types. The collection types of a formal specification language will be more abstract than programming collection types such as arrays. This abstractness allows us to write much more concise specifications, as the details of implementation can be omitted. The first collection type of VDM-SL that we will look at is the set type.

5.2 Sets for System Modelling

We have already come across the mathematical concept of a set in Chapter 2. A set is an *unordered* collection of objects in which *repetition is not significant*. So, if we are modelling a collection of objects that are considered unique, and in which ordering is unimportant, the set type is a good candidate. For example, consider a collection of patients registered on the books of a doctor's surgery. A set might be used to model this collection, as patients are considered unique in the register and the ordering of patients in this register will not be relevant. If repetition and ordering are relevant, however, a set may not be an appropriate type to use. For example, a set would not be the appropriate way to model the queue of patients waiting for a doctor, as ordering is important here. Also, a set may not be an appropriate way to model the patients seen by a doctor over a given period, as a patient may have seen a doctor more than once. We will look at suitable VDM-SL types for such scenarios in later chapters.

5.3 Declaring Sets in VDM-SL

To indicate a value to be of the set type in VDM-SL, the type constructor **-set** is appended to the type associated with the *elements* of the set. A **type constructor** creates a new type from an old. For example, consider the following familiar VDM-SL declaration:

aNumber: $\mathbb{N}$

This records the fact that *aNumber* is an item of data that may be used to hold a natural number. To declare an item of data to hold a *collection* of numbers the following declaration can be used:

someNumbers: $\mathbb{N}$-**set**

This records the fact that *someNumbers* is an item of data that will hold zero, one or more natural numbers. If negative whole numbers are to be allowed then the integer type, not the natural number type, is the appropriate base type of the set elements.

someOtherNumbers: $\mathbb{Z}$-**set**

As a further example, assume that a *Day* type has already been defined as follows:

types

$Day = <\text{MON}> \mid <\text{TUE}> \mid <\text{WED}> \mid <\text{THU}> \mid <\text{FRI}> \mid <\text{SAT}> \mid <\text{SUN}>$

We might declare an item of data, *importantDays* say, to hold a collection of days as follows:

importantDays: *Day*-**set**

Once a set has been declared in VDM-SL its values can be defined.

5.4 Defining Sets in VDM-SL

One way in which to define the value of a set is to list the elements individually, separated by commas and enclosed in braces. This is known as **enumerating** the elements of a set. So we could define the values in the sets *someNumbers* and *importantDays* as follows:

someNumbers = *{2, 4, 28, 19, 10}*
importantDays = {$<\text{FRI}>$, $<\text{SAT}>$, $<\text{SUN}>$}

Of course, the ordering of the elements in these sets is unimportant. So the above sets could just as equally be presented as follows:

someNumbers = *{28, 2, 10, 4, 19}*
importantDays = {$<\text{SUN}>$, $<\text{FRI}>$, $<\text{SAT}>$}

Also, as repetition is not significant in sets, the above sets are equivalent to the sets given below:

someNumbers = *{28, 2, 10, 2, 4, 19, 2}*
importantDays = {$<\text{SUN}>$, $<\text{FRI}>$, $<\text{SAT}>$, $<\text{FRI}>$, $<\text{FRI}>$}

However, since repetition is not significant in a set, it is common to list sets without such repetitions.

A second way of defining a set in VDM-SL is to use **subranges**. This method can be used when a set of continuous integers is required. For example:

someRange = {5, ... ,15}

A subrange returns the set of all numbers from the first to the last number inclusive. So this subrange is equivalent to the following enumerated set definition:

someRange = {*5, 6, 7, 8, 9, 10, 11, 12, 13, 14, 15*}

When the second number in the range is smaller than the first, the empty set is returned. The empty set is represented in VDM-SL as an empty pair of braces.[1] For example:

{*7, ... ,6*} = { }

The third and most powerful way to define a set is by **comprehension**. This allows a set to be defined by means of an expression and/or a test that each element in the set must satisfy. Here is an example (assuming the existence of an *isEven* function for determining whether or not a number is even):

someNumbers = {*x* | *x* ∈ {*2, ... ,6*} • *isEven*(*x*)}

This produces a set of all elements that are drawn from the set {2, ...,6} and are also even numbers. In other words it produces the set {2, 4, 6}.

In general, set comprehension takes the following form:

someSet = {*expression* (*x*) | *binding* (*x*) • *test*(*x*)}

Here the bar | is read 'such that'. The binding and the test to the right of this bar determine acceptable values for the free variable (*x* in this case). The bullet (•) separates the binding from the test. This free variable is then used in the expression to the left of the bar to determine the final value of elements in the new set. The expression can be extremely simple, as in the *someNumbers* example where the expression was the bound variable itself. Here is an example that employs a slightly more complex expression:

someOtherNumbers = {x^2 | *x* ∈ {*2, ... ,6*}}

In this case the expression squares the value of the bound variable. In a case such as this, where the binding has no associated test, the test is assumed to evaluate to TRUE for all values of the bound variable. So in this case, all numbers from 2 to 6 are squared, producing the following set:

$$someOtherNumbers = \{2^2, 3^2, 4^2, 5^2, 6^2\}$$

$$= \{4, 9, 16, 25, 36\}$$

Finally, note that a type can be used in the binding instead of a set. When using a type the 'is of type' symbol (:) is to be used rather than the 'is an element of' symbol used on sets (∈). Here is an example of the use of a type binding.

smallNumbers = {*x* | *x*: ℕ • 1 ≤ *x* ≤ 10}

This set comprehension produces a set of all natural numbers that lie within the range 1–10.

---

1 In maths texts that cover standard set theory, the symbol Ø will usually be used to represent an empty set.

5.4.1 FINITE AND INFINITE SETS IN VDM-SL

All of the sets defined above are **finite sets** – they contain a clearly defined number of elements. However, sets such as the set of all integers or the set of all real numbers have an infinite number of elements and so are described as **infinite sets**. Eventually, sets defined in specifications need to be implemented on a machine. As infinite sets are impossible to implement on a machine, a requirement on sets used in VDM-SL is that they be finite. This is not such an issue when defining sets using enumeration (or subranges) as listing the elements individually clearly implies the sets are finite. However, it is important to ensure sets are finite when defining them using comprehension. Consider the following set for example:

$$infiniteSet = \{x \mid x: \mathbb{Z} \bullet x < 0\}$$

This defines a set of all negative integers and as such is an infinite set that is not permissible in VDM-SL.

5.5   Set Operations

In this section we will explore the various operations that we can perform on one or more sets.

5.5.1 SET UNION, INTERSECTION AND DIFFERENCE

There are three set operators that take two sets from which one new set is returned. They are set **union**, set **intersection** and set **difference**. In each case, the types of elements in each set are assumed to be the same.

The **union** of two sets, j and k returns a set that contains all the elements of the set j *and* all the elements of the set k. It is denoted by:

$$j \cup k$$

This is read as j *union* k. For example:

if $j = \{<\text{MON}>, <\text{TUE}>, <\text{WED}>, <\text{SUN}>\}$
and $k = \{<\text{MON}>, <\text{FRI}>, <\text{TUE}>\}$
then $j \cup k = \{<\text{MON}>, <\text{TUE}>, <\text{WED}>, <\text{SUN}>, <\text{FRI}>\}$

Notice that the union operator returns a result *whether or not* the two sets have common elements. If, as in this case, the two sets do have common elements, then it is usual to list the element only once in the union of the two sets – as explained in section 5.4, to list them more than once would be redundant. So, for example, $<\text{MON}>$ and $<\text{TUE}>$ appear in both the sets j and k. They are listed only once in the resulting union of the two sets, however.

The next operator to consider is **intersection**. The intersection of two sets j and k returns a set that contains all the elements that are common to both j and k. It is denoted by:

$$j \cap k$$

This is read *j intersection k*. For example:

if $j = \{<\text{MON}>, <\text{TUE}>, <\text{WED}>, <\text{SUN}>\}$
and $k = \{<\text{MON}>, <\text{FRI}>, <\text{TUE}>\}$
then $j \cap k = \{<\text{MON}>, <\text{TUE}>\}$

The **difference** of *j* and *k* is the set that contains all the elements that belong to *j* but do not belong to *k*. It is denoted by:

$j \setminus k$

This is read *j difference k*. For example:

if $j = \{<\text{MON}>, <\text{TUE}>, <\text{WED}>, <\text{SUN}>\}$
and $k = \{<\text{MON}>, <\text{FRI}>, <\text{TUE}>\}$
then $j \setminus k = \{<\text{WED}>, <\text{SUN}>\}$

As with set union and set intersection, set difference requires two *sets*. It would not be correct to use the following notation:

$\{<\text{MON}>, <\text{TUE}>, <\text{WED}>\} \setminus <\text{TUE}>$

Here, the second operand of the set difference operator is given as an element, $<\text{TUE}>$, when it should be a set. The correct way to formulate this expression would be to make this element into a set containing just that element:

$\{<\text{MON}>, <\text{TUE}>, <\text{WED}>\} \setminus \{<\text{TUE}>\}$

A set containing just a single element is referred to as a **singleton** set.

Note that set union and set intersection are what is known as **commutative** operators. A commutative operator returns the same result regardless of the order of the parameters. For example, in arithmetic, the addition operator is commutative i.e.

$x + y = y + x$

In a similar way, set union and set intersection return the same result regardless of the order of the two parameters:

$j \cup k = k \cup j$
$j \cap k = k \cap j$

However, set difference is not commutative: the order of the parameters is significant to the result. In general:

$j \setminus k \neq k \setminus j$

This is clear from the values of *j* and *k* given earlier where:

$j = \{<\text{MON}>, <\text{TUE}>, <\text{WED}>, <\text{SUN}>\}$
$k = \{<\text{MON}>, <\text{FRI}>, <\text{TUE}>\}$

Given these values it can be seen that $j \setminus k$ gives

{<WED>, <SUN>}

Whereas $k \setminus j$ gives:

{<FRI>}

5.5.2 SUBSETS

In Chapter 2 we met two set operators that return boolean results, that is set membership ($\in$) and set non-membership ($\notin$). These operators check whether or not a particular *element* is present in a particular set. Another set operator that returns a boolean result is the **subset** operator ($\subseteq$). Unlike the set membership operators, this operator takes *two* sets. It returns TRUE if *all* the elements in the first set are also elements of the second set and FALSE otherwise. So the following evaluates to TRUE:[2]

$\{a, d, e\} \subseteq \{a, b, c, d, e, f\}$

The following, however, evaluates to FALSE:

$\{a, b, c, d, e, f\} \subseteq \{a, d, e\}$

as some elements of the first set (namely b, c and f) are not elements of the second set. The subset operator also returns TRUE if both sets are *equal* (that is, share exactly the same elements). Thus the following evaluates to TRUE:

$\{a, d, e\} \subseteq \{d, a, e\}$

If you wish to exclude this possibility then the **proper subset** operator can be used ($\subset$). Thus, although the following evaluates to TRUE:

$\{a, d, e\} \subset \{a, b, c, d, e, f\}$

the following evaluates to FALSE:

$\{a, d, e\} \subset \{d, a, e\}$

Striking a line through the subset operators reverses the logic so that the operator returns TRUE when one set is *not* a subset of another. Thus the following evaluates to TRUE:

$\{a, d, e\} \not\subseteq \{a, x, y, k\}$

---

2   In the example given, and throughout this text, we are using italics for variable names.

5.5.3 CARDINALITY

The cardinality operator of VDM-SL (**card**) returns the number of elements in a given set. Here are some examples:

> **card** {7, 2, 12} = 3
> **card** {4, ... ,10} = 7
> **card** { } = 0

Note that, as repetition is not significant in sets, repeated elements are counted only once when calculating the cardinality. For example

> **card** {7, 2, 12, 2, 2} = **card** {7, 2, 12} = 3

5.6 The Patient Register

To illustrate the use of sets in a formal specification we will consider a system that registers patients at a doctor's surgery. We will assume that the surgery can deal with a maximum of 200 patients on its register. It will be necessary to add and remove patients from the register. As well as this, the register must be able to be interrogated so that the list of patients and the number of patients registered can be returned. Also, a check can be made to see if a given patient is registered. The UML diagram for the *PatientRegister* class is given in Figure 5.1.

Here we have used the UML collection syntax ([*]), to indicate a collection of values. For example, the type of the *reg* attribute is not a single patient but a collection of zero or more patients.

reg: Patient [*]

Similarly, the *getPatients* operation does not return a single patient but many (zero or more) patients:

getPatients( ): Patient [*]

PatientRegister
reg: Patient [*]
addPatient(Patient) *removePatient(Patient)* *getPatients( ): Patient[*]* *isRegistered (Patient): Boolean* *numberRegistered():Integer*

Figure 5.1   The UML specification of the *PatientRegister* class

None of the methods of the *PatientRegister* class requires us to interrogate the details of a patient, so the *Patient* type itself does not need to be analysed further.

Having clarified the nature of the system we can now specify it formally in VDM-SL.

5.7   Modelling the *PatientRegister* Class in VDM-SL

Clearly the class centres around recording of information about a collection of patients. You can see from Figure 5.1 that we have identified a *Patient* type but that it was decided that it was not necessary to analyse this type further. Types whose internal details are not relevant to the specification can be declared to be TOKEN types in VDM as follows:

---

types

  Patient = TOKEN

The number of patients that can be registered at the surgery is said to be limited to 200. This can be recorded as a constant value in our specification:

---

values

  LIMIT: $\mathbb{N}$ = 200

Returning to the single attribute, *reg*, we have already seen that in UML this has been specified to be a collection of patients. Since ordering of patients on the register is not significant, and since patients are considered unique in the register, a set is a good way to model this collection formally:

---

state *PatientRegister* **of**

  reg: *Patient*-**set**

As we have seen, a restriction on this model is that the number of patients in the register can never exceed the limit of 200. The cardinality operator can be used to express this constraint in the invariant.

---

inv mk-*PatientRegister* (*r*) $\underline{\Delta}$ **card** *r* $\leq$ *LIMIT*

Initially, the register will be empty:

---

init mk-*PatientRegister* (*r*) $\underline{\Delta}$ *r* = { }

Here is the complete state definition.

---

types

  Patient = TOKEN

values

  LIMIT: $\mathbb{N}$ = 200

state *PatientRegister* **of**

  reg: *Patient*-**set**

 inv mk-*PatientRegister* (*r*) $\underline{\Delta}$ **card** *r* ≤ *LIMIT*

 init mk-*PatientRegister* (*r*) $\underline{\Delta}$ *r* = { }

end

Now for the operation specifications. We will start by considering the *addPatient* operation. Here is its interface from the UML specification:

addPatient(Patient)

You can see that this operation takes one input (of type *Patient*) and does not return a value. Remembering to give a name to the input variable, this gives us the following VDM operation header:

---

addPatient (patientIn: Patient)

Since this operation will modify the list, the state attribute needs to be given read and write access.

---

ext wr *reg*: *Patient*-**set**

We will consider the postcondition before returning to think about the pre-condition. The postcondition has to capture the fact that the given patient is now recorded within the register. Set union allows us to capture the notion of adding to the register:

---

post $reg = \overline{reg} \cup \{patientIn\}$

Note the need to enclose the element *patientIn* in braces in order to make it a set. It is often useful to reconsider the **ext** clause once the postcondition is completed, to ensure state access has been specified correctly. In this case the postcondition makes clear that the *reg* attribute will be modified, so **wr** access was the correct type of access to choose.

Now consider any restrictions that might need to be placed on this operation. These restrictions will be recorded in the precondition. There are two restrictions that are worth recording. It is sensible to record a patient in the register only if that patient has not yet been recorded. This has nothing to do with the use of the union operator in the postcondition, as the union operator allows two sets with common elements to be joined. However, it is a real-world consideration that is worth recording. Second, in order to preserve the invariant, we should ensure the register is not full before an extra patient is recorded. This gives us the following precondition:

---

pre $patientIn \notin reg \wedge$ **card** $reg < LIMIT$

The complete specification for this operation is presented below:

---

addPatient (*patientIn*: *Patient*)

ext wr *reg*: *Patient*-**set**

pre $patientIn \notin reg \wedge$ **card** $reg < LIMIT$

post $reg = \overline{reg} \cup \{patientIn\}$

The *removePatient* operation is structurally the same as the *addPatient* operation, except its logic is reversed. The patient should have been registered before her record can be removed, and once complete the new register will be the same as the old but for the fact that the given record has been *removed*. The set difference operator can be used:

---

removePatient (*patientIn*: *Patient*)

ext wr *reg*: *Patient*-**set**

pre $patientIn \in reg$

post $reg = \overline{reg} \setminus \{patientIn\}$

It is worth noting how concise this specification is when compared to the complex algorithm that might be required in software to remove a patient's record from a store of information. This abstractness captures the essence of the operation, namely that all occurrences of the given patient are removed from the register, without having to deal with the complexities of the implementation.

We now turn our attention to the *getPatients* operation. Here again is the operation's interface from the UML specification:

getPatients( ): Patient[*]

This operation has no inputs but returns a collection of patient records as an output. Again, since records in this collection are unique and ordering of this collection is unimportant, the result can be modelled as a set of patient records. This operation need only read access to the register, giving the following VDM specification:

---

getPatients ( ) *output*: *Patient*-**set**

ext rd *reg*: *Patient*-**set**

pre   TRUE

post   *output = reg*

The *isRegistered* operation checks whether or not a given patient record is included in the register:

---

isRegistered (*patientIn*: *Patient*) *query*: $\mathbb{B}$

ext rd *reg*: *Patient*-**set**

pre   TRUE

post   *query* $\Leftrightarrow$ *patientIn* $\in$ *reg*

Finally, the *numberRegistered* operation returns the number of patients currently registered at the surgery. The UML specification for the operation interface indicates the return value is to be of type integer.

numberRegistered( ):Integer

In fact, the number registered will never be a negative number so the natural number type is the better choice in our specification. The number of patients registered can be retrieved by using the cardinality operator:

---

numberRegistered ( ) *total*: $\mathbb{N}$

ext rd *reg*: *Patient*-**set**

pre   TRUE

post   *total* = **card** *reg*

That completes the formal specification of the *PatientRegister* class. You can see that the set type and its associated operators provide us with a powerful mechanism for modelling system properties in a very concise way when dealing with collections of objects.

5.8   The *Airport* Class

We now turn our attention to a slightly more complex example of specification using sets. Consider a system that keeps track of aircraft that are allowed to land at a particular airport. Aircraft must apply for permission to land at the airport prior to landing. When an aircraft arrives to land at the airport it should only have done so if it had previously been given permission. When an aircraft leaves the airport its permission to land is also removed.

Aspects of this system description are oversimplified, but this will be improved upon in Chapter 7 when we have more data types available. From this description the following operations have been identified.

givePermission: records the fact that an aircraft has been granted permission to land at the airport.
recordLanding: records an aircraft as having landed at the airport.
recordTakeOff: records an aircraft as having taken off from the airport.
getPermission: returns the aircrafts currently recorded as having permission to land
getLanded: returns the aircrafts currently recorded as having landed
numberWaiting: returns the number of aircrafts granted permission to land but not yet landed.

Figure 5.2 shows the UML specification for the *Airport* class.

The internal details of the *Aircraft* type are not relevant to the *Airport* specification, so it is not analysed further. In the VDM specification of the *Airport* class, this *Aircraft* type can therefore be represented as a TOKEN type:

---

types

$\qquad$ *Aircraft* = TOKEN

The UML specification of Figure 5.2 indicated that two attributes are required and that both attributes are a collection of aircraft records. Since each aircraft record is unique, and ordering of records in either collection is not important here, sets of aircraft records can be used to model these collections in VDM-SL:

---

state *Airport* **of**

$\qquad$ *permission*: *Aircraft* **-set**

$\qquad$ *landed*: *Aircraft* **-set**

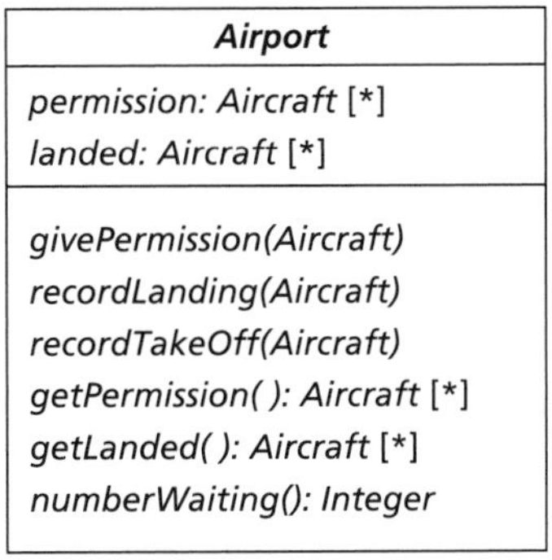

Figure 5.2   A UML specification of the *Airport* class

Now consider the state invariant. Only aircraft with permission can have landed. The subset operator allows us to express the fact that all landed aircraft must also be aircraft with permission:

inv mk-*Airport(p,l)* $\underline{\Delta}$ $l \subseteq p$

Notice that the proper subset operator ($\subset$) is not the appropriate one to use here, since all aircraft with permission to land might actually have landed; in other words the two sets of aircraft might be equal. Finally, consider the initial values of these attributes. No aircraft will have been given permission to land or will have landed so both sets should initially be empty:

init mk-*Airport* (p, l) $\underline{\Delta}$ $p = \{\;\} \wedge l = \{\;\}$

Here is the complete data specification.

types
      Aircraft = TOKEN
state *Airport* **of**
      permission: *Aircraft*-**set**
      landed: *Aircraft* -**set**
      inv   mk-*Airport(p,l)* $\underline{\Delta}$ $l \subseteq p$
      init   mk-*Airport* (p, l) $\underline{\Delta}$ $p = \{\;\} \wedge l = \{\;\}$
end

Now we can turn to the operation specifications. Here is the *givePermission* operation:

---

givePermission (*craftIn*: *Aircraft*)

ext wr *permission*: *Aircraft* **-set**

pre   *craftIn* $\notin$ *permission*

post   *permission* $= \overline{permission} \cup \{craftIn\}$

The precondition records the requirement that, before the operation, the given aircraft should not already have permission to land. The postcondition records the requirement that, after the operation, the given aircraft should be recorded in the set of aircraft given permission to land.

Next we will specify the *recordLanding* operation. This operation needs to modify the *landed* attribute, but it also needs to ensure that the landed aircraft had permission to do so – consequently it will need to read the set of aircraft with permission to land:

---

recordLanding (*craftIn*: *Aircraft*)

ext rd *permission*: *Aircraft* **-set**

     wr *landed*: *Aircraft* **-set**

pre   *craftIn* $\in$ *permission* $\wedge$ *craftIn* $\notin$ *landed*

post   *landed* $= \overline{landed} \cup \{craftIn\}$

The precondition records the restriction that the given aircraft needs to have been allocated permission to land and should not already be recorded as having landed. The postcondition records the modification that should have occurred to the set of landed aircraft upon completion.

Notice that if we did not record the precondition that the given aircraft already be recorded in the *permission* set, it is possible that the state invariant (which requires all landed aircraft be in the set *permission*) may be broken upon completion of this operation. Checking that operations preserve the state invariant often proves useful in spotting specification errors.

The *recordTakeOff* operation removes an aircraft record from the *landed* set and also removes the record from the *permission* set. So both attributes require write access. A precondition is required to ensure that the aircraft was previously recorded as having landed at the airport. Here is its specification:

---

recordTakeOff (*craftIn*: *Aircraft*)

ext wr *permission*: *Aircraft* **-set**

    wr *landed*: *Aircraft* **-set**

pre   *craftIn* $\in$ *landed*

post   *landed* = $\overleftarrow{landed} \setminus \{craftIn\} \wedge permission = \overleftarrow{permission} \setminus \{craftIn\}$

The *getPermission* operation returns the value of the *permission* attribute:

---

getLanded ( ) *out*: *Aircraft* **-set**

ext rd *permission*: *Aircraft* **-set**

pre   TRUE

post   *out* = *permission*

Similarly, the *getLanded* operation returns the value of the *landed* attribute:

---

getLanded( ) *out*: *Aircraft* **-set**

ext rd *landed*: *Aircraft* **-set**

pre   TRUE

post   *out* = *landed*

The final operation to look at is *numberWaiting*. The cardinality operator is used to count the number of aircraft that have been given permission to land but not yet landed:

---

numberWaiting( ) *total*: $\mathbb{N}$

ext rd *permission*: *Aircraft* **-set**

    rd *landed*: *Aircraft* **-set**

post   *total* = **card** (*permission* $\setminus$ *landed*)

This completes the *Airport* specification.

1. Consider the following sets:
   $a = \{1, 3, 5, 2\}$ $b = \{3, 2\}$ $c = \{5, 3, 7, 9\}$ $d = \{2, 3\}$
   Now evaluate the following expressions

   (i) $a \cup b$
   (ii) $a \cup \{\}$
   (iii) **card** $(b \cup c)$
   (iv) $c \cap d$
   (v) $\{\} \cap d$
   (vi) $c \setminus d$
   (vii) $c \setminus \{\}$
   (viii) $b \subset d$
   (ix) $a \subseteq b$
   (x) $b \subseteq a$
   (xi) $\{2x \mid x \in a \bullet x > 2\}$
   (xii) $\{\textbf{card } b, \dots, \textbf{card } c\}$

2. How would specification of the *Airport* system change if there were to be a limit (say 20) to the number of aircraft that could be landed at any one time?

3. Consider a system to monitor ambulances allocated to a hospital. All ambulances will either be at the hospital base or on call. The hospital can be responsible for a maximum of 25 ambulances. Figure 5.3 gives the UML specification of an *AmbulanceMonitor* class that tracks the location of ambulances.

   It is not necessary to analyse the details of the *Ambulance* type further. The operations identified are informally specified as follows:

addAmbulance: records an additional ambulance at the hospital base as long as there is capacity to do so.
removeAmbulance: removes an ambulance from the list of recorded ambulances as long as that ambulance is not out on call.
sendOnCall: records an ambulance, which should currently be recorded as being at the hospital base, as being sent out on a call.

AmbulanceMonitor
atBase: Ambulance[*]
onCall: Ambulance [*]
addAmbulance(Ambulance)
removeAmbulance(Ambulance)
sendOnCall(Ambulance)
backToBase(Ambulance)
getAtBase( ): Ambulance [*]
getOnCall( ): Ambulance [*]
ambulanceAvailable( ): Boolean
totalNumber( ):Integer

Figure 5.3   The UML specification for the *AmbulanceMonitor* class

backToBase: records an ambulance, which should currently be recorded as being out on call, returning back to the hospital base.

getAtBase: returns the ambulances currently recorded as being at the base.

getOnCall: returns the ambulances currently recorded as being out on call.

ambulanceAvailable: checks whether or not there are any ambulances at base to send out to a call.

totalNumber: returns the total number of ambulances.

Formally specify the *AmbulanceMonitor* class in VDM-SL.

CHAPTER 6

Implementing Sets

6.1 Introduction

We saw in Chapter 4 that the simple types of VDM-SL all have a representation in Java. Although the collection types available in Java are a fair approximation to the collection types available in VDM-SL, they do not completely model the VDM types. If these Java types were directly used in the final implementation then the differences between them and the VDM types would need to be borne in mind. The approach that we take in this book, however, is to provide our own Java classes that completely model the VDM-SL collection types. Our Java classes will make extensive use of the predefined collection classes already available in Java, but customize them so that all operators available in the corresponding VDM types are made available.

In this chapter we describe the `VDMSet` class that we have implemented to model the VDM-SL set type. This class can be downloaded from the website. We go on to use this class to develop Java implementations of the VDM specifications from Chapter 5.

6.2 The Collection Classes of Java

Java provides a large group of predefined collection classes known as the **collection framework.** These classes are found in the **`java.util`** package. The collection class we shall adopt for implementing the VDM-SL set type will be the `Vector` class.

6.2.1 THE `Vector` CLASS

A vector is an indexed collection of items. Like all of Java's collections, a vector is a **generic** collection class – meaning that it can be used to hold objects of any class. This is achieved by treating all elements in the collection as being of type `Object`. Since all classes in Java inherit from the `Object` class this allows objects of any type to be placed into the collection. Table 6.1 lists some of the more common methods available with the `Vector` class.

Elements in a vector need not be unique and the vector grows as more elements are added to it. Here is an example of a collection of strings being added to a vector and

Table 6.1 Some *Vector* methods

Method	Description
`Vector( )`	Creates a new empty vector.
`boolean add (object)`	Adds the given item to the end of the vector. This method always returns **true**.[1]
`boolean contains(Object)`	Returns **true** if the vector contains the given element, and **false** otherwise.
`Enumeration elements( )`	Returns an `Enumeration`[2] object that allows the values of a vector to be scanned.

then displayed:

```
// create empty vector
Vector someList = new Vector();
// add items
someList.add("RED");
someList.add("GREEN");
someList.add("YELLOW");
someList.add("GREEN");
// display vector
System.out.println(someList);
```

When these instructions are executed within a Java program the following vector is displayed:

[*RED, GREEN, YELLOW, GREEN*]

A vector can be displayed because it, like all collection classes in Java, has a `toString` method defined. In Java, a vector is displayed in square brackets. Although vectors can be used to hold *objects* of any type, they cannot hold values of primitive types such as **int** and **double**. Instead, wrapper classes such as `Integer` and `Double` must be used to wrap primitive values inside an object before placing into the collection. For example:

```
// create empty vector
Vector someNumbers = new Vector();
// add primitive integers by wrapping up in Integer objects
someList.add(new Integer(3));
```

---

1 The `add` methods of other collection classes return a **boolean** value to indicate whether or not an element was added successfully to the collection. To be consistent with these add methods, the `Vector add` method also returns a **boolean** value, but because an item can always be added into a vector the value returned is always **true**.

2 `Enumeration` objects provide a standard way of scanning the elements of a collection. Such objects provide two methods for this purpose: `hasMoreElements` (which returns true if there are more elements to scan) and `nextElement` (which returns the next element in the collection to process).

```
someList.add(new Integer(11));

someList.add(new Integer(9));

// display vector

System.out.println(someList);
```

This displays the following vector:

$[3, 11, 9]$

6.3   Using a Vector to Implement a Set

We have developed a class, VDMSet,[3] which models the VDM-SL set type. The single attribute of this class is a vector to hold the elements of the set:

```
import java.util.*;
class VDMSet

{

      private Vector theSet;
      // methods go here

}
```

This is a **private** attribute so is kept hidden, but we list it here for your information. If a set had been declared in a VDM specification, it can be declared as an object
of our VDMSet class in Java. For example:

VDM-SL	Java
someSet: *SomeType*-*set*	`VDMSet someSet;`

The methods of our VDMSet class allow for a set to be initialized in various ways (as
an empty set, by means of a range and so on) and to be examined by the set operators
(such as set union, set intersection and so on). We will discuss the use of these
methods in the following sections. They have been implemented to ensure that
repetition of elements is not significant in the set.

---

3   We have called our class VDMSet rather than Set as a class called Set has recently been added
    to newer versions of Java. The new Java Set class, however, is not a complete model of the VDM-
    SL set type, so we still need to develop our own class for this purpose.

6.3.1 THE CONSTRUCTORS

A number of constructors are provided to allow for a set to be initialized as empty or with a collection of values. They are summarized in Table 6.2. Table 6.3 provides examples of how these constructors are used.

We draw your attention to the use of the set constructor that creates a set from an array of elements sent as a parameter. The parameter to this constructor is overloaded to accept an array of primitive values as well as an array of objects. For example, an

Table 6.2 VDMSet constructors

Constructor	Description
VDMSet()	Empty set constructor.
VDMSet(Object[])	Explicit set constructor – creates a new set from an array of objects passed as a parameter. Overloaded for an array of primitive types (int, char and double). Repeated array elements are stored only once in the resulting set.
VDMSet(Object)	Singleton set constructor – creates a new set containing the single object passed in as a parameter. Overloaded for the primitive types int, char and double.
VDMSet (int, int)	Set range constructor – creates a new set of integers ranging from the first to the second integer parameter inclusive. As with the VDM-SL range operator, if the first range value is greater than the second an empty set is returned.

Table 6.3 VDMSet constructors – examples

VDM-SL example	Java example
Empty set constructor	
someSet = {}	someSet = new VDMSet();
Explicit set constructors	
someSet = {"RED", "BLUE"}	someSet = new VDMSet (new Object[] {"RED", "BLUE"});
someSet = {12, 9, 17]	someSet = new VDMSet (new int[] {12, 9, 17});
someSet = {5.5, 12.75, 0.75}	someSet = new VDMSet (new double[] {5.5, 12.75, 0.75});
someSet = {'A', 'B', 'C'}	someSet = new VDMSet (new char[] {'A', 'B', 'C'});
Singleton set constructors	
someSet = {"RED"}	someSet = new VDMSet("RED");
someSet = {12}	someSet = new VDMSet(12);
someSet = [12.75]	someSet = new VDMSet(12.75);
someSet = {'B'}	someSet = new VDMSet('B');
Set range constructor	
someSet = {1, ... , 10}	someSet = new VDMSet (1, 10};

array of integers is appropriate to create the set {12, 9, 17}. An **anonymous array**[4] is a convenient way of submitting this parameter:

```
new VDMSet (new int[] {12, 9, 17})
```

Note that the ordering of the elements within the array is irrelevant and any repeated elements in the array are recorded only once in the set.

6.3.2 THE SET OPERATORS

We have provided methods for all the set operators within the VDMSet class. These are summarized in Table 6.4. Table 6.5 provides examples of the use of these operators.

Table 6.4   VDMSet operators

Method	Description
int card()	Returns the cardinality of the set.
boolean contains(Object)	Returns **true** if the given object is a member of the set and **false** otherwise. This method is overloaded to accept a parameter of type int, double or char.
boolean doesNotContain(Object)	Returns **true** if the given object is not a member of the set and **false** otherwise. This method is overloaded to accept a parameter of type int, double or char.
VDMSet union(VDMSet)	Returns a VDMSet constructed from the union of the set and the set passed in as a parameter.
VDMSet intersection(VDMSet)	Returns a VDMSet constructed from the intersection of the set and the set passed in as a parameter.
VDMSet difference(VDMSet)	Returns a VDMSet constructed from the difference of the set and the set passed in as a parameter.
boolean isASubsetOf(VDMSet)	Returns **true** if the set is a subset of the set passed in as a parameter and **false** otherwise.
boolean isNotASubsetOf(VDMSet)	Returns **true** if the set is not a subset of the set passed in as a parameter and **false** otherwise.
boolean isAProperSubsetOf(VDMSet)	Returns **true** if the set is a proper subset of the set passed in as a parameter and **false** otherwise.
boolean isNotAProperSubsetOf (VDMSet)	Returns **true** if the set is not a proper subset of the set passed in as a parameter and **false** otherwise.

4   An anonymous array is one that is not assigned to a variable but is created and initialized in one line. If you are not already familiar with anonymous arrays you can find a more detailed overview in the appendix on the accompanying website.

Table 6.5   VDMSet operators – examples

VDM-SL	Java
card someSet	`someSet.card();`
i ∈ someSet	`someSet.contains(i);`
i ∉ someSet	`someSet.doesNotContain(i);`
setA ∩ setB	`setA.intersection(setB);`
setA ∩ {1,2}	`setA.intersection(new VDMSet (int[]` `{1,2}));`
setA ∪ setB	`setA.union(setB);`
setA ∪ {'C'}	`setA.union(new VDMSet ('C'));`
setA \ setB	`setA.difference(setB);`
setA \ {10, …,50}	`setA.difference(new VDMSet(10,50));`
setA ⊆ setB	`setA.isASubsetOf(setB);`
setA ⊄ setB	`setA.isNotASubsetOf(setB);`
setA ⊂ setB	`setA.isAProperSubsetOf(setB);`
setA ⊄ setB	`setA.isNotAProperSubsetOf(setB);`

Additional methods have been provided in order to simplify the process of testing and implementation. These are shown in Table 6.6.

Table 6.6   Additional VDMSet operators

VDMSet method	Description
`Object choice ( )`	Returns an arbitrary element from the set. If the set is empty, throws a `VDMException`.
`boolean equals(Object)`	Accepts an object, and returns **true** if this object is identical to the original set, otherwise returns **false**.
`String toString()`	Returns a string representation of the set.
`Enumeration getElements()`	Returns an enumeration object to allow the elements of the set to be scanned.
`boolean isEmpty()`	Returns **true** if the set is empty, otherwise returns **false**.

6.3.3 SET COMPREHENSION

Set comprehension allows a set to be defined by filtering the elements of some other set by means of a test and/or an expression.[5] We have provided a **class**

---

5   You will remember from Chapter 5 that VDM-SL allows types as well as sets to be used in set comprehension. Our set comprehension method cannot be used with types, it must always be used with a set. If a type is used in VDM-SL, you must replace it with a set of values in Java.

method, `setComp`, for this purpose. The general form of this method is given as follows:

```
someSet = VDMSet.setComp (Expression e, VDMSet other, Testable t);
```

Overloaded forms of this method allow either the expression or the test to be omitted. We have defined two interfaces for this purpose: `Testable` and `Expression`. The `Testable` interface ensures an implementation is provided for a `test` method. This method checks the value of an object to determine whether or not it should be added into the set:

```
interface Testable
{
        public boolean test (Object x);
}
```

The `Expression` interface ensures an implementation is provided for an `action` method. This method applies some function to an object before it is added into the set:

```
interface Expression
{
        public Object action (Object x);
}
```

These interfaces assume a set of *objects* is being filtered. Alternative interfaces exist for tests and expressions dealing with the primitive parameter types. These interface names end in the type name. `ExpressionInt` and `TestableInt`, for instance, allow expressions and tests to be created that process integer values rather than objects. The set comprehension method has been overloaded to allow parameters of these types to be passed. Here is an example of the use of set comprehension to initialize a set of integers by means of a test:

VDM-SL	Java

someSet = $\{ x \mid x \in \{2, 4, 7, 1, 11\} \bullet x > 5 \}$	`someSet = VDMSet.setComp(`
	`    new VDMSet(new int[]{2,4,7,1,11}),`
	`    new TestableInt(){`
	`     public boolean test (int x)`
	`      {return x > 5;}`
	`    } );`

Notice how an object from an **anonymous class**[6] is used to send a `TestableInt` object to this method. This anonymous class implements the `TestableInt` interface by providing a `test` method that accepts an integer and returns a boolean value:

```
new TestableInt()
{
        public boolean test (int x)
        {
                return x > 5;
        }
}
```

Our `setComp` method iterates through the given set (`new VDMSet(new int[] {2,4,7,1,11})`) and applies the test (x > 5) to all elements in the set. Those elements that satisfy the test are included in the new set, giving a final set as follows:

{7, 11}

Here is an example of a set comprehension that uses an expression rather than a test:

VDM-SL	Java
someSet = { 2 x | x ∈ {2, 4, 7, 1, 11} }	someSet = VDMSet.setComp(new ExpressionInt() { public Object action (int x) {return new Integer (2*x);}}, new VDMSet(new int[]{2,4,7,1,11}));

This set comprehension doubles the value of every element in the original set, giving a new set with the following value:

{4, 8, 14, 2, 22}

Notice that the `ExpressionInt` interface requires that the `action` method still return an object:

```
public Object action (int x)
```

---

6   Like an anonymous array, an anonymous class allows a class to be defined and used in one line without giving it a specific name. Further coverage of anonymous classes can be found in the appendix on the accompanying website.

So the integer returned needs to be wrapped up in an object by making use of the `Integer` class:

```
return new Integer (2*x);
```

Having discussed the `VDMSet` class we now go on to demonstrate how this class can be used to implement a VDM specification.

6.4 Implementing the *PatientRegister* Specification

In the previous chapter we presented the specification of the *PatientRegister* class. Here is the specified data model once again:

types

　　　　Patient = TOKEN

values

　　　　LIMIT: $\mathbb{N}$ = 200

state *PatientRegister* **of**

　　　　reg: *Patient*-**set**

inv mk-*PatientRegister* (*r*) $\underline{\Delta}$ **card** *r* $\leq$ *LIMIT*

init mk-*PatientRegister* (*r*) $\underline{\Delta}$ *r* = { }

end

This specification defines a token type, `Patient`.

　　Patient = TOKEN

We have not shown you how to implement a VDM specification that makes use of token types before, so we need to discuss this before returning to the `PatientRegister` class.

6.4.1 IMPLEMENTING TOKEN TYPES

A token type is one whose internal details are not relevant to the specification. However, when it comes to system implementation, a concrete representation for this token `Patient` type is required. This representation should be encapsulated in a `Patient` class.

The details of such a `Patient` class are not significant for the system being specified. All that is functionally required of values of a token type such as this is that they be distinguishable from each other, that is, it should be possible to check for equality. The simplest implementation of this type is therefore a `Patient` class that provides an `equals` method. Once again, for testing to be effective, a `toString` method should also be provided.

We have provided a class, `VDMToken` for this purpose. The class contains a single `String` attribute and a constructor is provided to set this attribute. If a concrete representation for a token type has not been decided upon prior to program implementation, you may simply extend our VDMToken type. Here for example is a suitable Patient type:

Implementing the token *Patient* type

```
class Patient extends VDMToken
{
   public Patient(String valueIn)
   {
      super(valueIn); // The constructor just needs to call the super constructor
   }
}
```

Values of this type can now be created by sending in an appropriate parameter to the Patient constructor. For example:

```
Patient somePatient = new Patient ("Madhu");
```

In the final system we may wish to revisit this implementation of the Patient class and provide more attributes and/or methods. But for testing purposes this class will be sufficient. We will consistently use this approach to implement token types if the final representation has yet to be decided upon. Let us return now to the PatientRegister class.

6.4.2 THE DATA MODEL

Returning to the formal specification, we will implement the *LIMIT* constant in the usual way:

```
class PatientRegister implements InvariantCheck
{
   public static final int LIMIT = 200;
   // rest of class goes here
}
```

Notice that we have marked this class as having implemented the InvariantCheck interface as we will be providing an invariant method.

The class has only one state attribute, *reg*. It is declared to be of the set type so the VDMSet class can be used in the Java implementation:

VDM-SL	Java
reg: *Patient*-**set**	`private VDMSet reg;`

The invariant checks the cardinality of the *reg* set, the `card` method of `VDMSet` can be used here.

VDM-SL	Java

inv mk-*PatientRegister* (*r*) $\underline{\Delta}$ **card** $r \leq LIMIT$	```public boolean inv ()```
	 ```{```
	     ```return reg.card() < = LIMIT;```
	 ```}```

The constructor for this class should ensure the patient register is empty. This can be achieved by calling the empty `VDMSet` constructor. As usual, we check the invariant before completing the method:

VDM-SL	Java

init mk-*PatientRegister* (*r*) $\underline{\Delta}$ $r = \{ \}$	```public PatientRegister ()```
	 ```{```
	     ```reg = new VDMSet();```
	     ```VDM.invTest(this);```
	 ```}```

Now, we can move on to look at the operations.

6.4.3 THE OPERATIONS

We begin with the *addPatient* method. Take a look at the translation before we analyse it:

VDM-SL	Java

addPatient (*patientIn*: *Patient*)
 ext wr *reg*: *Patient*-**set**
 pre   *patientIn* $\notin$ *reg* $\wedge$ **card** *reg* $< LIMIT$
 post *reg* = $\overline{reg}$ $\cup$ *{patientIn}*
	```public void addPatient(Patient patientIn)```
	 ```{```
	     ```VDM.preTest(reg.doesNotContain(patientIn)```
	                   ```&&reg.card()<LIMIT);```
	     ```reg = reg.union(new VDMSet(patientIn));```
	     ```VDM.invTest(this);```
	 ```}```

Looking at the header first, notice how the token *Patient* type appears in the Java implementation as well as the VDM specification. Even if we were later to modify the `Patient` class we would not need to modify this `PatientRegister` class.

The precondition requires a check for non-membership of a set. The `doesNotContain` method is used here to check for non-membership.

The postcondition contains a single equality. As we discussed in Chapter 4, an equality such as this can be satisfied by an assignment. The union method of VDMSet is required. The singleton set {*patientIn*} is implemented by calling the appropriate VDMSet constructor:

```
reg = reg.union(new VDMSet(patientIn));
```

As this method has write access to the state the invariant is checked before completion:

```
VDM.invTest(this);
```

The *removePatient* method follows a similar pattern:

VDM-SL	Java
removePatient (*patientIn*: *Patient*) **ext wr** *reg*: *Patient*-**set** **pre** *patientIn* ∈ *reg* **post** *reg* = $\overline{reg}$ \ { *patientIn*}	```public void removePatient(Patient patientIn)` `{`  ` VDM.preTest(reg.contains(patientIn));` ` reg = reg.difference(new VDMSet(patientIn));` ` VDM.invTest(this);`  `}```

The *getPatients* method has no precondition and returns the value of the *reg* set.

VDM-SL	Java
getPatients ( ) *output*: *Patient*-**set** **ext rd** *reg*: *Patient*-**set** **pre** TRUE **post** *output* = *reg*	```public VDMSet getPatients()` `{`  ` return reg;`  `}```

Again, notice the fact that the return type in the Java method is given as VDMSet. Unlike the VDM specification, the type of the elements of the set (Patient) is not specified in the Java header. Now, look at the translation of the *isRegistered* operation:

VDM-SL	Java
isRegistered (*patientIn*: *Patient*) *query*: 𝔹 **ext rd** *reg*: *Patient*-**set** **pre** TRUE **post** *query* ⇔ *patientIn* ∈ *reg*	```public boolean isRegistered(Patient patientIn)` `{`  ` return reg.contains(patientIn);`  `}```

The postcondition contains an equivalence. As we demonstrated in Chapter 4 this can be satisfied by evaluating and returning the appropriate test. In this case the test requires us to check whether or not the given patient is present in the set. The `contains` method of `VDMSet` allows us to do this. Finally, here is the translation of the `numberRegistered` method:

VDM-SL	Java
numberRegistered () *total*: $\mathbb{N}$	`public int numberRegistered()`
ext rd *reg*: *Patient*-**set**	`{`
pre TRUE	`    return reg.card();`
post *total* = **card** *reg*	`}`

That completes our discussion of the operations specified for the `PatientRegister` class. As we mentioned in Chapter 4, as well as the operations specified in VDM, it is useful to include a `toString` method for the final class. The complete code listing for the `PatientRegister` class, including a `toString` method, is given below:

The *PatientRegister* class

```
class PatientRegister implements InvariantCheck
{
  // constant value
  public static final int LIMIT = 20;

  // state attribute
  private VDMSet reg;

  // initialize the state
  public PatientRegister()
  {
    reg = new VDMSet();
    VDM.invTest();
  }
  // state invariant
  public boolean inv()
  {
    return reg.card() < = LIMIT;
  }

  // operations
  public void addPatient(Patient patientIn)
  {
    VDM.preTest(reg.doesNotContain(patientIn));
```

```
        reg = reg.union(new VDMSet(patientIn));
        VDM.invTest(this);
    }
    public void removePatient(Patient patientIn)
    {
        VDM.preTest(reg.contains(patientIn));
        reg = reg.difference(new VDMSet(patientIn));
        VDM.invTest(this);
    }
    public VDMSet getPatients()
    {
        return reg;
    }
    public boolean isRegistered(Patient patientIn)
    {
        return reg.contains(patientIn);
    }
    public int numberRegistered()
    {
        return reg.card();
    }
    // additional toString method
    public String toString()
    {
        return "the register: "+reg;
    }
}
```

6.5   Implementing the *Airport* Specification

In the previous chapter we presented the formal specification of an *Airport* class. Following the guidelines we have presented in this chapter and in Chapter 4, we present the Java implementation of this class. This specification also defined a token type:

Aircraft = TOKEN

As before, we implement this as an Aircraft class by extending the VDMToken type:

The *Aircraft* class

```
class Aircraft extends VDMToken
{
    public Aircraft (String valueIn)
```

```
  {
    super (valueIn);
  }
}
```

Here is the code for the `Airport` class. Examine it closely and compare it to the original specification:

The *Airport* class

```
class Airport
{

    // state attributes
    private VDMSet permission;

    private VDMSet landed;

    // initialize the state
    public Airport()
    {
      permission = new VDMSet();

      landed = new VDMSet();

      VDM.invTest(this);
    }

    // state invariant
    public boolean inv()
    {
      return landed.isASubsetOf(permission);
    }

    // operations
    public void givePermission(Aircraft craftIn)
    {
      VDM.preTest(permission.doesNotContain(craftIn));

      permission = permission.union(new VDMSet (craftIn));

      VDM.invTest(this);
    }
    public void recordLanding(Aircraft craftIn)
```

```
    {

      VDM.preTest(permission.contains(craftIn) && landed.doesNotContain(craftIn));

      landed = landed.union(new VDMSet (craftIn));

      VDM.invTest(this);

    }

    public void recordTakeOff(Aircraft craftIn)

    {

      VDM.preTest(landed.contains(craftIn));

      landed = landed.difference(new VDMSet(craftIn));

      VDM.invTest(this);

    }

    public int numberWaiting()

    {

      return (permission.difference(landed)).card();

    }

    public VDMSet getPermission()

    {

      return permission;

    }

    public VDMSet getLanded()

    {

      return landed;

    }

    public String toString() // additional toString method

    {

      return "Permission: " + permission + "\nLanded: "+ landed;

    }

}
```

Again, notice the addition of a `toString` method. We leave the testers for both this class and the `PatientRegister` class as exercises.

EXERCISES

1. In exercise 1 of the previous chapter you were given four sets to consider:

   a = {1, 3, 5, 2}   b = {3, 2}   c = {5, 3, 7, 9}   d = {2, 3}

   Write a tester program to implement these four sets and evaluate all the expressions from the same question.
2. Test the `PatientRegister` class by developing an appropriate tester program.
3. Make the amendments to the `Airport` class you considered in exercise 2 of the last chapter.
4. Test the `Airport` class by developing an appropriate tester program.
5. Implement the `AmbulanceMonitor` class you specified in exercise 3 of the last chapter.
6. Test the `AmbulanceMonitor` class by developing an appropriate tester program.

CHAPTER 7

Sequences

7.1 Introduction

In Chapter 5 you saw how the *set* type is used in VDM-SL specifications. In this chapter we will study a different type of collection, known as a **sequence**.

A sequence differs from a set in two principal ways:

- A sequence is an *ordered* collection of objects.
- In a sequence, repetitions *are* significant.

We begin by explaining the notation for using a sequence in VDM-SL, and then go on to explore the sequence operators. We then move on to look at two applications that make use of the sequence type.

7.2 Notation

A sequence is specified by enclosing its members in square brackets. In general terms we could define a particular sequence, *s*, as follows:

$$s = [\, a, d, f, a, d, d, c \,]$$

A sequence representing a queue of people, say, at a bus-stop could be defined as[1]

$$queue = [\, \text{MICHAEL, VARINDER, ELIZABETH, WINSTON, JUDITH}]$$

It is important to note that because a sequence is an *ordered* collection, then, for example:

$$[\, a, d, f \,] \neq [\, a, f, d \,]$$

The empty sequence is expressed as:

$$[\,]$$

The elements of a sequence are numbered, starting from 1, from left to right. We can refer to a particular element of a sequence by placing the position of the element

---

1   We are using small caps to represent values (as opposed to variables, which are italicized).

in brackets. For example, using the above sequences:

$s(3) = f$

$queue(4) = \text{WINSTON}$

If the position is invalid, then the value associated with that position is undefined. For example, referring to the sequence s above, $s(10)$ is undefined.

7.3   Sequence Operators

The **len** operator gives us the length of the sequence. Using the above examples:

len $s = 7$
len $queue = 5$

The **elems** operator returns a set that contains all the members of the sequence (it therefore removes the duplicates):

elems $s = \{a, d, f, c\}$
elems $queue = \{\text{MICHAEL, VARINDER, ELIZABETH, WINSTON, JUDITH}\}$

The *head* (**hd**) operator gives us the first element in the sequence; the *tail* (**tl**) operator gives us a sequence containing all but the first element:

hd $s = s(1) = a$
tl $s = [d, f, a, d, d, c]$

hd $queue = \text{MICHAEL}$
tl $queue = [\text{VARINDER, ELIZABETH, WINSTON, JUDITH}]$

The result of both **hd**[] and **tl**[] is undefined. Notice that **hd** returns an element, whereas **tl** returns a sequence.

The **concatenation** operator ($^\wedge$) operates on two sequences, and returns a sequence that consists of the two sequences joined together:

if **first** = [w, e, r, w]
and **second** = [t, w, q]
then
first $^\wedge$ **second** = [w, e, r, w, t, w, q]

The **override** operator, †, takes a sequence and gives us a new sequence with a particular element of the old sequence overridden by a new element. The generalized form of this expression is:

$s \dagger m$

where s is a sequence and m is a **map** – a VDM data type that you have not yet come across. Maps will be dealt with fully in Chapter 11; for now you can see from the following example how the override operator works:

$$[a, c, d, e] \dagger \{2 \mapsto x, 4 \mapsto y\} = [a, x, d, y]$$

In this example, the element at position 2 has been overridden with the value x, and the element at position 4 has been overridden with the value y. The override operator is undefined if any index is invalid.

The **inds** operator returns a set of all the indices of the sequence. Thus, using the previous examples:

> **inds** $s = \{1, 2, 3, 4, 5 , 6, 7\}$
> **inds** $queue = \{1, 2, 3, 4, 5\}$

A **subsequence** operator is defined to allow us to extract a part of a sequence between two indices. For example, using, s above:

$$subseq(s, 2, 5) = [d, f, a, d]$$

The language allows us to write this in the following, more convenient, way:

$$s(2, \ldots , 5) = [d, f, a, d]$$

With two exceptions, the subsequence operator is undefined if either index is out of range, or if the first index is greater than the second. The exceptions are defined especially for the boundaries, in order to enable us to extract empty sequences. So, again using the sequence s above (which has a length of 7):

$$s(1, \ldots ,0) = []$$

and

$$s(8, \ldots , 7) = []$$

You should also note that:

$$s(2, \ldots , 2) = [d]$$

7.4   Defining a Sequence by Comprehension

We saw in Chapter 5 that it is possible to define a set by comprehension. Similarly, we can define a sequence by comprehension. For example, if we were interested in the sequence of odd numbers from 1 to 20 we could define this implicitly as follows:

$$[\, a \mid a \in \{1, \ldots , 20\} \bullet is\text{-}odd(a)]$$

where $is\text{-}odd$ is a function that returns TRUE if a is odd and FALSE if a is even.

More generally sequence comprehension takes the following form:

$$[\, expression(a) \mid a \in SomeSet \bullet test\ (a)\ ]$$

where *SomeSet* must be a collection of numeric values. When constructing the sequence, these values are considered in order, smallest first.

Often sequence comprehension is used to 'filter' a sequence. For example, if the sequence *s1* were defined as follows:

$$s1 = [2, 3, 4, 7, 9, 11, 6, 7, 8, 14, 39, 45, 3]$$

and *s2* were defined as

$$s2 = [\, s1(i) \mid i \in \mathbf{inds}\ s1 \bullet s1(i) > 10]$$

then *s2* would evaluate to the sequence [11, 14, 39, 45].

7.5   Using the Sequence Type in VDM-SL

We saw previously that to declare a variable to be of a *set* type, we append the word **-set** to the type contained in the set. To declare a variable to be of type *sequence* we place an asterisk after the name of the type contained within the sequence.

For example, the statement

$$seq : \mathbb{Z}^*$$

declares a variable *seq* to be a sequence of integers.

If we had previously declared a type *SpaceCraft* then we could declare a variable *convoy*, for example, as follows:

$$convoy : SpaceCraft^*$$

7.6   Specifying a Stack

The first application of a sequence that we shall develop will be a simple stack. A stack is an important data structure in computer science, and, as you will be aware, is an ordered list that obeys a last-in-first-out (LIFO) protocol. Thus, items are added to the list, and when it comes to the time that an item is to be removed, then this item will be the last one that was added. We often conceptualize a stack as having a top and a bottom (see Figure 7.1), items entering at the top and leaving from the top.

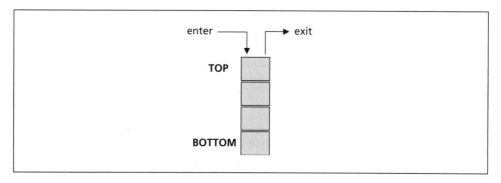

Figure 7.1   A stack

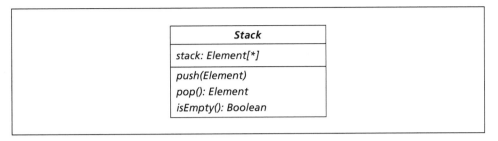

Figure 7.2   The UML specification for a *Stack* class

It is conventional to refer to the operations that add and remove items from a stack as *push* and *pop* respectively, and we shall follow that convention here. The *pop* operation that we will specify will also return the item that has been removed. We will also specify an *isEmpty* operation.

We begin, as usual, with the UML diagram, which is shown in Figure 7.2.

We are going to create a generic stack by specifying a token type called *Element* – this could be defined in detail at implementation time, but for the purposes of specification its internal details are not relevant. We can now proceed to the specification of the stack in VDM-SL.

7.7   Specifying the State of the Stack

Before specifying the state, we need, as usual, to identify any types that we will use in our specification. All we have to do is to define our 'base' type, *Element*:

types
Element = TOKEN

As you can see from the UML diagram, the stack must contain a collection of elements; as this must be an ordered collection we will choose the sequence type – be careful, by the way, not to confuse the UML notation for a collection (an asterisk in square brackets), with the VDM notation for a sequence (an asterisk after the type name).

Our state is specified as follows:

state *Stack* **of**
        stack : *Element**
        init mk-*Stack*(*s*) $\underline{\Delta}$ *s* = []
    end

The initialization clause states simply that the stack must be empty on creation. We have not placed any constraints on the stack (such as imposing a maximum length for example), nor are there any intrinsic constraints, thus making an invariant unnecessary.

We can now go on to specify the operations.

7.8   Specifying the Operations on the Stack

We will begin with the *push* operation, which we specify as follows:

---

push(*itemIn* : *Element*)
ext wr   *stack* : *Element**
pre   TRUE
post   *stack* = [*itemIn*] $^\wedge$ $\overline{stack}$

You can see that it is straightforward – in the postcondition we make use of the concatenation operator ($^\wedge$) to append the existing stack to the new item; after the operation is performed the new item will be at the head of the stack. Notice that the concatenation operator requires two *sequences* as arguments, so we must create a unitary sequence containing just our new item that is then concatenated with the old stack.

Now the *pop* operation:

---

pop() *itemRemoved* : *Element*
ext wr   *stack* : *Element**
pre   *stack* ≠ []
post   *stack* = **tl** $\overline{stack}$ ∧ *itemRemoved* = **hd** $\overline{stack}$

Here we have a precondition that records the restriction that items cannot be popped from an empty stack. The postcondition consists of two conjuncts. The first of these states that the new stack should be identical to the old stack, but with the head removed – that is, to the tail of the old stack. The second conjunct is concerned with reporting on which element has been removed; we state that the output value, *itemRemoved*, should be equal to the last element added, namely the head of the old sequence.

Finally we come to the *isEmpty* operation. Again, this is straightforward, and does not require further explanation, as you have seen operations of this type before.

---

isEmpty() *query* : $\mathbb{B}$
ext rd   *stack* : *Element**
pre   TRUE
post   *query* ⇔ *stack* = []

7.9   Rethinking our Airport System

Now that we have the benefit of a new type, we can revisit the airport system from Chapter 5, and can specify a new, more realistic system. In our new system, when an aircraft is to take off from its original airport, then at that time it requests permission to land at our airport. When it approaches the airport it is placed in a queue, and must circle the airport until a runway becomes available. Only aircraft that have permission to land are allowed to circle. The circling aircraft are landed on a first-come-first-served basis.

7.9.1 RESPECIFYING THE STATE

The state must be respecified with an additional component. Recall that we had previously defined the following types:

---

types
      $Aircraft = \text{TOKEN}$

We will call our new software system *Airport2*. Our new state definition becomes:

---

state *Airport2* **of**
        permission : *Aircraft*-**set**
        landed : *Aircraft*-**set**
        circling : *Aircraft**

You can see that we have added the component *circling*, which is declared as a sequence of *Aircraft*.

Now we also have to rethink our initialization clause and our invariant. The initialization clause is straightforward – we just have to ensure that the sequence starts off empty, as well as the other two components:

---

init mk-*Airport2*(*p, l, c*) $\underline{\Delta}$ $p = \{\ \} \wedge l = \{\ \} \wedge c = [\ ]$

The invariant is a little more complicated:

- In addition to the fact that the landed aircraft must have been granted permission to land, this now has to be true for the circling aircraft as well.
- There must never be an aircraft in the circling queue that is also in the set of landed aircraft.
- All aircraft must be unique – this did not present a problem before, because we used sets only, and duplicates are not counted in a set. But for a sequence this is not the case, and we have to add to our invariant to ensure that this is always the case.

In regard to the last point, it will be useful to define a function, *isUnique*, which receives a sequence of aircraft and reports on whether or not that sequence contains unique items only:

---

isUnique(*seqIn* : *Aircraft**) *query* : $\mathbb{B}$

pre   TRUE
post $query \Leftrightarrow \forall i_1, i_2 \in \textbf{inds } seqIn \bullet i_1 \neq i_2 \Rightarrow seqIn(i_1) \neq seqIn(i_2)$

The expression on the right-hand side of the equivalence operator in the postcondition looks a little complicated at first, but is actually quite easy to unravel. We are simply saying that for each pair of indices in the sequence – that is 1 and 1,

1 and 2, 2 and 1, 2 and 2, and so on – the items at that index must not be the same. We do, of course, have to exclude the case when the indices are equal, when obviously the items will also be equal!

We could actually have expressed our postcondition in the following way:

$$query \Leftrightarrow \textbf{card elems } seqIn = \textbf{len } seqIn$$

Remember that the **elems** operator returns a set of all the elements in the sequence, and therefore would remove the duplicates. Thus, if the cardinality of this set were equal to the length of the sequence this must mean that the sequence contained no duplicates.

Although the second method looks a little neater than the first, it is important that you understand the first method, as there will be occasions in future when you will have to use that approach – you will see the reason for this once you have covered composite objects in Chapter 9.

We can now use this function in our invariant:

> **inv mk**-*Airport 2*(p,l,c) $\underline{\Delta}$ $l \subseteq p$
>
> $\qquad \wedge$ **elems** $c \subseteq p$
>
> $\qquad \wedge$ **elems** $c \cap l = \{\ \}$
>
> $\qquad \wedge$ *isUnique*(c)

Note that we have had to use the **elems** operator to convert the sequence to a set in order to use the set operators.

7.9.2 RESPECIFYING THE OPERATIONS

The operations *givePermission, recordTakeOff, numberWaiting* and *atAirport*, as well as *getPermission* and *getLanded*, access only the *permission* and *landed* components, and do not therefore need to be changed. The meaning of *recordLanding* will change in light of our new specification, and we will describe this in a moment. However, before we do that, there is a need for two new operations. One is a simple *getCircling* operation, while the other is an operation that records the fact that an aircraft has been allowed to circle the airport. We will call this *allowToCircle*. Its specification is as follows:

> *allowToCircle* (*craftIn* : *Aircraft*)
>
> **ext wr**   *circling* : *Aircraft**
>
>   **rd**   *permission* : *Aircraft*-**set**
>
>   **rd**   *landed* : *Aircraft*-**set**
>
> **pre**   *craftIn* $\in$ *permission* $\wedge$ *craftIn* $\notin$ **elems** *circling* $\wedge$ *craftIn* $\notin$ *landed*
>
> **post**   *circling* = $\overline{circling}$ ⌢ [*craftIn*]

We can now consider the *recordLanding* operation. The process is that on completion of the operation the first item in the circling queue will have been removed from this queue, and will be contained in the set of aircraft that has landed. We no longer need to specify which aircraft to land, as it will always be the first one in the queue. Also, we no longer need to check whether the aircraft has permission – this was checked before it was allowed to circle, so it would not be in the circling queue if it did not have permission.

The operation is now specified as follows – notice how useful the **hd** and **tl** operators are:

---

recordLanding( )

ext wr   *circling* : *Aircraft**

  wr   *landed* : *Aircraft*-**set**

pre   *circling* $\neq$ []

post   *landed* = $\overline{landed}$ $\cup$ { **hd** $\overline{circling}$ } $\wedge$ *circling* = **tl** $\overline{circling}$

That completes the respecification of the airport software. We present the complete specification of the new software below:

---

types

  Aircraft = TOKEN

state *Airport2* **of**

  permission : *Aircraft*-**set**

  landed : *Aircraft*-**set**

  circling : *Aircraft**

  inv mk-*Airport2*(*p*,*l*,*c*) $\triangle$ $l \subseteq p$

              $\wedge$ **elems** $c \subseteq p$

              $\wedge$ **elems** $c \cap l = \{ \}$

              $\wedge$ *isUnique*(*c*)

  init mk-*Airport2*(*p*, *l*, *c*) $\underline{\triangle}$ $p = \{ \} \wedge l = \{ \} \wedge c = [\,]$

end

functions

  isUnique(*seqIn* : *Aircraft**) *query* : $\mathbb{B}$

  pre   *seqIn* $\neq$ []

  post   *query* $\Leftrightarrow$ $\forall i_1, i_2, \in$ **inds** *seqIn* $\bullet$ $i_1 \neq i_2 \Rightarrow seqIn(i_1) \neq seqIn(i_2)$

operations

getPermission() *permissionOut* : *Aircraft*-**set**

ext rd   *permission*: *Aircraft*-**set**

pre   TRUE

post   *permissionOut* = *permission*

getLanded() *landedOut* : *Aircraft*-**set**

ext rd   *landed* : *Aircraft*-**set**

pre   TRUE

post   *landedOut* = *landed*

getCircling() *circlingOut* : *Aircraft**

ext rd   *circling* : *Aircraft**

pre   TRUE

post   *circlingOut* = *circling*

givePermission (*craftIn* : *Aircraft*)

ext wr   *permission*: *Aircraft*-**set**

pre   *craftIn* $\notin$ *permission*

post   *permission* = $\overline{permisssion}$ $\cup$ {*craftIn*}

allowToCircle (*craftIn* : *Aircraft*)

ext wr   *circling* : *Aircraft**

　　rd   *permission* : *Aircraft*-**set**

　　rd   *landed* : *Aircraft*-**set**

pre   *craftIn* $\in$ *permission* $\land$ *craftIn* $\notin$ **elems** *circling* $\land$ *craftIn* $\notin$ *landed*

post   *circling* = $\overline{circling}$ ⌢ [*craftIn*]

recordLanding( )

ext wr   *circling* : *Aircraft**

　wr   *landed* : *Aircraft*-**set**

pre   *circling* $\neq$ []

post   *landed* = $\overline{landed}$ $\cup$ { **hd** $\overline{circling}$ } $\land$ *circling* = **tl** $\overline{circling}$

recordTakeOff (*craftIn* : *Aircraft*)

ext wr   *landed*: *Aircraft*-**set**

pre   *craftIn* $\in$ *landed*

$$\textbf{post } \textit{landed} = \overline{\textit{landed}} \setminus \{\textit{craftIn}\} \wedge \textit{permission} = \overline{\textit{permisssion}} \setminus \{\textit{craftIn}\}$$

$\textit{numberWaiting}(\ ) \textit{ total} : \mathbb{N}$

ext rd   *landed* : *Aircraft*-**set**

  rd   *permission* : *Aircraft*-**set**

pre   TRUE

post $\textit{total} = \textbf{card}(\textit{permission} \setminus \textit{landed})$

7.10   Some Useful Functions to Use with Sequences

You have seen that VDM-SL provides a *head* and a *tail* operator to use with sequences. There are sometimes occasions (in our *Stack* example for instance) when it would be useful to have a function that returns the last element in a sequence, and one that returns the sequence with the last element removed. We provide such functions below, using the generalized type *Element*. You should note of course that these are not standard VDM functions, and should you wish to use or adapt them in your specifications you must include them in your functions clause.

$\textit{last}(\textit{sequenceIn} : \textit{Element}^*) \textit{ elementOut} : \textit{Element}$
pre $\textit{sequenceIn} \neq [\ ]$
post $\textit{elementOut} = \textit{sequenceIn}(\textbf{len } \textit{sequenceIn})$

$\textit{allButLast}(\textit{sequenceIn} : \textit{Element}^*) \textit{ sequenceOut} : \textit{Element}^*$
pre $\textit{sequenceIn} \neq [\ ]$
post $\textit{sequenceOut} = \textit{sequenceIn}(1, \ldots, (\textbf{len } \textit{sequenceIn} - 1))$

Finally, it is very useful to have a *find* function, which will return the index of a particular element. The meaning of such a function could be slightly different depending on whether or not the sequence contains unique elements. In the case where the elements are unique, there is only one interpretation of a *find* function. It could be specified as:

$\textit{find}(\textit{sequenceIn} : \textit{Element}^*, \textit{element} : \textit{Element}) \textit{ position} : \mathbb{N}$
pre $\textit{element} \in \textbf{elems } \textit{sequenceIn}$
post $\textit{sequenceIn}(\textit{position}) = \textit{element}$

Consideration of the case where the elements are not necessarily unique brings home the non-algorithmic nature of implicit specification. The above function would be satisfied by an implementation that returned *any* position in which the chosen element was present. If, for example, we were referring to the position of *banana* in the sequence:

[APPLE, BANANA, PLUM, PEAR, BANANA, BANANA, MANGO]

then a program that returned any of the values 2, 5 or 6 would satisfy the postcondition of the *find* function. You should note that a function such as this, which can be satisfied by any one of a number of different values is referred to as an **underspecified** function.

Depending on the nature and purpose of the software being specified, the above definition may or may not be satisfactory – it would depend on the requirements. If the requirements specifically stated, for example, that the *first* position must be returned, then the function would need to be modified as follows:

findFirst(sequenceIn : Element, element : Element) position :* $\mathbb{N}$

pre *element* $\in$ *sequenceIn*

post *sequenceIn(position) = element* $\wedge$ $\forall i \in$ **inds** *sequenceIn* $\bullet$ *sequenceIn (i) =*
$$element \Rightarrow position \leq i$$

Here the second conjunct ensures that the position returned is the first matching item in the sequence.

EXERCISES

1. Given

   s1 = [10, 3, 2, 10, 3]   *s2* = [3]

   Write down values of the following:

   (a)   *s1* (3)
   (b)   *s2* (3)
   (c)   **inds** *s1*
   (d)   **elems** *s1*
   (e)   *s2* ^ *s1*
   (f)   **len** (*s1* ^ *s2*)
   (g)   *s2* ^ [ ]
   (h)   *s1*(3, ... ,5)
   (i)   *s1*(6, ... ,5)
   (j)   *s1* † {4 $\mapsto$ 20}
   (k)   **hd** *s2*
   (l)   **tl** *s2*

2. Make the following changes to the *Stack* application that we specified in this chapter:

   (a) Specify an invariant that restricts the number of elements on the stack to 20.
   (b) Make any changes to the operations that are necessary in light of the above invariant.
   (c) Specify an *isFull* operation.

3. Write the specification for a queue of elements (that is a list obeying a first-in-first-out (FIFO) protocol).

4. A **priority queue** is a specialized version of a regular queue. It therefore operates on a FIFO protocol but with a difference. Each item in the queue has a priority – either HIGH or LOW – associated with it. When it is time to remove an item from the queue, the item to be removed will be the first high-priority item in the queue. Only when there are no high-priority items in the queue should a low-priority item be removed.

One way to think of a priority queue is to consider it as consisting of two queues – a high-priority queue and a low-priority queue. As long as there are items in the high-priority queue then items are always removed from this queue; only when the high-priority queue is empty are items removed from the low-priority queue.

(a) Write the specification for a priority queue in VDM-SL. You should include operations *add, remove* and *showNext*.

(b) Modify your specification so that duplicates (for the system overall) are not allowed.

(c) Write a *changePriority* operation that accepts an element, together with its current priority, and changes it to the opposite priority; in so doing it places the element at the end of the appropriate queue. You will find that utilizing a *find* function as described in Section 7.10 is very helpful.

CHAPTER 8

Implementing Sequences

8.1 Introduction

In Chapter 6 we described the VDMSet class that we developed to facilitate the implementation of sets in Java. In this chapter we do the same thing with a VDMSequence class, which once again makes use of the Vector class that we discussed in Chapter 6. This class can be downloaded from the website. We begin by describing the methods of the VDMSequence class, and then go on to use this class, along with the VDMSet class, to implement the enhanced Airport application that we specified at the end of Chapter 7.

8.2 The *VDMSequence* Class

As we have indicated, the class contains a single attribute, a Vector, which holds the elements of the sequence:

```
import java.util.*;
class VDMSequence
{

        private Vector theSequence;
        // methods go here

}
```

Thus, if a sequence has been declared in a VDM specification, it can be declared as an object of the VDMSequence class in Java. For example:

VDM-SL	Java
*someSequence : SomeType**	VDMSequence someSequence;

8.2.1 THE CONSTRUCTORS

A number of constructors is provided, similar to those provided for the VDMSet class described in Chapter 6. They are summarized in Table 8.1.

Table 8.1 VDMSequence constructors

Constructor	Description
VDMSequence()	Empty sequence constructor.
VDMSequence(Object[])	Explicit sequence constructor – creates a new sequence from an array of objects passed as a parameter. Overloaded for an array of scalar types int, char and double.
VDMSequence(Object)	Singleton sequence constructor – creates a new sequence containing the single object passed in as a parameter. Overloaded for the scalar types int, char and double.

Table 8.2 provides examples of how these constructors are used.

Table 8.2 VDMSequence constructors – examples

VDM-SL	Java
Empty sequence constructor	
someSeq = []	someSeq = new VDMSequence();
Explicit sequence constructors	
someSeq = ["RED", "BLUE", "RED"]	someSeq = new VDMSequence (new Object[] {"RED", "BLUE", "RED"});
someSeq = [1, 1, 3]	someSeq = new VDMSequence (new int[] {1, 1, 3});
someSeq = [1.1, 2.39, 0.8]	someSeq = new VDMSequence (new double[] {1.1, 2.39, 0.8});
someSeq = ['A', 'B', 'C']	someSeq = new VDMSequence (new char[] { 'A', 'B', 'C'});
Singleton sequence constructors	
someSeq = ["RED"]	someSeq = new VDMSequence("RED");
someSeq = [2]	someSeq = new VDMSequence(2);
someSeq = [1.1]	someSeq = new VDMSequence(1.1);
someSeq = ['C']	someSeq = new VDMSequence('C');

8.2.2 THE SEQUENCE OPERATORS

Just as we did with the VDMSet, we have provided methods for all the sequence operators within the VDMSequence class. These are summarized in Table 8.3.

Table 8.3 The VDMSequence operators

Method	Description
int len()	Returns the length of the sequence.
VDMSet elems()	Returns a VDMSet constructed from the sequence as prescribed by the *elems* operator.
VDMSequence concat (VDMSequence)	Accepts a VDMSequence, and returns a new VDMSequence constructed by concatenating the received sequence onto the original sequence.
VDMSequence override (VDMMap)	Accepts a VDMMap and returns a sequence with its elements overridden as determined by the elements of the map (you should return to this after you have studied maps in Chapters 11 and 12).

Table 8.3 *(continued)*

`Object hd()`	Returns the head of the sequence. Throws a `VDMException` if the sequence is empty.
`VDMSequence tl()`	Returns the tail of the sequence. Throws a `VDMException` if the sequence is empty.
`VDMSet inds()`	Returns a `VDMSet` of Integer objects representing the indices of the sequence.
`VDMSequence subseq (int, int)`	Accepts two integers representing the first and second index of a subsequence, which it constructs from the original sequence and returns. Throws a `VDMException` if either index is out of bounds.
`Object index(int)`	Accepts an integer representing an index, and returns the element at that index. Throws a `VDMException` if the index is invalid.

Table 8.4 provides examples of the use of these operators.

Table 8.4 VDMSequence operators – examples

VDM-SL	Java
len *someSeq*	`someSeq.len();`
elems *someSeq*	`someSeq.elems();`
seqA ^ seqB	`seqA.concat(seqB);`
someSeq † {2 ↦ "RED"}	`someSeq.override(new VDMMap(new Maplet(2,"red")));`
	(The VDMMap and Maplet classes will be discussed in Chapter 12)
hd *someSeq*	`someSeq.hd();`
tl *someSeq*	`someSeq.tl();`
inds *someSeq*	`someSeq.inds();`
someSeq(5,9)	`someSeq.subSeq(5,9);`
someSeq(6)	`someSeq.index(6);`

As with the VDMSet class from Chapter 6, additional methods have been provided in order to simplify the process of testing and implementation. These are shown in Table 8.5.

Table 8.5 Additional VDMSequence operators

VDMSequence method	Description
`boolean equals(Object)`	Accepts an `Object` as a parameter, and returns **true** if this object is identical to the original sequence, otherwise returns **false**.
`String toString()`	Returns a string representation of the sequence.
`Enumeration getElements()`	Returns an enumeration object to allow the elements of the sequence to be scanned.
`boolean isEmpty()`	Returns **true** if the sequence is empty, otherwise returns **false**.

8.2.3 SEQUENCE COMPREHENSION

You will recall from Chapter 7 that sequence comprehension takes the following form:

$$[\, expression(a) \mid a \in SomeSet \bullet test\,(a)\,]$$

where *SomeSet* must be a collection of numeric values.

We have provided a number of overloaded methods called `sequenceComp` that allow sequences to be constructed in this way, just as we did for sets. If *SomeSet* is a set of integers, for example, then one of the following methods can be used:

```
VDMSequence sequenceComp(VDMSet, TestableInt)
VDMSequence sequenceComp(ExpressionInt, VDMSet)
VDMSequence sequenceComp(ExpressionInt, VDMSet,TestableInt)
```

These are all `static` methods, and are therefore called in conjunction with the class name, `VDMSequence`.

As an example, consider the following sequence:

$$s1 = [2, 3, 4, 7, 9, 11, 6, 7, 8, 14, 39, 45, 3]$$

If *s2* were defined as

$$s2 = [\, s1(i) \mid i \in \textbf{inds}\ s1 \bullet s1(i) > 10]$$

then we could implement this as:

```
s2 = VDMSequence.sequenceComp(
            new ExpressionInt() // the expression
            {
              public Object action(int i)
              {
                  return s1.index(i);
              }
            },
            s1.inds(), // the set
            new TestableInt() // the test
            {
              public boolean test( int i)
              {
                  Integer localInt = (Integer) s1.index(i);
                  return localInt.intValue() > 10;
              }
            });
```

Similar methods are provided for the other primitive types, `char` and `double`; methods are not provided for `Objects`, since the set in question must be able to be ordered.

8.3   Implementing the Enhanced *Airport* Specification

You will recall from Chapter 7 that once we had learnt about the sequence type in VDM-SL we were able to rethink the airport software from the previous chapters to make it more complex and closer to a real-life system.

The implementation – which once again uses an `Aircraft` class, which will have at least the basic implementation described in Chapter 6 – is for the most part straightforward; the same principles apply to the implementation of sequences as to that of sets. The only really complex aspect to this implementation is the `isUnique` function, which requires some explanation. Study the code shown below, and we will discuss it afterwards.

The *Airport2* class

```
class Airport2 implements InvariantCheck
{
// state attributes
private VDMSet permission;
private VDMSet landed;
private VDMSequence circling;

// initialize the state
public Airport2()
{
        permission = new VDMSet();
        landed = new VDMSet();
        circling = new VDMSequence();
        VDM.invTest(this);
}
//invariant test
public boolean inv()
{
    return landed.isASubsetOf(permission)
        && circling.elems().isASubsetOf(permission)
        && circling.elems().intersection(landed).isEmpty()
        && isUnique(circling);
}
// function
private boolean isUnique(final VDMSequence seqIn)
{
    return VDM.forall(seqIn.inds(), new TestableInt() //outer forall
      {
       public boolean test (final int i1) // first anonymous inner class
        {
         return VDM.forall(seqIn.inds(), new TestableInt() // inner forall
          {
           public boolean test(int i2) // second anonymous inner class
            {
             return i1 != i2 && !seqIn.index(i1). equals(seqIn.index(i2))
                            ||
                        i1 == i2;
```

```
                }
            } );
        }
    } );
}

// operations
public VDMSet getPermission()
{
    return permission;
}

public VDMSet getLanded()
{
    return landed;
}

public VDMSequence getCircling()
{

    return circling;
}

public void givePermission(Aircraft craftIn)
{

    VDM.preTest(permission.doesNotContain(craftIn));
    permission = permission.union(new VDMSet(craftIn));
    VDM.invTest(this);
}
public void allowToCircle(Aircraft craftIn)
{
    VDM.preTest(permission.contains(craftIn)
            && circling.elems().doesNotContain(craftIn)
            && landed.doesNotContain(craftIn));
    circling = circling.concat(new VDMSequence(craftIn));
    VDM.invTest(this);
}

public void recordLanding()
{
    VDM.preTest(!circling.isEmpty());
    landed = landed.union(new VDMSet(circling.hd()));
    circling = circling.tl();
    VDM.invTest(this);
}

public void recordTakeOff(Aircraft craftIn)
{
    VDM.preTest(landed.contains(craftIn));
    landed = landed.difference(new VDMSet(craftIn));
    permission = permission.difference(new VDMSet(craftIn));
    VDM.invTest(this);
}

public int numberWaiting()
{

    return permission.difference(landed).card();
```

```
}
public String toString()
{
  return "Permission: " + permission + "\nCircling: " + circling + "\nLanded: " + landed;
}
}
```

8.4 Analysis of the *Airport2* Class

As we have said, the implementation of the *isUnique* function could do with some explanation. At first glance it looks rather cumbersome and needs some unravelling.

First, however, we must introduce a method of our VDM class that you have not previously seen in action, namely the `forall` method, which implements the 'forall' quantifier, ∀. This takes the form:

```
public static boolean forall(VDMSet set, Testable obj)
```

The `Testable` interface was discussed in the Chapter 6 – you saw there how it is used with an anonymous inner class. The `forall` method uses the same technique – each element of a set is subjected to a test, and the method returns **true** if all elements pass the test, or **false** otherwise. The test is defined by means of an anonymous inner class that implements a test method.

As mentioned in Chapter 4, as well as the `forall` method, the VDM class contains an `exists` method and a `uniqueExists` methods which operate in a similar way; all three methods have been overloaded to accept objects of the types `TestableInt`, `TestableChar` and `TestableDouble`.

Now to return to our `isUnique` function. In order to understand this, we need to re-examine the original VDM specification of the function:

isUnique(*seqIn* : *Aircraft**) *query* : $\mathbb{B}$

pre   TRUE

post   *query* ⇔ ∀ i_1 ,i_2 ∈ **inds** *seqIn* • $i_1 \neq i_2 \Rightarrow$ *seqIn*(i_1) ≠ *seqIn*(i_2)

When we introduced this function in the last chapter, we explained it by saying that for each pair of indices in the sequence, the items at that index must not be the same (excluding the case when the indices are equal). In actual fact, the right-hand side of the equivalence expression in the postcondition is really a short-hand for a longer expression:

$$\forall\, i_1 \in \textbf{inds}\ seqIn \bullet$$
$$\forall\, i_2 \in \textbf{inds}\ seqIn \bullet i_1 \neq i_2 \Rightarrow seqIn(\,i_1) \neq seqIn(\,i_2)$$

In a sense this can be thought of as a 'nested' forall ($\forall$) expression, containing an outer and an inner statement. Thinking of it in this way makes the implementation a little easier to understand:

```
private boolean isUnique(final VDMSequence seqIn)
{
   return VDM.forall(seqIn.inds(), new TestableInt() // outer forall
    {
     public boolean test (final int i1) // first anonymous inner class
      {
       return VDM.forall(seqIn.inds(), new TestableInt() // inner forall
        {
          public boolean test(int i2) // second anonymous inner class
           {
             return i1 !5 i2 && !seqIn.index(i1).equals(seqIn.index(i2))
                                 ||
                               i1 = 5 i2;
           }
        } );
      }
   } );
}
```

You should note that any local variables that are used within an inner class but declared outside of that class must have been declared as **final**. Thus, *seqIn* has been declared **final** as it has been referenced within both inner classes; i1 has been declared **final** as it has been referenced within the second inner class.

The other methods of the Airport2 class are straightforward, and you should have no difficulty understanding them. You should note once again how the precondition and the invariant are, where appropriate, tested at the beginning and end of each operation; you will see how useful this is when you implement a tester as required in the exercises that follow.

EXERCISES

1. In exercise 1 of the previous chapter you were given two sequences to consider:

    s1 = [10, 3, 2, 10, 3]   *s2* = [3]

    Write a tester program to implement these sequences and evaluate all the expressions from the same question.
2. Write a program that tests out the `Airport2` class. You might wish to use a menu-driven program such as the following:

AIRPORT TESTER

    1. Give permission

    2. Allow to circle

    3. Record Landing

    4. Record take off

    5. Get number waiting

    6. Show all

    7. Quit

    Each menu option can test a method of the `Airport2` class – the 'Show all' method can simply make use of the `toString` method of `Airport2`.
    Look back at the example in chapter 4 to see how the potential exceptions are caught by means of a **try…catch** block within the menu loop.
3. Implement the specification of the *Stack* developed in Chapter 7.
4. Test the `Stack` class by developing an appropriate tester program.
5. Implement the priority queue that you specified in exercise 4 of the last chapter.
6. Test the `PriorityQueue` class by developing an appropriate tester program.

CHAPTER 9

Composite Objects

So far, we have always associated a *single* type with each item of data in our VDM specifications. For example, the value of the temperature in the incubator was allocated an integer type, the status of a robot the *Status* type, the collection of aircraft landed at the airport an *Aircraft*-**set** type.

There will be occasions, however, when you need to associate *more than one* type with an object. This will occur when the object consists of several pieces of data, each potentially having a different type. For example, if we were developing a software system for a car dealership, it might not be possible to associate a single type with a record for an individual car. The car record might consist of a registration number, a year of manufacture and a price, and each of these items of data would have their own individual type. The appropriate type for the object as a whole would then be a *composite* of all the types of its internal data. We call such a type a *composite object type* in VDM-SL.

9.1 Defining Composite Object Types

Composite objects are very similar to the concept of *records* in a database. In fact, they are very often referred to as *record* types in VDM-SL. To define a type to be composite (that is to be composed of more than one type) we use a **composite type definition**. Composite types are defined as follows:

>*TypeName* :: *fieldname1* : *Type1*
>   *fieldname2* : *Type2*
>   :

where the symbol '::' is read '*is composed of*'.

For example, consider a type *Time*, which may be useful in many applications. Assume that a time value consists of an hour, minute and second value. Now the composite object type *Time* would need to combine the types for hour, minute and second into a single type, *Time*. This can be achieved as follows (also under the **types** clause)

>*Time*:: *hour*: $\mathbb{N}$
>   *minute*: $\mathbb{N}$
>   *second*: $\mathbb{N}$

Here, the composite type *Time* is composed of appropriate types for an *hour* value, a *minute* value and a *second* value. These individual components of a composite type are referred to as the *fields* of the composite object so this *Time* type has three fields. In this case the appropriate type for all these fields is natural number. Generally, a composite type may have any number of fields and the types of these fields may well be different from each other.

This *Time* type can now be used like any other type in your specification. For example, you could define a set of important times as follows:

> *importantTimes* : *Time*-**set**

At the moment, all we have done is to look at how composite object types are *defined*. We have not created or used any objects from these type definitions yet. To do so we need to look at the composite object operators.

9.2   Composite Object Operators

The most important composite object operator is the **make** function (**mk**-*TypeName*) that creates a new object of a given composite type. We have already been using **make** functions in our state initialization and invariant clauses. Here, for example, is the initialization and invariant clause of our *Airport2* model from Chapter 7:

> **inv**   **mk**-*Airport2(p, c, l)* $\underline{\Delta}$ $l \subseteq p \wedge$ **elems** $c \subseteq p \wedge$ **elems** $c \cap l = \{\} \wedge isUnique(c)$
> **init**   **mk**-*Airport2(p, c, l)* $\underline{\Delta}$ $p = \{\} \wedge l = \{\} \wedge c = [\ ]$

In this example, the type name associated with the **make** function is the name of the system that we are modelling (*Airport2*). Any system that we model, be it an *Incubator* or an *Airport*, is itself a user-defined type. Since states that we model in VDM may consist of many fields, the type of the state is itself a *composite* type, composed of the types of all the state fields. To construct an object of such a type therefore requires a **make** function.

The standard template for a **make** function is as follows:

> **mk**-*CompositeObjectTypeName* (*parameter list*)

where the order of items in the parameter list matches the order of fields defined for the composite object. Clearly there is not a single **make** function in VDM-SL, but one per composite object type. The signature of each function will therefore differ. The *Airport2* type consisted of three fields: the first and second are both a set of aircraft, the third is a sequence of aircraft; so the **make** function of *Airport2* has the following signature:

> **mk**-*Airport2*: *Aircraft*-**set** $\times$ *Aircraft*-**set** $\times$ *Aircraft** $\rightarrow$ *Airport2*

The *Time* type also has three fields, but to construct a *Time* object the types of the three fields (hour, minute and day) differ from that of *Airport2*:

> **mk**-*Time*: $\mathbb{N} \times \mathbb{N} \times \mathbb{N} \rightarrow$ *Time*

Here is an example of the use of a **mk**-*Time* function to create a *Time* object:

someTime = **mk**-*Time* (16, 20, 44)

Of course not all combinations of hour/minute/time are valid. For example, we would not want to allow the following:

strangeTime = **mk**-*Time* (36, 20, 44)

This time should not be allowed as there are only 24 hours in a day! Just as states can have invariants defined on them, so can any composite object types you define. Here is an appropriate invariant added to the *Time* type definition:

Time:: *hour*: $\mathbb{N}$
         minute: $\mathbb{N}$
         second: $\mathbb{N}$
inv mk-*Time* $(h, m, s) \underline{\Delta}$ $h < 24 \wedge m < 60 \wedge s < 60$

As you can see from the invariant, we are assuming the use of a 24-hour clock and we are allowing values from 0 to 23 for the hour, 0 to 59 for the minute and 0 to 59 for the second. When specifying systems informally, the use of a 12- or 24-hour timing system may not be made clear. The invariant of the composite object, however, removes any ambiguity by recording the choice formally, and makes clear to engineers developing code from this specification the restrictions that need to be observed for all objects of this type.

Once an object has been generated using a **make** function, its values can be interrogated. We can refer to a particular field of a composite object by using a **selector operator**. Individual fields are selected (read) in much the same way as object fields in programming languages, by the dot operator '.' followed by the name of a field. For example:

someTime.minute = 20
someTime.hour = 16

The only other composite object operator is a **mu** (μ) function. The **mu** function returns one composite object from another but with one or more fields changed. The fields to modify, and their new values, are specified by one or more *maplets*. Maplets will be discussed in detail in Chapter 11, but for now be aware that a maplet consists of a pair of values separated by a special maplet arrow ($\mapsto$). For example, to change the hour of a particular time we may use the function as follows:

newTime = μ (*someTime, hour* $\mapsto$ 15)

This returns an object identical to *someTime* but with the hour field changed to 15. To change the hour and the minute value the following **mu** function could be used:

thisTime = μ (*someTime, minute* $\mapsto$ 0, *second* $\mapsto$ 0)

Although **mu** functions can be useful, they can always be replaced by an expression involving a **make** function and selectors. For example the object *thisTime*, defined above using a **mu** function, could also have been defined as follows:

thisTime = **mk**-*Time*(*someTime.hour*,0,0)

The fields of the old object that are to be left unchanged are selected in the **make** function, and the new values of the remaining fields are given explicitly.

A variable in a formal specification is rarely a *single* composite object. More often than not attributes are *collections* of composite objects. So far we have met sets and sequences as means of specifying collections in VDM-SL, so you will find sets and sequences of composite objects will be very common models.

9.3   A Specification of a Disk Scanner

Consider a piece of software designed to keep track of damaged blocks on the surface of a disk. A disk is divided into a number of tracks and each track into a number of sectors. A block is identified, therefore, by giving both a track and sector number. Figure 9.1 gives a simplified UML specification of the *DiskScanner* class.

You can see in Figure 9.1, that the *DiskScanner* class is specified as being a collection of *Block* records. The details of this *Block* type need to be analysed further. A block consists of a *track* and a *sector* number. Figure 9.2 gives the UML specification of an appropriate *Block* type.

Now, consider the VDM specification of the *DiskScanner* class. A *Block* type has been identified in the UML diagram of Figure 9.1 and informally specified in Figure 9.2.

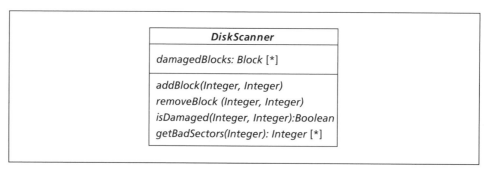

Figure 9.1   UML specification of the *DiskScanner* class

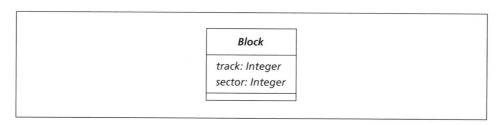

Figure 9.2   UML specification of the *Block* type

A type with several fields such as this can be specified as a composite type in VDM-SL:

---
types
$Block :: track: \mathbb{N}$
$\qquad\qquad sector: \mathbb{N}$

Note that the natural number type is appropriate for track and sector numbers, as these values can never be non-negative (though they can be zero). In this simplified version of the system we will not place a restriction on the number of tracks and sectors (this is left as an exercise at the end of this chapter).

A single attribute, *damagedBlocks*, is also identified in Figure 9.1. This represents a collection of blocks recorded as damaged. The collection has no ordering and no repetition, so a set of blocks will suffice here:

---
state *DiskScanner* **of**
$\qquad\qquad damagedBlocks: Block\text{-}\mathbf{set}$

Initially no damaged blocks will be recorded:

---
init mk-*DiskScanner* $(dB) \; \underline{\Delta} \; dB = \{\;\}$

Notice that no invariant is required on this model so we can move on to the operation specifications. First the *addBlock* operation. This operation receives two parameters, representing the track and sector number of a block to be recorded as damaged. Here is the specification:

$addBlock \; (trackIn: \mathbb{N}, sectorIn: \mathbb{N})$
ext wr $\qquad damagedBlocks: Block\text{-}\mathbf{set}$
pre $\qquad\quad \mathbf{mk}\text{-}Block \; (trackIn, sectorIn) \notin damagedBlocks$
post $\qquad\; damagedBlocks = \overline{damagedBlocks} \cup \{\mathbf{mk}\text{-}Block \; (trackIn, sectorIn)\}$

The precondition ensures that a block record, composed of the given track and sector number, is not currently recorded as damaged. A **make** function is required to compose the track and sector number into a *Block* object. Similarly a **make** function is required in the postcondition to record the fact that, upon completion of this operation, the block record composed of the given track and sector number should have been added to the old collection of damaged blocks.

The next operation we will specify is *removeBlock*. This operation receives a track and sector number, and removes the given block record from the collection of damaged blocks:

$removeBlock \; (trackIn: \mathbb{N}, sectorIn: \mathbb{N})$
ext wr $\qquad damagedBlocks: Block\text{-}\mathbf{set}$
pre $\qquad\quad \mathbf{mk}\text{-}Block \; (trackIn, sectorIn) \in damagedBlocks$
post $\qquad\; damagedBlocks = \overline{damagedBlocks} \setminus \{\mathbf{mk}\text{-}Block \; (trackIn, sectorIn)\}$

As you can see this is very similar to the *addBlock* operation, except that the precondition ensures the given block is initially recorded as damaged, and the postcondition ensures the given block record is removed from the set *damagedBlocks*.

The *isDamaged* operation also receives the track and sector number of a block. Upon completion, it reports on whether or not the given block is damaged. Read access only is required here, as the state is not being modified:

---

isDamaged (*trackIn*: $\mathbb{N}$, *sectorIn*: $\mathbb{N}$) *query*: $\mathbb{B}$
ext rd   *damagedBlocks*: *Block*-**set**
pre   TRUE
post   *query* $\Leftrightarrow$ **mk**-*Block* (*trackIn, sectorIn*) $\in$ *damagedBlocks*

The query returns TRUE when the block record, composed of the given track and sector number, is contained within the *damagedBlocks* set, and FALSE otherwise.

Finally, the *getBadSectors* operation returns the sector numbers associated with damaged blocks within a given track. These sector numbers have no ordering or repetition so a set is appropriate here. Again, this operation requires only read access to the record of damaged blocks:

---

getBadSectors (*trackIn*: $\mathbb{N}$) *list*: $\mathbb{N}$-**set**
ext rd   *damagedBlocks*: *Block*-**set**
pre   TRUE
post   *list* = {*b.sector* | *b* $\in$ *damagedBlocks* $\bullet$ *b.track* = *trackIn*}

The postcondition uses set comprehension to define a set of appropriate sector numbers. An object selector is used here to examine the *track* field of each damaged block. If the *track* field matches the track sent in as a parameter it is a block we are interested in:

b$\in$*damagedBlocks* $\bullet$ *b.**track*** = *trackIn*

We wish to record only the sector number of the block, so a selector is used to extract this number from the given block and place it into this set of sector numbers:

*b.**sector***

Here is the complete specification for the *DiskScanner* class:

---

types
Block : :   *track*: $\mathbb{N}$
            sector: $\mathbb{N}$
state   *DiskScanner* **of**
            damagedBlocks: *Block*-**set**
init mk-*DiskScanner* (*dB*) $\underline{\Delta}$ *dB* = { }
end

---

operations
addBlock (*trackIn*: $\mathbb{N}$, *sectorIn*: $\mathbb{N}$)
ext wr   *damagedBlocks*: *Block*-**set**
pre mk-*Block* (*trackIn, sectorIn*) $\notin$ *damagedBlocks*
post *damagedBlocks* = $\overline{damagedBlocks}$ $\cup$ {**mk**-*Block* (*trackIn, sectorIn*)}

removeBlock (*trackIn*: $\mathbb{N}$, *sectorIn*: $\mathbb{N}$)
ext wr   *damagedBlocks*: *Block*-**set**
pre mk-*Block* (*trackIn, sectorIn*) $\in$ *damagedBlocks*
post *damagedBlocks* = $\overline{damagedBlocks}$ \ {**mk**-*Block* (*trackIn, sectorIn*)}

isDamaged (*trackIn*: $\mathbb{N}$, *sectorIn*: $\mathbb{N}$) *query*: $\mathbb{B}$
ext rd   *damagedBlocks*: *Block*-**set**
pre TRUE
post   *query* $\Leftrightarrow$ **mk**-*Block* (*trackIn, sectorIn*) $\in$ *damagedBlocks*

getBadSectors (*trackIn*: $\mathbb{N}$) *list*: $\mathbb{N}$-**set**
ext rd   *damagedBlocks*: *Block*-**set**
pre TRUE
post *list* = {*b.sector* | *b* $\in$ *damagedBlocks* $\bullet$ *b.track* = *trackIn*}

In this example we illustrated the use of a set of composite objects. We now turn our attention to a slightly more complex example that allows us to explore a model involving a sequence of composite objects.

9.4   A Process Management System

Consider a process management system for a multitasking operating system. Processes are identified by a unique *process identification number* (*pid*). When a process is created it joins the list of waiting processes and will initially be in the READY state.

Various algorithms exist for determining the order in which processes are allocated to the CPU – these include shortest-job-first, round-robin and others. Here we will specify a simple first-in-first-out policy – this is not the most efficient of scheduling policies, but a good one to use for illustrative purposes.

When the CPU becomes available, the first READY process in the queue is allocated to the CPU and removed from the waiting list. Each running process is allotted a fixed amount of CPU time (a quantum). If a process uses up its allotted time before it terminates, it is placed back at the end of the waiting queue with a READY status; if it has finished, then it is not placed back in the list but is removed from the system.

If the process did not time out, but could not proceed for some reason (such as waiting for an input/output operation), it is placed back at the end of the waiting queue with a BLOCKED status. When a blocked process is ready to be processed again it is woken up from its BLOCKED status and is once again in a READY state. Figure 9.3 gives a state transition diagram summarizing the allowed changes of state for any particular process.

Figure 9.4 gives the UML specification for the *ProcessManagement* class. Note that an operation is provided to cover each state transition.

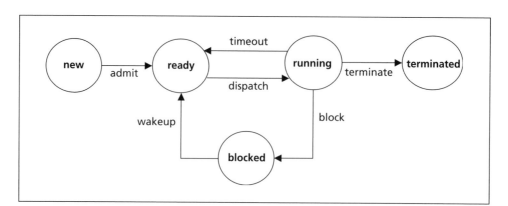

Figure 9.3 A state transition diagram for a process

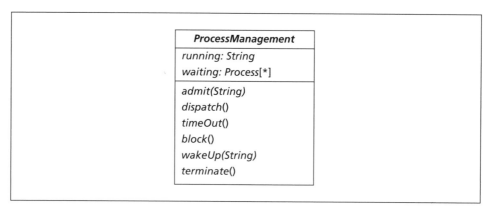

Figure 9.4 UML specification of the *ProcessManagement* class

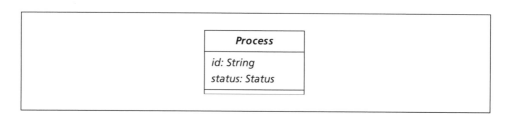

Figure 9.5 UML specification of the *Process* type

Two types are identified in the UML diagram of Figure 9.4: *String* and *Process*. The *String* type is predefined in UML. The *Process* type needs further analysis. A process consists of an *id* and a *status*. Figure 9.5 gives the UML specification of this type.

Before we proceed to formally specify the *ProcessManagement* class, the *Status* type used in Figure 9.5 needs further analysis. The status of a process is either *ready* or *blocked*. An enumerated type is appropriate here (Figure 9.6).

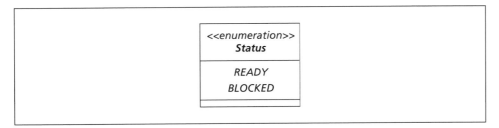

Figure 9.6   UML specification of the *Status* type

9.4.1 MODELLING THE DATA IN VDM-SL

The *String* type is predefined in UML but not in VDM-SL. We can define such a type in VDM-SL as a *sequence* of characters:

types
    String = Char*

The *Process* type of Figure 9.5 will need to be a composite, consisting of the *pid* and the process *status*. Before we define this type, a *Status* type must be defined from Figure 9.6 as follows:

Status = <READY> | <BLOCKED>

We can now define a *Process* type as follows:

Process :: *id* : *String*
            status : *Status*

As indicated in Figure 9.4, the state consists of two attributes, the identification number of the running process and the collection of waiting processes. The ordering of these waiting processes is important so we will use a sequence to model this collection:

state *ProcessManagement* **of**
            running : [*String*]
            waiting : *Process**

Notice the square brackets around the *String* type for the running process. Remember that this allows a value of **nil** to be given to this variable. Such a value would indicate no running process.

The invariant needs to record two restrictions. First, if there is a running process its identification number should not be the identification number of any process in the waiting queue. Secondly, no two processes in the waiting queue should have the same identification number. Here is its specification:

$$\textbf{inv mk-}\textit{ProcessManagement (run, wait)} \underline{\Delta} \textit{ (run = } \textbf{nil} \lor \neg\exists i \in \textbf{inds } \textit{wait} \bullet \textit{wait}(i).id = run)$$

$$\land$$

$$\forall\, i, j \in \textbf{inds } \textit{wait} \bullet i \neq j \Rightarrow \textit{wait}(i).id \neq \textit{wait}(j).id$$

In this model we have a sequence of composite objects. As you can see, this means that we have to combine the syntax for sequences and composite objects in order to express properties of our model. For example, in the invariant above, we needed to say that no two processes in the waiting queue should have the same id:

$$\forall\, i, j \in \textbf{inds } \textit{wait} \bullet i \neq j \Rightarrow \textit{wait}(i).id \neq \textit{wait}(j).id$$

The quantifier names two arbitrary waiting process indices, i and j. The process identification number of the two processes at these indices are then compared by looking up the processes in the sequence at those positions and then selecting their id field:

select the id field of the given process

$$\textit{wait}(i).id \neq \textit{wait}(j).id$$

look up the process at sequence position i

Initially no process will be running and no processes will be waiting to run, giving the following initialization function:

$$\textbf{init mk-}\textit{ProcessManagement (run, wait)} \underline{\Delta} \textit{ run} = \textbf{nil} \land \textit{wait} = [\,]$$

Here is the complete data model:

```
types
    String = Char*
    Status = <READY> | <BLOCKED>
    Process :: id : String
              status : Status
state ProcessManagement of
        running : [String]
        waiting : Process*
inv mk-ProcessManagement (run, wait) Δ (run = nil ∨ ¬∃i∈inds wait • wait(i).id = run)
                                        ∧
                          ∀ i, j ∈ inds wait • i ≠ j ⇒ wait(i).id ≠ wait(j).id
init mk-ProcessManagement (run, wait) Δ run = nil ∧ wait = [ ]
end
```

In order to simplify the specification of the operations, a few auxiliary functions will prove useful, as is often the case with a relatively complex model such as this.

9.4.2 SOME USEFUL FUNCTIONS

When a process is woken up it will need to have its status changed from BLOCKED to READY. The process to wake will be determined by submitting a process identification number. A function, *findPos* say, that returns the position of a process within a sequence given the *pid* of a process, will be useful here. Its specification is very similar to the *find* function specified in Chapter 7, except that the sequence being searched contains composite objects and these objects need to be interrogated with an object selector to identify the correct process. Here is its specification:

$findPos(qIn : Process^*, idIn : String) \; pos : \mathbb{N}$
pre $\exists p \in$ **elems** $qIn \bullet p.id = idIn$
post $qIn(pos).id = idIn$

The precondition records the fact that a process with the given *pid* should exist within the sequence. The postcondition indicates that the process at the returned position must have the same *pid* as that submitted to the function. Because process identification numbers are unique we know that only one process will have this *pid*. Once again, notice how sometimes a composite object has to be selected from a sequence before its field can be interrogated. For example:

$qIn(pos). \; id = idIn$

When dispatching a process, the relevant process in the waiting queue needs to be identified. A variation of the *findPos* function, *findNext* say, will be useful here to return the position of the correct process to dispatch. Here is its specification:

$findNext(qIn : Process^*) \; pos : \mathbb{N}$
pre $\exists p \in$ **elems** $qIn \bullet p.status = \text{<READY>}$
post $qIn(pos).status = \text{<READY>} \wedge \neg \exists i \in \{1, \ldots, pos\text{-}1\} \bullet qIn(i).status = \text{<READY>}$

The precondition records the requirement that a process exists in the sequence which is in the READY state. The postcondition indicates that the position returned is the index of a process in the READY state, and that no processes before this index position should be in the READY state.

Finally, when a process is dispatched, the waiting queue of processes needs to be compressed to remove the given process. A *remove* function can be specified for this purpose:

$remove(qIn : Process^*, posIn : \mathbb{N}) \; qOut : Process^*$
pre $posIn \in$ **inds** qIn
post $qOut = qIn(1, \ldots, posIn\text{-}1) \; ^\frown \; qIn(posIn + 1, \ldots, \text{len } qIn)$

Here, the precondition records the requirement that the position of the process to remove be a legal index. The postcondition indicates that the compressed sequence will consist of the subsequence that comes before the element to remove, concatenated to the subsequence that comes after the element to remove.

Taking the time to define extra functions in this way is not essential but it does greatly reduce the complexity of operation specifications, as you will see in the next section.

9.4.3 SPECIFYING THE OPERATIONS IN VDM-SL

The first operation we will look at will be the *admit* operation. This operation takes a process identification number and adds it to the waiting queue. The identification number should not already be in the queue or be the current running process identification number.

> *admit(idIn: String)*
> **ext**   **wr**   *waiting: Process**
>   **rd**   *running: [String]*
> **pre**   *(running =* **nil** $\lor$ *idIn* $\neq$ *running* $) \land \forall p \in$ **elems** *waiting* $\bullet$ *p.id* $\neq$ *idIn*
> **post** *waiting =* $\overline{waiting}$ $^\frown$ [**mk**-*Process(idIn,* <READY>)]

Notice the use of the **make** function in the postcondition to make an appropriate process to add to the waiting queue. This process will have the given identification number and will have its status set to READY. Now the *dispatch* operation. This operation takes the next READY process and records it as the running process:

> *dispatch( )*
> **ext wr** *running: [String]*
>   **wr** *waiting: Process**
> **pre**   *running =* **nil** $\land$ $\exists p \in$ **elems** *waiting* $\bullet$ *p.status =* <READY>
> **post** *running =* $\overline{waiting}$ *(findNext(*$\overline{waiting}$*)).id*
> $\land$ *waiting = remove(*$\overline{waiting}$*, findNext(*$\overline{waiting}$ *))*

The precondition records the requirement that that there should be no current running process and that there should be a waiting process in the READY state. The postcondition records the fact that, after the operation is executed, the appropriate process should be running and that this process is removed from the old *waiting* queue. Notice how the use of the *findNext* and *remove* functions greatly simplified the specification of this operation.

The *timeOut* operation returns the running process to the waiting queue and records its status as READY:

> *timeOut( )*
> **ext wr** *running: [String]*

> **wr** *waiting: Process**
>
> **pre**   *running* ≠ **nil**
>
> **post**   *waiting* = $\overline{waiting}$ ⁀ [**mk**-*Process*($\overline{running}$, <READY>)] ∧ *running* = **nil**

The precondition records the requirement that, prior to the operation, a process must be running. The postcondition then ensures that, after the operation, no process will be recorded as running and this process is added to the waiting queue.

The *block* operation is very similar to the *timeOut* operation except that when the process is returned to the *waiting* queue, its status is not recorded as READY but as BLOCKED:

---

block( )

ext wr *running:* [*String*]

    wr *waiting: Process**

pre   *running* ≠ **nil**

post   *waiting* = $\overline{waiting}$ ⁀ [**mk**-*Process*($\overline{running}$, <BLOCKED>)] ∧ *running* = **nil**

The *wakeUp* operation takes the *pid* of a BLOCKED process and changes its status back to READY. Here is its specification:

---

wakeUp(idIn: String)

ext wr *waiting: Process**

pre   *waiting(findPos(waiting, idIn)).status* = <BLOCKED>

post   *waiting* = $\overline{waiting}$ † {*findPos*($\overline{waiting}$, *idIn*) ↦ **mk**-*Process*(*idIn*, <READY>)}

The precondition records the requirement that the given process is recorded as BLOCKED before the operation is invoked. Notice the use of the *findPos* function to determine the position of the given process in the waiting sequence.

The postcondition uses the sequence override operator (†) to override the given process with a process that has a READY state. Again, notice the use of the *findPos* function to determine the position of the process to overwrite.

Finally, the terminate operation removes the current running process from the system:

---

terminate( )

ext wr *running:* [*String*]

pre   *running* ≠ **nil**

post   *running* = **nil**

9.4.4 THE LET … IN CLAUSE

The complexity of operation specifications in the last section was greatly reduced by the use of additional functions such as *findNext* and *remove*. Even with the use of such functions, however, pre- and postconditions can still involve cumbersome expressions that can be difficult to follow. For example, look again at the postcondition of the *dispatch* operation:

$$
\begin{aligned}
\textbf{post} \quad & running = \overline{waiting}\ (findNext\ (\overline{waiting})).id \\
& \wedge waiting = remove(\overline{waiting}, findNext(\overline{waiting}))
\end{aligned}
$$

The use of functions allowed this postcondition to be simplified but still produced a longwinded expression. To improve readability of such expressions, local names can be given to sub-expressions and these names can then be used in place of the longer sub-expression throughout the rest of the given pre- or postcondition.

These local names are created in **let … in** clauses. A **let … in** clause takes the following general form

let   *name = sub-expression*
in   *expression(name)*

Returning to the postcondition of the *dispatch* operation, we could formulate it using a **let … in** as follows:

$$
\begin{aligned}
\textbf{post} \quad \textbf{let} \quad & next = findNext\ (\overline{waiting}) \\
\textbf{in} \quad & running = next.id \\
& \wedge waiting = remove(\overline{waiting}, next)
\end{aligned}
$$

Here, a local name (*next*) is given to a sub-expression (*findNext(*$\overline{waiting}$*)*). This name is then used in place of the sub-expression throughout the postcondition. This was particularly useful here because the sub-expression repeats in the postcondition, so replacing it with a short name greatly reduces the complexity of the final expression. However, **let … in** clauses might be useful even if sub-expressions are not repeated, just to simplify the final expression. Here, for example, is the original precondition of the *wakeUp* operation:

$$
\textbf{pre} \quad waiting(findPos(waiting, idIn)).status = <\text{BLOCKED}>
$$

To reduce the complexity of this expression we might wish to give a simple name to the position of the process that is to be woken as follows:

$$
\begin{aligned}
\textbf{pre} \quad \textbf{let} \quad & pos = findPos(waiting, idIn) \\
\textbf{in} \quad & waiting(pos).status = <\text{BLOCKED}>
\end{aligned}
$$

You should be aware that the named **let…in** value, *pos*, has a scope that is restricted to the precondition. This value cannot be referenced in the postcondition. If such a value is required in the postcondition another **let…in** must be used. So, for example, the original postcondition of *wakeUp*

$$\textbf{post} \quad waiting = \overline{waiting} \dagger \{findPos(\overline{waiting}, idIn) \mapsto \textbf{mk-}Process(idIn, <\text{READY}>)\}$$

would also benefit by using the *pos* value created in the precondition, but this needs to be recreated with another **let … in** clause in the postcondition:

$$
\begin{aligned}
\textbf{post} \quad &\textbf{let} \quad pos = findPos(\overline{waiting}, idIn) \\
&\textbf{in} \quad waiting = \overline{waiting} \dagger \{pos \mapsto \textbf{mk-}Process(idIn, <\text{READY}>)\}
\end{aligned}
$$

Many **let … in** clauses may be used in a single expression such as a postcondition. While this might lengthen the specification it may help to make it more readable. Here, again, is a reformulated postcondition of the *wakeUp* operation:

$$
\begin{aligned}
\textbf{post} \quad \textbf{let} \quad &pos = findPos(\overline{waiting}, idIn) \\
\textbf{in} \quad \textbf{let} \quad &wakeProcess = \textbf{mk-}Process(idIn, <\text{READY}>) \\
\textbf{in} \quad &waiting = \overline{waiting} \dagger \{pos \mapsto wakeProcess\}
\end{aligned}
$$

Here two **let … in** clauses are used, but the final expression becomes much clearer as a result.

EXERCISES

1. Consider a collection of sensors (numbered 1 to 10). Sensors are one of two types, temperature and pressure. Each sensor, as well as having a number and a type has a reading. Initially no readings will be recorded for sensors. Pressure sensors can only have positive readings but temperature sensors can have negative and positive readings.

   (i) Declare a composite type *Sensor*, defining any additional types and composite type invariant you think necessary.
   (ii) Declare a state attribute *sensors* to be a set of sensors.
   (iii) Using set comprehension, initialize this state attribute so that it contains 10 sensors numbered from 1 to 10, sensors from 1 to 6 are temperature sensors, the others are pressure sensors. Initially all sensor readings will be set to **nil**.

2. Amend the *DiskScanner* specification by imposing a maximum track and sector number on the disk surface. Assume 80 tracks and 9 sectors.
3. Use **let…in** clauses to improve the readability of operation specifications in the *ProcessManagement* class specification.

4. Consider a system to monitor the relationship between the maximum temperature of a blast furnace during the day, and whether or not an emergency occurred during that day. Readings are to be taken for a period of 30 consecutive days. Figure 9.7 gives the UML specification for the *Readings* class. The *Reading* type is specified in figure 9.8.

The operations are informally defined as follows:
addReading: takes the maximum temperature for a day, and whether or not there was an emergency that day and records this information in the system.
wasEmergency: takes a day number and reports on whether or not an emergency occurred during that day.
getTemperatures: returns a collection of temperatures on all days there was an emergency (this collection should allow for repetitions).
numberOfEmegencies: returns the number of emergencies recorded so far.

Specify this class formally in VDM-SL.

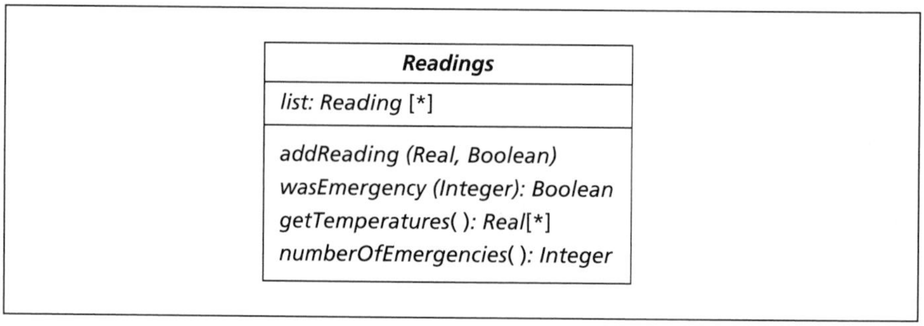

Readings
list: Reading [*]
addReading (Real, Boolean) wasEmergency (Integer): Boolean getTemperatures( ): Real[*] numberOfEmergencies( ): Integer

Figure 9.7 UML specification of the *Readings* class

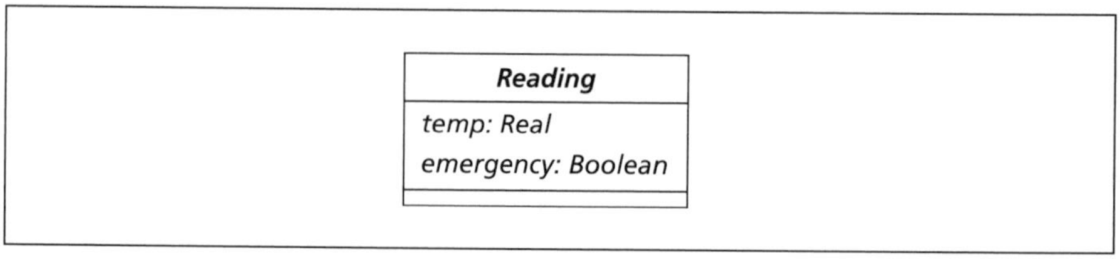

Reading
temp: Real emergency: Boolean

Figure 9.8 UML specification of the *Reading* type

CHAPTER 10

Implementing Composite Objects

10.1 Introduction

In previous chapters we have encountered two of the collection types of VDM-SL (sets and sequences) and discussed two Java classes (`VDMSet` and `VDMSequence`) that we developed to model these types. We now turn our attention to the implementation of specifications involving composite objects. Specific composite object types are specified as and when they are required in VDM specifications. The number and type of fields associated with these composite types will almost always vary so we cannot provide a standard composite object implementation in Java. Instead, you will need to define a suitable type for any composite objects you have in your specification. We discuss how to go about defining such types in Java and then go on to develop implementations of specifications involving composite objects.

10.2 Implementing the *Time* Type

In the previous chapter we introduced you to composite objects by specifying a `Time` type. Here, again is its definition:

Time:: *hour*: $\mathbb{N}$

     minutes: $\mathbb{N}$

     seconds: $\mathbb{N}$

inv mk-*Time* (h, m, s) $\underline{\Delta}$ $h < 24 \ \wedge \ m < 60 \ \wedge \ s < 60$

A composite object type in VDM, such as `Time`, consists of a collection of publicly accessible fields of data. We can model such a composite object type in Java by developing a `Time` class with publicly accessible attributes corresponding to the fields of the composite object. Care has to be taken here, however. The composite object operators, as with all VDM-SL operators, have no *side-effects*. That is, they do not alter the original object. This is identical to the concept of an *immutable* object in Java. An immutable object is one whose attributes cannot be modified once initialized. As we have made the attributes of this object **public**, we should also declare them to be **final** so that they cannot be modified:

```
class Time
{
        public final int hour;
        public final int minute;
        public final int second;
        // more code here
}
```

Now, if a variable is declared to be of type Time in the VDM specification, it can be declared to be of type *Time* in the Java code too. For example:

VDM-SL	Java
someTime: *Time*	`Time someTime;`

Composite objects are created by passing appropriate values for each object field to a **make** function. This corresponds to the idea of a constructor in a class. The order of the values sent to the **make** function is the order in which the fields are declared so we will stick to this in our constructor for the Time class:

```
public Time(int hourIn, int minuteIn, int secondIn)
{
    hour = hourIn;
    minute = minuteIn;
    second = secondIn;
}
```

Now, when reference is made to a **mk**-*Time* function in VDM-SL we can call the Time constructor. For example:

VDM-SL	Java
someTime: **mk**-*Time(10, 45, 05)*	`someTime = ` **new** `Time (10,45,05)`

Of course, some composite object types (such as this Time type) can have an invariant associated with them. We can implement this invariant within the Time class just as we did with invariants in previous classes: by defining an inv method and marking the class as implementing the `InvariantCheck` interface. As we said in Chapter 4, we have to be careful here, as we are using the **int** type of Java to model the natural number type of VDM-SL. Natural numbers must be non-negative so we must add this requirement into our invariant:

```
class Time implements InvariantCheck

{

    // other code here

    public boolean inv()

    {

        // check integers are non-negative and check specified invariant

        return hour >= 0 && minute >= 0 && second >= 0

        && hour < 24 && minute < 60 && second < 60;

    }

}
```

It is important that objects that break the object invariant are not created. As before, we should monitor for this by checking the invariant within the constructor. So a better constructor would be given as follows:

```
public Time(int hourIn, int minuteIn, int secondIn)

{

    hour = hourIn;

    minute = minuteIn;

    second = secondIn;

    VDM.invTest(this); // check invariant of this composite object

}
```

Now, the following attempt at creating an invalid composite `Time` object would fail and a `VDMException` would be thrown:

```
someOtherTime = new Time (32, 45, 10); // invalid hour causes VDMException
```

The publicly accessible fields of a `Time` object can be accessed in the same way as those of a VDM-SL object – by the dot operator:

VDM-SL	Java
someTime.hour < 12	`someTime.hour < 12`

A **mu** function is provided in VDM-SL for returning a copy of an object but with one or more fields modified. There is no simple way to provide such a method within a Java class so we will translate the **mu** function to the appropriate **mk** function (as demonstrated in the previous chapter) and implement this **mk** function as a call to a constructor in Java. For example:

VDM-SL	Java

thisTime =
 	
    μ *(someTime, minute* $\mapsto$ *0, second* $\mapsto$ *0)*
	`thisTime =`
	
	    `new Time (someTime.hour,0,0)`

As with all classes, the methods `equals` and `toString` are required for this class to be useful. The complete code listing for the `Time` class is now given below:

The *Time* class

```
class Time implements InvariantCheck
{
  public final int hour;
  public final int minute;
  public final int second;
  public Time(int hourIn, int minuteIn, int secondIn)
  {
    hour = hourIn;
    minute = minuteIn;
    second = secondIn;
    VDM.invTest(this);
  }
public boolean inv()
  {
    return hour > = 0 && minute > = 0 && second > = 0
      && hour < 24 && minute < 60 && second < 60;
  }
```

```
// next two methods should be provided with every Java class

public boolean equals(Object objIn)

{

  Time timeIn  = (Time) objIn;

  return hour = = timeIn.hour && minute  = = timeIn.minute && second  = = timeIn.second;

}

public String toString()

{

  return "mk-Time("+ hour +","+ minute +","+ second +")";

}

}
```

The `toString` method allows a `Time` object to be displayed in an output statement such as the following:

```
System.out.println(new Time (12, 30, 22));
```

This would call the `toString` method of `Time` and display the following:

```
mk-Time (12, 30, 22)
```

The procedure we followed for implementing the composite `Time` class will be the same procedure we follow throughout the rest of this book for implementing any composite object type. We look now at the implementation of the specifications in the previous chapter.

10.3   Implementing the *DiskScanner* Specification

The *DiskScanner* specification of the previous chapter included the definition of a composite `Block` type:

Block : : *track*: $\mathbb{N}$

  sector: $\mathbb{N}$

Following the guidelines of the previous section this composite type can be implemented as a `Block` class as follows:

The *Block* class

```
class Block implements InvariantCheck
{
  public final int track;
  public final int sector;
  public Block(int trackIn, int sectorIn)
  {
    track = trackIn;
    sector = sectorIn;
    VDM.invTest(this);
  }
// need to add invariant as integers are being used to model natural numbers
  public boolean inv()
  {
    return track >= 0 && sector >= 0;
  }
  public boolean equals(Object objectIn) // redefine equals method
  {
    Block blockIn = (Block) objectIn;
    return (track == blockIn.track) && (sector == blockIn.sector);
  }
  public String toString() // add a toString method
  {
   return "mk-Block("+ track +","+ sector +")";
  }
}
```

Notice that, although the original VDM specification had no invariant on this type, we have had to add an invariant into the `Block` class. The reason for this is that the natural number attributes of VDM-SL have been modelled using integers in Java and we must ensure that negative integer values are disallowed.

Returning to the *DiskScanner* specification, the state can be implemented in the usual way as follows:

VDM-SL	Java

state *DiskScanner* **of**
 	
 damagedBlocks : *Block*-**set**
 init **mk**-*DiskScanner* (*dB*) $\underline{\Delta}$ *dB* = { }
	``
	class DiskScanner
	{
	    private VDMSet damagedBlocks;
	    public DiskScanner()
	    {
	        damagedBlocks = new VDMSet();
	    }
	``

Turning to the operations now, take a look at the translation of `addBlock`:

VDM-SL
addBlock (*trackIn*: $\mathbb{N}$, *sectorIn*: $\mathbb{N}$)
ext **wr** *damagedBlocks*: *Block*-**set**
pre   **mk**-*Block* (*trackIn, sectorIn*) $\notin$ *damagedBlocks*
post   *damagedBlocks* = $\overline{damaged\,Blocks}$ $\cup$ {**mk**-*Block* (*trackIn, sectorIn*)}

Java

``
public void addBlock(int trackIn, int sectorIn)
{
  VDM.preTest(damagedBlocks.doesNotContain (new Block(trackIn, sectorIn)));
  damagedBlocks = damagedBlocks.union(new VDMSet (new Block(trackIn, sectorIn)));
  VDM.invTest(this);
}
``

Notice how the **mk**-*Block* function of VDM-SL is translated into a call to the `Block` constructor. The `Block` constructor checks that the track and sector numbers are both natural numbers. In the postcondition of the VDM operation, this **mk** function is used within a singleton set definition, so the equivalent Java expression places the call to the `Block` constructor within the call to the appropriate `VDMSet` constructor:

VDM-SL	Java
....{ **mk**–*Block* (*trackIn, sectorIn*) }	...new VDMSet(new Block(trackIn, sectorIn))

We look now at the translation of the *getBadSectors* operation. Here, once again, is the VDM specification:

getBadSectors (*trackIn*: ℕ) *list*: ℕ-**set**

ext   **rd**   *damagedBlocks*: *Block*-**set**

pre   TRUE

post *list* = {*b.sector* | *b* ∈ *damagedBlocks* • *b.track* = *trackIn*}

The postcondition here employs set comprehension. This comprehension consists of a range, a test and an expression. The range is the set *damagedBlocks*. So the following form of set comprehension is required in the Java method:

```
VDMSet.setComp( new Expression(){public Object action (Object x) {// some code here}},

        damagedBlocks, // range

        new Testable(){public boolean test (Object x){// some code here}});
```

Both the action and the test method receive a parameter of type `Object`. This has to be type-cast to be of type `Block` in each case, then the appropriate action and test can be coded. Here is the translation of the `action` method:

VDM-SL	Java

b.sector	```public Object action (Object x)```
	```{```
	``` Block b = (Block)x; // type-cast to Block```
	``` return new Integer(b.sector); // return as object```
	```}```

Notice that we have to ensure that the item returned is an object, not a primitive type. So, we create an `Integer` object from the sector number. Here now is the translation of the `test` method:

VDM-SL	Java

b.track = trackIn	```
	public boolean test (Object x)
	{
	    Block b = (Block) x;
	    return b.track = = trackIn;
	}
	``

The complete `DiskScanner` class is now presented below. Examine it closely and compare it to the original specification.

The *DiskScanner* class

```
class DiskScanner
{
   private VDMSet damagedBlocks; // attribute
   public DiskScanner() // initialization
   {
      damagedBlocks = new VDMSet();
   }
   // operations
   public void addBlock(int trackIn, int sectorIn)
   {
     VDM.preTest(damagedBlocks.doesNotContain(new Block(trackIn, sectorIn)));
     damagedBlocks = damagedBlocks.union(new VDMSet(new Block (trackIn, sectorIn)));
   }
   public void removeBlock(int trackIn, int sectorIn)
   {
     VDM.preTest(damagedBlocks.contains(new Block(trackIn, sectorIn)));
     damagedBlocks = damagedBlocks.difference(new VDMSet(new Block(trackIn, sectorIn)));
   }
   public boolean isDamaged(int trackIn, int sectorIn)
   {
     return damagedBlocks.contains(new Block(trackIn, sectorIn));
   }
   public VDMSet getBadSectors(final int trackIn)
```

```
{

  return VDMSet.setComp(new Expression()

                        {

                            public Object action (Object x)

                            {

                                    Block b = (Block)x;

                                    return new Integer(b.sector);

                            }

                        },

                        damagedBlocks,

                        new Testable()

                        {

                                public boolean test (Object x)

                                {

                                        Block b = (Block) x;

                                        return b.track = = trackIn;

                                }

                        }

                    );

}

public VDMSet getDamagedBlocks()

{

  return damagedBlocks;

}

// additional toString method

public String toString()

{

    return "damaged blocks:\t" + damagedBlocks;

  }

}
```

10.4   Implementing the *ProcessManagement* System

To end this chapter we consider an implementation of the *ProcessManagement* class.
The implementation of this class allows us to discuss how **nil** values can be dealt with
in respect to objects. Also, we will look at the issues raised when implementing highly

implicit postconditions and show you how **let ... in** clauses can be incorporated into Java methods.

10.5   The Data Model

Here is a reminder of the original specification of the data:

types

String = char*

Status = <READY> | <BLOCKED>

Process :: id : String

　　　　　status : Status

state *ProcessManagement* **of**

　　　　　running : [String]

　　　　　waiting : Process*

inv　　**mk-***ProcessManagement (run, wait)* $\underline{\Delta}$
　　　　　　　　　　　*(run = **nil** $\vee \neg \exists i \in$ **inds** wait • wait(i).id = run)*

　　　　　　　　　$\wedge$

　　　　　　　　　$\forall i,j \in$ **inds** *wait • i ≠ j $\Rightarrow$ wait(i).id ≠ wait(j).id*

init　　**mk-***ProcessManagement (run, wait)* $\underline{\Delta}$ *run = **nil** $\wedge$ wait = [ ]*

end

The `String` type is already available in Java. The *Status* type will be implemented as a `Status` class following the guidelines given in Chapter 4:

The *Status* class

```
class Status
{
    private int value;
    public static final Status READY = new Status(0);
    public static final Status BLOCKED = new Status (1);

    private Status(int x)
    {
        value = x;
    }
```

```
public boolean equals(Object objectIn)

{

     Status s = (Status) objectIn;

     return value = = s.value;

}

public String toString()

{

   switch(value)

   {

     case 0: return "READY";

     default:return "BLOCKED";

   }

  }

}
```

The composite *Process* type will be implemented as the following `Process` class following the guidelines given earlier in this chapter:

The *Process* class

```
class Process

{

   public final String id;

   public final Status status;

   public Process (String idIn, Status statusIn)

   {

     id = idIn;

     status = statusIn;

   }

   public boolean equals (Object processIn)

{

     Process p = (Process)processIn;
```

```
      return p.id.equals(id) && p.status.equals(status);
  }
   public String toString()
   {
      return "mk-Process("+ id +", "+ status +")";
   }
}
```

Returning to the `ProcessManagement` class, the attributes are coded in the obvious way from the VDM specification:

VDM-SL	Java

state *ProcessManagement* **of**
running : [*String*]
waiting : *Process**
	`class ProcessManagementSystem implements InvariantCheck`
	`{`
	`  private String running;`
	`  private VDMSequence waiting;`
	`  // more code here`
	`}`

The class is marked as implementing the `InvariantCheck` interface as we will be including an invariant method. Notice that the fact that the *running* attribute was specified as being of type *String* or **nil**, in the Java class we just declare it as being of type `String`.

VDM-SL	Java
running : [*String*]	`private String running;`

We will use the `null` value of Java to represent the **nil** value of VDM-SL for objects such as the *running* attribute. All objects in Java can take the `null` value without needing to modify the object type.

The initialization clause contains two conjuncts, the first requiring the *running* attribute to be equal to **nil**, the second requiring the *waiting* attribute to be equal to the empty sequence. This can be satisfied by two assignments:

VDM-SL	Java

init mk-*ProcessManagement* (*run, wait*) $\underline{\Delta}$
 	
run = **nil** $\wedge$ *wait* = [ ]
	``
	public ProcessManagementSystem()
	{
	    running = null;
	    waiting = new VDMSequence();
	    VDM.invTest(this);
	}
	``

Notice the invariant test at the end of this constructor as this class contains an invariant method.

Turning to the implementation of the invariant, there are two conjuncts to code in the Java method. Here is the first:

run = **nil** $\vee$ $\neg\exists i \in$**inds** *wait* $\bullet$ *wait*(*i*).*id* = run

This disjunction can be coded as a disjunction in Java but we have to be careful about the ordering of the Java expression. The ordering of the VDM-SL expression is unimportant and could have been given as follows:

$\neg\exists i \in$**inds** *wait* $\bullet$ *wait*(*i*).*id* = *run* $\vee$ *run* = **nil**

If the running process is equal to **nil**, however, the first disjunct will be undefined in Java and may cause program termination during evaluation. For this reason, as we stated in Chapter 4, we must place the potentially undefined expression second in the disjunction:

```
running == null || // translation of second disjunct here
```

Notice that we use the **null** value of Java to represent the **nil** value here, and the standard equality (==) operator is used in Java to check for this value, not an `equals` method. The second disjunct is an existential quantifier:

$\neg\exists i \in$**inds** *wait* $\bullet$ *wait*(*i*).*id* = *run*

We use the `exists` method of our VDM class here. This quantifier is quantifying over the indices of the `waiting` sequence. The set of indices will always be a set of integers so the associated test is a test on an integer value. `TestableInt` is the appropriate interface to implement here:

VDM-SL	Java

¬∃*i*∈**inds** *wait* ●
 	
    wait(*i*) .*id* = *run*
	```!VDM.exists (waiting.inds(), // range```
	``` new TestableInt()```
	``` { public boolean test (int i) // test```
	``` {```
	``` Process p = (Process) (waiting.index(i));```
	``` return p.id.equals(running);```
	``` }```
	``` });```

The `test` method takes an index and retrieves the object at that index in the waiting sequence. The `index` method of `VDMSequence` returns an item of type `Object` so this first needs to be type-cast to a `Process` object:

```
Process p = (Process)(waiting.index(i)); //type-cast returned item to a Process
```

The *id* field of this object can then be examined and compared to the *id* of the running process:

```
return p.id.equals(running);
```

The second conjunction is a two-placed quantifier:

$$\forall \; i,j \in \textbf{inds} \; wait \bullet i \neq j \Rightarrow wait(i).id \neq wait(j).id$$

We demonstrated in Chapter 8 how two-placed quantifiers can be implemented in Java as a pair of nested quantifiers. Here is the complete state translation including this two-placed quantifier:

```
class ProcessManagementSystem implements InvariantCheck
{
  private String running;

  private VDMSequence waiting;

  public ProcessManagementSystem()

  {
```

```
    running = null;

  waiting = new VDMSequence();

  VDM.invTest(this);

}

public boolean inv()

{

  return (running == null || !VDM.exists

                              (waiting.inds(),

                                new TestableInt()

                                {

                                  public boolean test (int i)

                                  {

                                    Process p = (Process)(waiting.index(i));
                                    return p.id.equals(running);

                                  }

                                }

                              )

          )

          &&

          // two placed quantifier implemented as a pair of nested quantfiers
          VDM.forall

              (waiting.inds(),

                      new TestableInt ()

                      {

                        public boolean test (final int i)
                          // remember to declare i final

                        {

                      return VDM.forall // test contains a second quantifier

                          (waiting.inds(),

                          new TestableInt()

                          {

                            public boolean test (int j)

                            {

                                // type cast two objects

                              Process first = (Process) (waiting.index(i));

                              Process second = (Process) (waiting.index(j));
```

```
                    // check predicate
                return VDM.implies (i! = j,!first.id.equals(second.id));
            }
        }
      );
    }
  }
 );
}
// rest of class here
}
```

10.6   The Functions

Before we consider the operations, the *ProcessManagement* specification included a number of function definitions. These can also be implemented as methods of the ProcessManagement class. For example, here is the specification of the *remove* function:

remove(*qIn* : *Process**, *posIn* : $\mathbb{N}$) *qOut* : *Process**

pre *posIn* $\in$ **inds** *qIn*

post *qOut* = *qIn*(1,..., *posIn*-1) $\wedge$ *qIn*(*posIn* + 1,...,**len** *qIn*)

VDM functions do not form part of the public interface of the class so they should be declared as **private** methods of the class. Here is the equivalent Java method:

```
private VDMSequence remove (VDMSequence qIn, int posIn)
{
  VDM.preTest(posIn > = 0 && qIn.inds().contains(posIn));
  return qIn.subseq(1, posIn-1).concat(qIn.subseq(posIn+1, qIn.len())) ;
}
```

Notice how the precondition has to be extended to ensure that the integer received as parameter is non-negative, as the VDM specification indicates it must be a natural number:

```
VDM.preTest(posIn >= 0 && qIn.inds().contains(posIn));
```

The postcondition is fairly explicit in the sense that an obvious sequence concatenation is suggested:

```
return qIn.subseq(1, posIn-1).concat(qIn.subseq(posIn + 1, qIn.len())) ;
```

In fact all the postconditions we have met so far have suggested quite obvious implementations. The postconditions for the remaining two functions, however, are very implicit and declarative – they succinctly say *what* is required of the final result without indicating in anyway *how* to achieve that result. For example, here again is the specification for the *findPos* function that returns the index of a process within a sequence with a given ID:

findPos(*qIn* : *Process**, *idIn* : *String*) *pos* : $\mathbb{N}$

pre $\exists p \in$ **elems** *qIn* $\bullet$ *p.id* = *idIn*

post *qIn(pos).id* = *idIn*

The header and the precondition are straightforward to translate:

```
private int findPos(VDMSequence qIn, final String idIn)

{

      VDM.preTest(VDM.exists(qIn.elems(),

                 new Testable()

                 {

                   public boolean test (Object pIn)

                   {

                        Process p = (Process)pIn;

                        return p.id.equals(idIn);

                   }

                 } ));

      // implement postcondition here

}
```

Notice that the `idIn` parameter has to be declared final in order to reference it within the inner class of the precondition test:

```
private int findPos(VDMSequence qIn, final String idIn)
```

The postcondition specifies the requirement that if the position returned were used to look up a `Process` object in the sequence, the ID of that process should match the ID submitted as a parameter. No clue is given, however, as to how this ID is to be found.

The implementation of this function will require a search of the given sequence to find the appropriate process. The precondition ensures that such a process exists. A common search algorithm employs a **boolean** flag and a loop to examine each item in turn until the correct item is found. This algorithm can be expressed in pseudocode as follows:

```
SET pos to 1

SET found to FALSE

WHILE not found

BEGIN

    IF current item meets search criteria

            SET found to TRUE

    ELSE

            increment pos

    ENDIF

END
```

At the end of this loop the variable `pos` will be the position of the correct item in the list. We will use this algorithm for implementing the `findPos` postcondition as follows:

```
int pos = 1;

boolean found = false;

while (!found)
```

```
    {
        Process p = (Process) (qIn.index(pos)); // type-cast current item to a Process

        if (idIn.equals(p.id)) // check ID

        {
            found = true;
        }

        else

        {
            pos++;
        }
    }

    return pos; // return result
```

If we were developing our code totally formally we would need to prove that this design and consequent implementation satisfied the original postcondition. In our lightweight approach to formal program development we will rely upon run-time integrity checks to monitor the correctness of the code.

One run-time check that we have shown you is that of consistently checking the system invariant. When a postcondition is particularly implicit, as in this case, it may be worthwhile adding an extra check to ensure that each time the function is called the postcondition is satisfied. We can do this by adding a postcondition check in much the same way we added a precondition check. We do this by calling the postTest method of our VDM class following the implementation of the postcondition:

```
    private int findPos(VDMSequence qIn, final String idIn)
    {
        VDM.preTest( /* pre test here */ )

        // code to implement postcondition here

        VDM.postTest(((Process)qIn.index(pos)).id.equals(idIn)); // check postcondition test

        return pos; // return position if postcondition test holds

    }
```

Now, if the software was tested and the findPos method called, the postcondition test would be evaluated before returning the value of *pos*. If there was an error in the implementation the test would fail and a VDMException would be thrown, alerting us of this mistake. If no mistake were made the method would continue and return the appropriate value of *pos*.

Such a test is clearly useful during testing. If, after the testing process was complete, we were reasonably confident that the final code was correct, we might choose to remove this test. Since testing can never guarantee correctness, however, we might choose to leave in this test to guard against any future failure.

We leave the implementation of the last function (`findFirst`) as an exercise and turn now to the implementation of the operations.

10.7   The Operations

Here is the translation of the `admit` operation, take a look at it and then we will discuss it:

VDM-SL

---

admit (*idIn* : *String*)

ext   **wr**   *waiting* : *Process**

        rd   *running* : [*String*]

pre   (*running* = **nil** ∨ *idIn* ≠ *running*) ∧ ∀*p* ∈ **elems** *waiting* • *p.id* ≠ *idIn*

post   *waiting* = $\overline{waiting}$ ^ [**mk-**Process(idIn, <READY>)]

Java

```java
public void admit(final String idIn)
{
     VDM.preTest((running = = null || !idIn.equals(running)) &&
                 (VDM.forall(waiting.elems(),
                   new Testable()
                   {
                      public boolean test (Object pIn)
                      {
                         Process p = (Process) pIn;
                         return !(p.id.equals(idIn));
                      }
                   })
                 )
              );
     waiting = waiting.concat(new VDMSequence(new Process(idIn, Status.READY)));
     VDM.invTest(this);
}
```

Notice that the parameter, `idIn` once again needs to be declared as **final** as it is accessed within an inner class:

```java
public void admit(final String idIn)
```

The precondition and the implementation of the postcondition then follow directly from the specification. Since this method has write access to the state, an invariant check is added at the end of the method.

Here is the translation of *block* operation:

VDM-SL

block( )

ext   **wr**   *running*: *[ID]*

wr   *waiting*: *Process**

pre   *running* ≠ **nil**

post   *waiting* = *waiting* ^ [**mk**-*Process*(*waiting*), <BLOCKED>)] ∧ *running* = **nil**

Java

```
public void block()

{

        VDM.preTest(running ! = null);

        waiting = waiting.concat(new VDMSequence(new Process(running,

                                        Status.BLOCKED)));

        running = null;

        VDM.invTest(this);

}
```

The precondition test follows directly from the specification. Again notice that, when checking for the **null** value in Java, the standard comparison operators (! =) are used not the `equals` method.

The postcondition consists of two conjuncts that are satisfied by two assignments. Care has to be taken here. Although the ordering of the conjuncts is unimportant in VDM-SL, the ordering of the assignments clearly is. The following would be incorrect:

```
// ordering of assigments important, this would be incorrect

running = null; // resets the value of 'running'

waiting = waiting.concat(new VDMSequence(new Process(running, Status.BLOCKED)));
```

The value of an attribute, such as *running*, should not be reset if its old value is still required. The old value of *running* is required when updating the *waiting* attribute, as made clear in the post-condition:

$$waiting = \overline{waiting} \ \hat{} \ [\textbf{mk-}Process(\overline{running}, <\text{BLOCKED}>)]$$

This old value of *running* will be lost if its old value is overwritten, so the assignment to the waiting attribute needs to be carried out first. Again, this method needs to check the invariant before completion.

Finally, we consider the `wakeUp` operation. Here is the specification of the method that made use of the **let ... in** clause:

---

wakeUp (idIn : String)

ext   **wr**   *waiting : Process**

pre   **let**   *pos = findPos (waiting, idIn)*

         in   *waiting (pos) . status =* $<$BLOCKED$>$

post   **let**   *pos = findPos ($\overline{waiting}$, idIn)*

         in   *waiting = $\overline{waiting}$ (pos)* † **mk**-*Process(idIn,* $<$READY$>$*)*

When implementing an operation that employs a **let ... in** clause, the local variable that is implicitly created in the VDM operation can also be created in the associated Java method. Whereas in VDM the scope of the **let ... in** variable is a given pre- or postcondition, the scope of such a variable in the Java method can be the whole method. You can see from the specification above that the variable defined, *pos*, has the same value in both the pre- and postcondition, so we will create one variable and make reference to it in both the `preTest` and the implementation of the postcondition. The type of this variable is not declared in the VDM specification but can be determined as being of type $\mathbb{N}$. We can create an equivalent variable in our Java method:

```
public void wakeUp (String idIn)

{

    int pos = findPos(waiting, idIn); // create local variable;

    // rest of method here

}
```

This variable is now used in the remainder of the method:

```
VDM.preTest(((Process)waiting.index(pos)).status.equals(Status.BLOCKED));

waiting = waiting.override(pos,new Process(idIn, Status.READY));
```

The implementation of the remaining operations of this `ProcessManagement` class we leave as an exercise.

EXERCISES

1. Why did the implementation of the `Block` class in section 10.2 include an invariant, when no invariant was associated with the composite Block type in the VDM specification?

2. In exercise 1 of the last chapter you considered the specification of a composite Sensor type. Implement this as a class in Java, then write a tester program to initialize and display a set of sensors as described in the same question.

3. Implement the `DiskScanner` class, including the amendments you considered to this class in exercise 2 of the last chapter.

4. Test the `DiskScanner` class by developing an appropriate tester program.

5. In exercise 3 of the last chapter, you rewrote the operation specifications of the `ProcessManagement` class by making use of **let ... in** clauses. Rewrite the `Process Management` class to incorporate these changes.

6. Test the `ProcessManagement` class by developing an appropriate tester program.

7. Implement the `Readings` class you specified in exercise 4 of the previous chapter.

8. Test the `Readings` class by developing an appropriate tester program.

Maps

11.1 Introduction

Computing systems often involve relating two types of value together. In Chapter 3 you were introduced to the idea of a function; you saw that a function is a set of assignments from one set to another. A map is closely related to the concept of functions. A map is a special sort of set, one which contains a set of **maplets**. Each maplet connects an element of one set to an element of another set; the first set is referred to as the **domain**, the second is referred to as the **range**.

11.2 Notation

Consider Table 11.1, which shows the state of a number of different temperature sensors that monitor the condition of various items in a laboratory. The condition of each item can be either LOW, NORMAL or HIGH.

We can express the Table 11.1 as a map, which we might call *sensors*. This will be a mapping from a set of sensors to the set of possible conditions. We do this as follows.

$$sensors = \{A \mapsto \text{<LOW>}, B \mapsto \text{<NORMAL>}, C \mapsto \text{<NORMAL>}, D \mapsto \text{<HIGH>},$$
$$E \mapsto \text{<NORMAL>}, F \mapsto \text{<NORMAL>}\}$$

You can see that a map is defined by listing the maplets within a pair of curly brackets; the association is represented by the special arrow, $\mapsto$.

In general terms, a particular map, m, might be specified as follows:

$$m = \{a \mapsto y, b \mapsto x, c \mapsto x, d \mapsto z\}$$

Table 11.1 A look-up table for a set of sensors

Sensor	Condition
A	LOW
B	NORMAL
C	NORMAL
D	HIGH
E	NORMAL
F	NORMAL

Two important points should be noted here:

- By definition, all the domain elements in a map are unique.
- The ordering of the maplets is not significant – the map m above could be specified, without changing the meaning, as:

$$m = \{d \mapsto z, a \mapsto y, c \mapsto x, b \mapsto x\}$$

You should also note that the empty map is written as: $\{\mapsto\}$.

11.3   Map Operators

In order to illustrate the use of the various map operators that exist, we will define the following three maps, all of which map from some previously defined set (the members of which are represented here by lower case letters) to the set of natural numbers.

$$m1 = \{a \mapsto 1, b \mapsto 2, c \mapsto 2, d \mapsto 3, e \mapsto 4\}$$
$$m2 = \{a \mapsto 2, f \mapsto 1, c \mapsto 7\}$$
$$m3 = \{f \mapsto 2, g \mapsto 6\}$$

The *domain* operator, **dom**, returns the set of all the domain elements of the maplets. The *range* operator, **rng**, returns the set of all the range elements.

$$\textbf{dom } m1 = \{a, b, c, d, e\}$$
$$\textbf{rng } m1 = \{1, 2, 3, 4\}$$

$$\textbf{dom } m2 = \{a, f, c\}$$
$$\textbf{rng } m2 = \{1, 2, 7\}$$

The **union** operator, $\cup$, behaves in a similar way as it does with sets. So

$$m1 \cup m3 = \{a \mapsto 1, b \mapsto 2, c \mapsto 2, d \mapsto 3, e \mapsto 4, f \mapsto 2, g \mapsto 6\}$$

The union operator is defined only if no two domain elements are the same; if this is not the case, then union is undefined (otherwise we would lose the uniqueness of the keys). Thus the following two expressions are undefined:

$$m1 \cup m2$$
$$m2 \cup m3$$

In the case where two or more domain elements are the same in both maps, we can use the **override** operator ($\dagger$). This behaves in the same way as the union operator, but if the domain element of a maplet is the same in both sets, then the second maplet wins. Thus

$$m1 \dagger m2 = \{a \mapsto 2, b \mapsto 2, c \mapsto 7, d \mapsto 3, e \mapsto 4, f \mapsto 1\}$$
$$m3 \dagger m2 = \{f \mapsto 1, g \mapsto 6, a \mapsto 2, c \mapsto 7\}$$

A **domain restriction** operator, $\lhd$, is defined with two operands (parameters). The first is a set and the second is a map. The result yields a map that contains only those maplets whose domain element is in the set. For example

$\{a, c, e\} \lhd m1 = \{a \mapsto 1, c \mapsto 2, e \mapsto 4\}$
$\{e, f\} \lhd m2 = \{f \mapsto 1\}$
$\{\} \lhd m3 = \{\mapsto\}$

The **domain deletion** operator, $\lhd\!\!-$, behaves in a similar way, but in this case deletes the maplet in question:

$\{a, c, e\} \lhd\!\!- m1 = \{b \mapsto 2, d \mapsto 3\}$
$\{e, f\} \lhd\!\!- m2 = \{a \mapsto 2, c \mapsto 7\}$
$\{\} \lhd\!\!- m3 = \{f \mapsto 2, g \mapsto 6\}$

The **range restriction** operator, $\rhd$, and the **range deletion** operator, $\rhd\!\!-$, are similar to the above, but apply to the last elements of the maplets. Thus

$m1 \rhd \{1, 2\} = \{a \mapsto 1, b \mapsto 2, c \mapsto 2\}$
$m3 \rhd \{6, 2\} = \{\mapsto\}$

11.4 Map Application

Applying a map is the same as applying a function, and we use the same notation. Thus if we apply our map to a particular domain element, then the result is the range element. For example, once again using the above maps:

$m1(d) = 3$
$m2(f) = 1$
$m3(f) = 2$
$m3(x)$ is undefined

Using the *sensors* example from section 11.2:

$sensors(\text{A}) = <\text{LOW}>$

11.5 Using the Map Type in VDM-SL

To declare a variable to be of type *Map* we use a special arrow $\xrightarrow{m}$. For example, to declare a variable m that maps characters to natural numbers we would write:

$m : Char \xrightarrow{m} \mathbb{N}$

11.6 Specifying a High-Security Building

The first example we will specify is a system that controls entry and exit to a high-security building. We start with the requirements definition.

11.6.1 REQUIREMENTS DEFINITION

Only authorized employees are allowed entry to the building and each one consists of a user name (which is unique) and a password, both of which must be supplied when the individual wishes to enter the building. If the details are correct, a signal is sent to the hardware instructing it to open the door, and the member of staff is recorded as being inside the building.

When the member of staff wishes to leave the building, the individual supplies his or her user name, and as long as the user is recorded as being currently inside the building, a signal is sent to the hardware to open the door, and the employee is recorded as having left.

The UML diagram for the system is shown in Figure 11.1.

You can see that we have identified two attributes. The first we have specified to be a collection of *Employees*. The second will be a collection of names – the names of those employees currently inside the building.

Two user-defined types are identified in Figure 11.1, *Employee* and *Signal*. They both need to be analysed further. An employee consists of name–password pair. The UML specification of an *Employee* type is given in Figure 11.2.

As will be seen in a moment, there are two possible signal values, either OPEN_DOOR or ACTIVATE_ALARM. An appropriate enumerated type can be specified in UML (Figure 11.3).

Four operations have been identified, and these are described below:

addEmployee
Accepts a name and password, and adds this pair to the collection of authorized personnel.

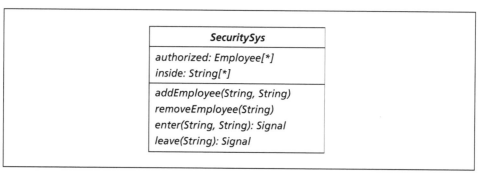

Figure 11.1 The UML diagram for the security system

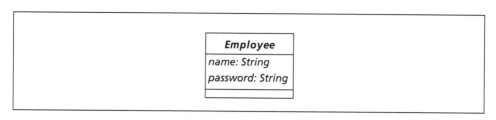

Figure 11.2 The UML specification of the *Employee* type

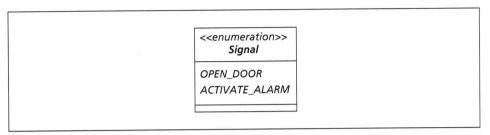

Figure 11.3   The UML specification of the *Signal* type

removeEmployee
Removes a specified employee from the list of authorized employees, providing that
that person is not currently inside the building.

enter
Accepts a name and password. If these details match an entry in the authorized list,
then a signal is sent to the hardware, telling it open the door, and the entry of the individual is recorded. If the details are incorrect the signal sent instructs the hardware to
set off an alarm.

leave
Accepts a name of an employee and if this individual is currently inside the building,
then a signal is sent to the hardware telling it to open the door, and the departure of
the individual is recorded. If the employee is not inside the building, the signal sent
instructs the hardware to set off an alarm.

11.6.2 THE VDM-SL SPECIFICATION

We begin with the types clause. A *String* and *Signal* type can be specified in the obvious way:

types

String = Char*

Signal = $<$OPEN_DOOR$>$ $|$ $<$ACTIVATE_ALARM$>$

The UML analysis also suggested an *Employee* type. Figure 11.2 identified that such
a type would need to consist of a name and password pair. A composite type could be
declared here, and the collection of employees modelled as a *set*. But we note from the
analysis that the names of employees are to be unique. Rather than use a set and
impose this restriction on the model as an invariant, we can use a map from names to
passwords. Such a map would guarantee the uniqueness of names and so avoid the
need to capture this in an invariant. A map would also simplify the final model by
removing the need for a composite type.

Figure 11.2 indicates that both name and password are strings so the following map
would be appropriate:

authorized : String $\xrightarrow{m}$ *String*

We now define the state as follows – it consists of a collection of employees (name–password mappings), representing the authorized employees, and a set of names of those employees currently inside the building. A set of names is appropriate as ordering and repetition are not significant here:

state *SecuritySys* **of**
     authorized : *String* $\xrightarrow{m}$ *String*
     inside : *String*-**set**

The invariant records the constraint that the set of employees that are inside the building comprise only those people who are authorized.

inv mk-*SecuritySys*(*a,i*) $\underline{\Delta}$ *i* $\subseteq$ **dom** *a*

Initially, the collection of authorized staff and the set of staff inside the building will both be empty:

init mk-*SecuritySys*(*a,i*) $\underline{\Delta}$ *a* = {$\mapsto$} $\wedge$ *i* = {}

Now we come to the operations.

The *addEmployee* operation is straightforward. Notice how in the precondition we have to use the **dom** operator to check that the name is not in the domain of the employee map. Notice also the use of the union operator in the postcondition to add the name–password pair into the map.

addEmployee(*nameIn* : *String*, *passwordIn* : *String*)
ext wr   *authorized* : *String* $\xrightarrow{m}$ *String*
pre *nameIn* $\notin$ **dom** *authorized*
post   *authorized* = $\overline{authorized}$ $\cup$ {*nameIn* $\mapsto$ *passwordIn*}

removeEmployee is also straightforward – notice the use of the domain deletion operator in the postcondition. Notice also how the precondition checks not only that the employee is an authorized member of staff, but also that he or she is not currently in the building.

removeEmployee(*nameIn* : *String*)
ext wr   *authorized* : *String* $\xrightarrow{m}$ *String*
    rd   *inside* : *String*-**set**
pre   *nameIn* $\in$ **dom** *authorized* $\wedge$ *nameIn* $\notin$ *inside*
post   *authorized* = {*nameIn*} $\vartriangleleft$ $\overline{authorized}$

The *enter* operation not only records the fact that a person is entering the building, but also signals the hardware to open the door – as long as the name and password are correct, and the individual is not already recorded as being inside the building. In the event that either of these two conditions is not met, then the state remains unchanged and the signal that is output sets off the alarm.

---

enter(*nameIn* : *String*, *passwordIn* : *String*) *signal* : *Signal*

ext rd *authorized* : *String* $\xrightarrow{m}$ *String*
      wr *inside* : *String*-**set**
pre   TRUE
post   (*authorized*(*nameIn*) = *passwordIn* ∧ *nameIn* ∉ $\overline{inside}$)
                    ∧ (*inside* = $\overline{inside}$ ∪ {*nameIn*} ∧ *signal* = <OPEN_DOOR>)

         ∨ (*authorized*(*nameIn*) ≠ *passwordIn* ∨ *nameIn* ∈ $\overline{inside}$)

               ∧ (*inside* = $\overline{inside}$ ∧ *signal* = <ACTIVATE_ALARM>)

In the *leave* operation, an alarm is raised if the employee wishing to leave is not currently recorded as being inside the building:

---

leave(*nameIn* : *String*) *signal* : *Signal*
ext wr *inside* : *String*-**set**
pre   TRUE
post   *nameIn* ∈ $\overline{inside}$ ∧ *inside* = $\overline{inside}$\{*nameIn*} ∧ *signal* = <OPEN_DOOR>

         ∨ *nameIn* ∈ *inside* ∧ $\overline{inside}$ = $\overline{inside}$ ∧ *signal* = <ACTIVATE_ALARM>

11.7   A Robot Monitoring System

Our second example in this chapter will model a software system that monitors a number of robots working at a space station. The requirements of the software are described informally below.

11.7.1 THE REQUIREMENTS OF THE ROBOT MONITORING SOFTWARE

Each robot will have a unique name and a mode, which can be WORKING, IDLE or BROKEN. There are two sectors, A and B, in which a robot can be set to work. The following operations are required:

- **addRobot:** accepts the name of a new robot and records the fact that this robot has been added to the collection. Its mode is set to idle and it is therefore not allocated a sector to work in.
- **removeRobot:** accepts the name of a robot and records the removal of this robot from the system.

- **setToWork:** accepts the name of a robot, that must currently be idle, and records the fact that it has been set to work in a given sector.
- **finishWork:** accepts the name of a robot, and records the fact that this robot has been removed from the sector and that its mode has been set to idle.
- **needsRepair:** as above but records its mode as broken.
- **fixed:** accepts the name of a broken robot and records that that its mode has been set to idle.
- **inSector:** accepts a given sector and returns the names of those robots in that sector.
- **numberToRepair:** returns the number of broken robots.

Figure 11.4 shows the UML specification of the robot monitor software.

Two types in this UML specification need further analysis: *Sector* and *Robot*. A robot can be in one of two sectors, A or B. An enumerated *Sector* type can be defined in UML for this purpose (Figure 11.5).

Turning to the *Robot* type, each robot will have a unique *name*, be in a particular *mode* and be associated with a particular *sector*. Figure 11.6 provides a UML specification for this type.

Figure 11.6 introduces yet another new type: *Mode*. A robot's mode will either be WORKING, IDLE or BROKEN. Once again, an enumerated type can be specified in UML (Figure 11.7). Now, we turn to the formal specification.

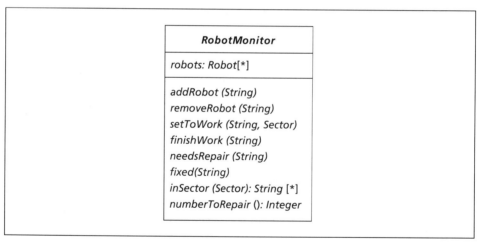

Figure 11.4   The UML specification of the *RobotMonitor* class

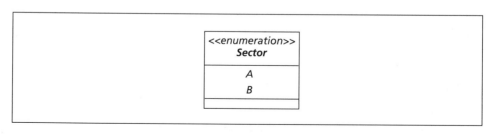

Figure 11.5   The UML specification of the *Sector* type

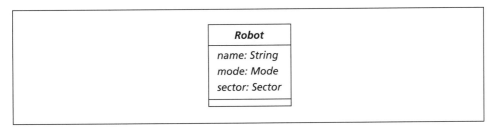

Figure 11.6   The UML specification of the *Robot* type

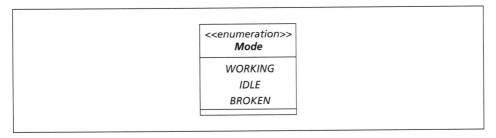

Figure 11.7   The UML specification of the *Mode* type

11.7.2 THE FORMAL SPECIFICATION OF THE ROBOT MONITORING SOFTWARE

First, the **types** definition needs to consider the types identified in the analysis stage. The *String, Mode* and *Sector* types are specified as follows:

> **types**
> $\quad$ *String = Char**
> $\quad$ *Mode* = <WORKING> | <IDLE> | <BROKEN>
> $\quad$ *Sector* = <A> | <B>

Now consider the *Robot* type of Figure 11.6. The type suggests a composite type is required in the VDM specification. Looking ahead to the state specification, a collection of robots is required in the *RobotMonitor* system. A map will be useful here with the robot name (specified to be a *String*) acting as the domain element. This will deal with the uniqueness of names as identified in the analysis stage.

We could map this robot name onto a composite object consisting of the remaining fields of a robot (*mode* and *sector*). However, we believe that in a case like this it is more natural and more useful to map to a 'whole' object such as a robot, rather than to split it up and create an 'artificial' composite object consisting just of the *sector* and *mode* fields. This gives us:

$$\textit{robots}: \textit{String} \xrightarrow{\;m\;} \textit{Robot}$$

As you will see in the state definition, this does mean that we need to specify an invariant to ensure that each name in the domain is the same as the name field of the object with which it is associated. Returning to the **types** definition, we now add a composite *Robot* type, with fields corresponding to the fields identified in Figure 11.6:

> *Robot* :: *name*: *String*
>   *mode*: *Mode*
>   *sector*: [*Sector*]
> **inv mk**-*Robot*(-, *m*, *s*) $\underline{\Delta}$ *m* = WORKING $\Leftrightarrow$ *s* $\neq$ **nil**

Important details about this *Robot* type, that are not made obvious in the informal UML specification, are captured in the formal specification. First, the sector type can be a *sector* value or it could be **nil** (indicating a robot is allocated to no sector). Second, a constraint on a robot type is recorded in an invariant. The constraint indicates that the *mode* cannot be **nil** if the robot is recorded as being in WORKING mode. Our state definition is now given as follows:

> **state** *RobotMonitor* **of**
>   *robots*: *String* $\xrightarrow{m}$ *Robot*
> **inv mk**-*RobotMonitor*(*r*) $\underline{\Delta}$ $\forall$ *n* $\in$ **dom** *r* $\bullet$ *n* = *r*(*n*).*name*
> **init mk**-*RobotMonitor*(*r*) $\underline{\Delta}$ *r* = {$\mapsto$}
> **end**

As we mentioned above, the state invariant records the fact that the names of robots in the domain must be the same as the corresponding names in the range. In the next section we present the complete specification, with the complete set of operations. The operations are reasonably straightforward, and comments have been added for extra clarity.

11.8 The Complete Specification of the Robot Monitoring Software

> **types**
>   *String* = *Char**
>   *Mode* = <WORKING> | <IDLE> | <BROKEN>
>   *Sector* = <A> | <B>
>   *Robot* :: *name*: *String*
>   *mode*: *Mode*
>   *sector*: [*Sector*]

-- the type invariant ensures that a working robot is allocated to one of
-- the two sectors

inv mk-*Robot*(-, *m*, *s*) $\underline{\Delta}$ *m* = WORKING $\Leftrightarrow$ *s* $\neq$ **nil**

state *RobotMonitor* **of**

$\quad$ *robots* : *String* $\xrightarrow{\;m\;}$ *Robot*

$\quad$ -- the state invariant ensures that each name in the domain is equal to the
$\quad$ -- corresponding name field in the object to which it maps

$\quad$ **inv mk**-*RobotMonitor*(*r*) $\underline{\Delta}$ $\forall$ *n* $\in$ **dom** *r* $\bullet$ *n* = *r*(*n*).*name*

$\quad$ **init mk**-*RobotMonitor*(*r*) $\underline{\Delta}$ *r* = {$\mapsto$}

end

operations

addRobot (*nameIn*: *String*)

ext wr$\quad$*robots*: *String* $\xrightarrow{\;m\;}$ *Robot*

pre$\qquad$*nameIn* $\notin$ **dom** *robots*

post$\qquad$*robots* = *robots* $\cup$ {*nameIn* $\mapsto$ **mk**-*Robot* (*nameIn*, <IDLE>, **nil**)}

removeRobot (*nameIn*: *String*)

ext wr$\quad$*robots*: *String* $\xrightarrow{\;m\;}$ *Robot*

-- the second part of the precondition ensures that we are not removing a

-- working robot

pre$\qquad$*nameIn* $\in$ **dom** *robots* $\wedge$ *robots*(*nameIn*).*mode* $\neq$ <WORKING>

post$\qquad$*robots* = {*nameIn* } $\lhd\!\!\!-$ *robots*

setToWork (*nameIn*: *String*, *sectorIn Sector*)

ext wr *robots*: *String* $\xrightarrow{\;m\;}$ *Robot*

-- the second part of the precondition ensures that the robot is currently idle

pre$\qquad$*nameIn* $\in$ **dom** *robots* $\wedge$ *robots*(*nameIn*).*mode* = <IDLE>

post$\qquad$*robots* = *robots* $\dagger$ { *nameIn* $\mapsto$ **mk**-*Robot*(*nameIn*, <WORKING>, *sectorIn*) }

finishWork (*nameIn*: *String*)

ext wr   *robots*: *String* $\xrightarrow{m}$ *Robot*

pre   *nameIn* $\in$ **dom** *robots* $\land$ *robots*(*nameIn*)*.mode* $=$ $<$WORKING$>$
$--$ note the use of the map override operator here – the second part of the maplet is
$--$ overridden with the a robot object containing the new details
post   *robots* $=$ $\overline{robots}$ † {*nameIn* $\mapsto$ **mk-Robot**(*nameIn*, $<$IDLE$>$, **nil**)}

needsRepair (*nameIn*: *String*)
ext wr   *robots*: *String* $\xrightarrow{m}$ *Robot*
pre   *nameIn* $\in$ **dom** *robots*
post   *robots* $=$ $\overline{robots}$ † {*nameIn* $\mapsto$ **mk-Robot**(*nameIn*, $<$BROKEN$>$, **nil**)}

fixed (*nameIn*: *String*)
ext wr   *robots*: *String* $\xrightarrow{m}$ *Robot*
pre   *nameIn* $\in$ **dom** *robots* $\land$ *robots*(*nameIn*)*.mode* $=$ $<$BROKEN$>$
$--$ we have used a μ-function here to change the value of one of the fields in the
$--$ robot object. A *make* function could have been used as an alternative, as above.
post   *robots* $=$ $\overline{robots}$ † {*nameIn* $\mapsto$ $\mu(\overline{robots}$ (*nameIn*), *mode* $\mapsto$ $<$IDLE$>$)}

inSector (*sectorIn Sector*) *result* : *String*-**set**
ext rd   *robots* : *String* $\xrightarrow{m}$ *Robot*
pre   TRUE
$--$ note the use of set comprehension to construct the correct set
post   *result* $=$ {*r.name* | *r* $\in$ **rng** *robots* $\bullet$ *r.sector* $=$ *sectorIn*}

numberToRepair() *number* : $\mathbb{N}$
ext rd   *robots* : *String* $\xrightarrow{m}$ *Robot*
pre   TRUE
post   *number* $=$ **card** {*r* | *r* $\in$ **rng** *robots* $\bullet$ *r.mode* $=$ $<$BROKEN$>$}

EXERCISES

1. Given the following maps:

$$m1 = \{a \mapsto x, b \mapsto y, c \mapsto x\} \qquad m2 = \{b \mapsto y, c \mapsto y, d \mapsto y\}$$

write down the value of:
(a) $m1\ (a)$
(b) $m2\ (x)$
(c) **dom** $m1$
(d) **rng** $m2$
(e) $m1 \dagger m2$
(f) $m2 \dagger m1$
(g) $m1 \cup m2$
(h) $\{a, d\} \lhd m1$
(i) $\{b, c\} \ntriangleleft m2$
(j) $m1 \rhd \{x\}$
(k) $m2 \ntriangleright \{y\}$

2. Study the scenario below, and answer the questions that follow.

'A space station allows certain authorized craft to take up orbit around it in order to undertake repairs or to transfer staff to and from the station. Each shuttle is identified by a unique identity number, and will carry staff who are also uniquely identified by a security number.

When a craft wishes to take up orbit, it announces its identity number together with a list of all staff on board. Permission will be granted only if the identity number of the craft is amongst those authorized, and all the staff on board are also authorized.

The system must be capable of recording a list of authorized craft and authorized staff, as well as recording each orbiting craft together with the staff on board'.

(a) Specify the state of the system in VDM-SL, including an invariant and an initialization clause.
(b) Based on your state specification, write specifications for the following operations:

addAuthorizedCraft: accepts an identity number of a craft and records the fact that this craft has been added to the list of authorized crafts.
addAuthorizedStaff: accepts an identity number of a member of staff and records the fact that this individual has been added to the list of authorized staff.
allowOrbit: accepts an identity number of a craft and a list of staff security numbers on board the craft, and, as long as the craft and all the staff are authorized, records the addition of this craft to the list of orbiting craft.
checkCraft: accepts an identity number of a craft and checks whether that craft is currently in orbit around the station.
removeCraftAuthority: accepts an identity number of a craft, and records the removal of that craft from the list of authorized craft; a craft should not be removed if it is currently in orbit.
removeStaffAuthority: accepts an identity number of a member of staff, and records the removal of that member of staff from the list of authorized staff; an individual should not be removed if he or she is currently aboard an orbiting craft.
listOrbitingCraft: outputs a list of identity numbers of all craft currently in orbit around the station.
listStaff: accepts an identity number of an orbiting craft, and outputs a list of the staff on that craft.

Implementing Maps

12.1 Introduction

In previous chapters we described how the VDMSet class and a VDMSequence class can be used to implement VDM specifications. In this chapter we do the same thing with a VDMMap class. This time we make use of the Hashtable class available in the java.util library, and we start with a brief description of the methods of that class. We then go on to describe the VDMMap class, and use it to implement the RobotMonitor software from the last chapter.

The VDMMap class can be downloaded from the website.

12.2 The *Hashtable* Class

As we did with the Vector class we will briefly describe the Hashtable class. In fact, this class is effectively the concrete representation of a map. A hash table contains pairs of objects, closely corresponding to a maplet. The first object, which in VDM-SL we would refer to as the domain element, is referred to as the *key* in Java. The second object – the range element – is referred to as the *value*. As with a map, the keys are unique, thus enabling a value to be looked up by submitting a key. Table 12.1 explains some of the commonly used Hashtable methods.

It must be pointed out that any object that is used as the key in a hashtable has to have a special method, hashCode (inherited from the Object class), overridden.

Table 12.1 Some *Hashtable* methods

Method	Description
Hashtable()	Creates a new empty hash table.
Object put(Object,Object)	Adds the given key and value pair to the hash table. This method returns the previous value of the specified key in this hash table, or **null** if it did not have one.
Object get(Object)	Returns the value associated with the given key. Returns **null** if this key is not in the hash table.
Object remove(Object)	Removes the given key (if it exists) and its corresponding value from this hash table. Like the put method, this method returns the previous value of the specified key in this hash table, or **null** if it did not have one.
boolean containsKey (Object)	Returns **true** if the specified object is a key in this hash table, and **false** otherwise.

The hashCode method is used in conjunction with the equals method when searching for a key that matches a particular object. For the two objects to be deemed identical then in addition to the equals method returning **true**, the hashCode method of the two objects must return the same integer. Objects of classes such as String, Integer, Double and Char will already have had the hashCode method overwritten, so you don't have to worry about this issue in such cases. But if you are using an object of a class that you have written yourself, then you must overwrite the hashCode method of that class. You will see an example of this in Chapter 14.

12.3   The *VDMMap* Class

As we have indicated, the class contains a single attribute, a Hashtable, which holds the elements of the map:

```
import java.util.*;

class VDMMap

{

    private Hashtable theMap;

    // methods go here

}
```

Thus, if a map had been declared in a VDM specification, it can be declared as an object of the VDMMap class in Java. For example:

VDM-SL	Java
someMap : *Type A* $\xrightarrow{m}$ *TypeB*	VDMMap someMap;

12.3.1 THE *MAPLET* CLASS

As you are aware from the last chapter, a map in VDM consists of a set of *maplets*. In order to facilitate the implementation of maps in Java we have therefore defined a Maplet class which has two attributes, representing the domain element and the range element:

```
class Maplet

{

  private Object domainElement;

  private Object rangeElement;

  // methods go here

}
```

Constructors have been provided for this class that allow the creation of a maplet from any combination of the primitive types (**int**, **char** and **double**) and objects. The class also has methods `getDomainElement` and `getRangeElement` which allow read access to the two components of the class.

12.3.2 THE CONSTRUCTORS OF THE *VDMMAP* CLASS

As with sets and sequences, a number of constructors have been provided to construct an empty map, a singleton map and to construct maps explicitly. They are summarized in Table 12.2.

Table 12.3 provides examples of how these constructors are used – you will see how useful the `Maplet` class is here, as any overloading of methods has already been taken care of in this class.

12.3.3 THE MAP OPERATORS

Just as we did with the `VDMSet` and `VDMSequence` classes, we have provided methods for all the map operators within the `VDMMap` class. These are summarized in Table 12.4.

Table 12.5 provides examples of the use of these operators.

As with the `VDMSet` and `VDMSequence` classes, additional methods have been provided in order to simplify the process of testing and implementation. These are shown in Table 12.6.

Table 12.2 VDMMap constructors

Constructor	Description
`VDMMap()`	Empty map constructor.
`VDMMap(Maplet[])`	Explicit map constructor – creates a new map from an array of maplets passed as a parameter.
`VDMMap(Maplet)`	Singleton map constructor – creates a new map containing the single maplet passed in as a parameter.

Table 12.3 VDMMap constructors – examples

VDM-SL example	Java example
Empty map constructor $someMap = \{\mapsto\}$	`someMap = new VDMMap();`
Explicit map constructors $someMap = \{\text{'a'} \mapsto 2,$ $\text{'b'} \mapsto 5\}$	`VDMMap someMap = new VDMMap(new Maplet[]` `    {new Maplet('a', 2), new Maplet('b', 5)});`
Singleton map constructors $someMap = \{\text{'x'} \mapsto 6.7\}$	`VDMMap someMap = new VDMMap(new Maplet('x', 6.7));`

Table 12.4 VDMMap operators

Method	Description
`VDMSet dom()`	Returns a `VDMSet` that is the domain of the map.
`VDMSet rng()`	Returns a `VDMSet` that is the range of the map.
`VDMMap override(VDMMap mapIn)`	Accepts a `VDMMap` and returns an identical `VDMMap` to the original map, but with its elements overridden as prescribed by the override operator.
`VDMMap union(VDMMap mapIn)`	Accepts a `VDMMap` and returns a `VDMMap` constructed by taking the union of the original map and the new map; throws a `VDMException` if the two maps contain any of the same domain elements.
`VDMMap domRestrict(VDMSet setIn)`	Accepts a `VDMSet` and returns a `VDMMap` identical to the original map, but containing only those maplets whose domain elements are contained within the set.
`VDMMap domDelete(VDMSet setIn)`	Accepts a `VDMSet` and returns a `VDMMap` identical to the original map, but containing all but those maplets whose domain elements are contained within the set.
`VDMMap rangeRestrict(VDMSet setIn)`	Accepts a `VDMSet` and returns a `VDMMap` identical to the original map, but containing only those maplets whose range elements are contained within the set.
`VDMMap rangeDelete(VDMSet setIn)`	Accepts a `VDMSet` and returns a `VDMMap` identical to the original map, but containing all but those maplets whose range elements are contained within the set.
`Object applyTo (Object domainElementIn)`	Accepts an `Object` representing the domain element and returns the associated range element; throws a `VDMException` if the domain element does not actually exist within the map.

Table 12.5 VDMMap operators – examples

VDM-SL	Java
dom *someMap*	`someMap.dom();`
rng *someMap*	`someMap.rng();`
someMap $\dagger$ $\{1 \mapsto 2\}$	`someMap.override(new Maplet(1, 2));`
someMap $\cup$ $\{'a' \mapsto 3\}$	`someMap.union(new Maplet('a', 3));`
$\{1, 2, 3\} \lhd$ *someMap*	`someMap.domRestrict(new VDMSet(new int[] {1,2,3}));`
$\{'a', 'b'\} \nleftarrow$ *someMap*	`someMap.domDelete(new VDMSet(new char[] {'a','b'}));`
someMap $\rhd$ $\{2\}$	`someMap.rangeRestrict(new VDMSet(2));`
someMap $\nrightarrow$ $\{"BLUE"\}$	`someMap.rangeDelete(new VDMSet("BLUE"));`
someMap(*x*)	`someMap.applyTo(x);`

Table 12.6   Additional VDMMap operators

VDMMap method	Description
`boolean equals(Object)`	Accepts an `Object` as a parameter and returns **true** if this object is identical to the original map, otherwise returns **false**.
`String toString()`	Returns a string representation of the map.
`boolean isEmpty()`	Returns **true** if the map is empty, otherwise returns **false**.

12.4   Implementing the *RobotMonitor* Software

The final example that we looked at in Chapter 11 was the specification for software that monitors a number of working robots. Take a look at this specification again to refresh your memory.

In this section we will implement that specification. You will see from the *types* clause that a *Robot* is specified as a composite object consisting of name, a mode and a sector. The first of these was specified as a *String*, the other two as quote types. It will therefore be necessary to define classes for these quote types (as we explained in Chapter 4), and then to define a `Robot` class to represent our composite object.

So first of all we define a `Mode` and a `Sector` class as follows:

The *Mode* class

```
class Mode
{

    private int value;

    public final static Mode WORKING = new Mode(0);

    public final static Mode IDLE = new Mode(1);

    public final static Mode BROKEN = new Mode(2);

    private Mode(int x)
    {

        value = x;

    }

    public boolean equals(Object modeIn)
    {

        Mode m = (Mode) modeIn; // type cast

        return m.value == value;

    }
```

```
public String toString()

{

    switch(value)

    {

        case 0 : return "WORKING";

        case 1 : return "IDLE";

        default : return "BROKEN";

    }

  }

}
```

The *Sector* class

```
class Sector
{
    private int value;

    public final static Sector A = new Sector(0);
    public final static Sector B = new Sector(1);

    public Sector(int x)
    {
       value = x;
    }
    public boolean equals(Object sectorIn)
    {
        Sector s = (Sector) sectorIn; // type cast
        return s ! = null && s.value == value;
    }
     public String toString()
    {
       switch(value)
       {
          case 0  : return "A";
          default : return "B";
       }
    }
}
```

Take a look at the `equals` method – notice that we have an additional conjunct in the **return** statement, to test if the sector is **null**. We need to make this check, because our specification of a robot allows for the possibility of the *Sector* field being **nil**. This will be implemented in Java using the **null** value, and it is important that we do not try to access an attribute of such a value as is done in the second conjunct, as this would raise an exception. You will recall that fortunately Java does not proceed with the test of the second conjunct once the first one has evaluated to **false**.

Now we are in a position to define our `Robot` class.

The *Robot* class

```java
class Robot implements InvariantCheck
{
    public final String name;
    public final Mode mode;
    public final Sector sector;

    public Robot(String nameIn, Mode modeIn, Sector sectorIn)
    {
        name = nameIn;
        mode = modeIn;
        sector = sectorIn;
        VDM.invTest(this);
    }
    public boolean inv()
    {
        return (mode == Mode.WORKING) == (sector == null);
    }
    public boolean equals(Object robotIn)
    {
        Robot robot = (Robot) robotIn;
        return name.equals(robot.name)
            && mode.equals(robot.mode)
            && (sector == null && robot.sector == null)
                || (sector != null && sector.equals(robot.sector));
    }
```

```
    public String toString()
    {
        return "mk-Robot("+ name +","+ mode +","+ sector +  ")";
    }
}
```

The last conjunct of the `equals` method needs some explanation. Once again we have the possibility that the sector of any robot could be equal to **null**, and once again we must avoid calling a method of a **null** object. Inspection of this conjunct will show that we have taken account of any situation where a sector could be **null** before allowing the `equals` method to be invoked.

Now we can define the `RobotMonitor` class. We present the code below, and as usual you should study it carefully before moving on to the next section where we provide an explanation of some of the more complex aspects of the class.

The *RobotMonitor* class

```
class RobotMonitor implements InvariantCheck
{
    // state attributes
    private VDMMap robots;
    // initialize the state
    public RobotMonitor()
    {
        robots = new VDMMap();
        VDM.invTest(this);
    }
    //invariant test
    public boolean inv()
    {
      return VDM.forall(robots.dom(), // the set whose elements are to be tested
            new Testable() // the test
            {
                public boolean test(Object nameIn)
                {
```

```
        String n = (String) nameIn;

        Robot robot = (Robot) robots.applyTo(n);

        return n.equals(robot.name);

      }

    } );

}
```

// operations

```
public void addRobot(String nameIn)

{

    VDM.preTest(robots.dom().doesNotContain(nameIn));

    robots

      = robots.union(new VDMMap(new Maplet(nameIn, new Robot(nameIn, Mode.IDLE, null))));

    VDM.invTest(this);

}

public void removeRobot(String nameIn)

{

    Robot rob = (Robot) robots.applyTo(nameIn);

    VDM.preTest(robots.dom().contains(nameIn) && !rob.mode.equals(Mode.WORKING));

    robots = robots.domDelete(new VDMSet(nameIn));

    VDM.invTest(this);

}

public void setToWork(String nameIn, Sector sectorIn)

{

    Robot rob = (Robot) robots.applyTo(nameIn);

    VDM.preTest(robots.dom().contains(nameIn)

                              && rob.mode.equals(Mode.IDLE));

    robots = robots.overwrite

            (new VDMMap(new Maplet(nameIn, new Robot(nameIn, Mode.WORKING, sectorIn))));

    VDM.invTest(this);

}

public void finishWork(String nameIn)

{

    Robot rob = (Robot) robots.applyTo(nameIn);

    VDM.preTest(robots.dom().contains(nameIn) && rob.mode.equals(Mode.WORKING));
```

```
      robots
        = robots.overwrite(new VDMMap(new Maplet(nameIn, new Robot(nameIn, Mode.IDLE, null))));
      VDM.invTest(this);
   }
   public void needsRepair(String nameIn)
   {
      VDM.preTest(robots.dom().contains(nameIn));
      robots
        = robots.overwrite(new VDMMap(new Maplet(nameIn, new Robot(nameIn, Mode.BROKEN, null))));
      VDM.invTest(this);
   }
   public void fixed(String nameIn)
   {
      Robot rob = (Robot) robots.applyTo(nameIn);
      VDM.preTest(robots.dom().contains(nameIn)
                                    && rob.mode.equals(Mode.BROKEN));
      robots = robots.overwrite
                (new VDMMap(new Maplet(nameIn, new Robot(nameIn, Mode.IDLE, rob.sector))));
      VDM.invTest(this);
   }
   public VDMSet inSector(final Sector sectorIn)
   {
      return VDMSet.setComp(new Expression() // the expression
          {
            public Object action(Object elementIn)
              {
                Robot rob = (Robot) elementIn;
                return rob.name;
              }
          }
          robots.rng(), //the set from which the elements are drawn
          new Testable() // the test
          {
                  public boolean test(Object elementIn)
```

```
                    {
                        Robot rob = (Robot) elementIn;

                        return sectorIn.equals(rob.sector);

                    }
                } );
    }
    public int numberToRepair()

    {
        VDMSet set = VDMSet.setComp(robots.rng(), // the set from which the elements are drawn

                    new Testable() // the test

                        {
                            public boolean test(final Object elementIn)

                            {
                                Robot rob = (Robot) elementIn;

                                return rob.mode.equals(Mode.BROKEN);

                            }
                        } );
        return set.card();

    }
    public String toString()

    {
        return robots.toString() + '\n';

    }
}
```

12.5   Analysis of the *RobotMonitor* Class

You are familiar with all of the techniques used in the above implementation, so we simply draw your attention to some of the more complex methods.

First, take a look at the invariant:

```
public boolean inv()

{
    return VDM.forall(robots.dom(), new Testable()

        {
            public boolean test(final Object nameIn)
```

```
                {
                    String n = (String) nameIn;
                    Robot robot = (Robot) robots.applyTo(n);
                    return n.equals(robot.name);
                }
            } );
    }
```

As a reminder, here is the original specification from which this was derived:

inv mk-*RobotMonitor*(*r*) $\underline{\Delta}$; $\forall\, n \in$ **dom** $r \bullet n = r(n).name$

Once again we see the use of the `forall` method of the VDM class. The set whose values are being tested is the domain of the robot map – implemented as `robots.dom()`, the first parameter to the `forall` method. The second parameter is the test, which requires that the domain element of the map (the name) is the same as the name component of the range element (a whole robot). You can see how this has been implemented by means of an object of the `Testable` class in which the test method is defined. Notice the need to type cast (the `test` method receives an `Object`, not a `Robot`) and notice the use of the `applyTo` method to obtain the range element associated with the name.

The other interesting methods are the ones that involve set comprehension. Let's remind ourselves of the specification for one of these, namely *inSector*:

inSector (*sectorIn: Sector*) *result* : *String*-**set**

ext rd *robots* : *String* $\xrightarrow{m}$ *Robot*

pre   TRUE

post   *result* = {*r.name* | *r* $\in$ **rng** *robots* $\bullet$ *r.sector* = *sectorIn*}

Now look at the way this has been implemented:

```
public VDMSet inSector(final Sector sectorIn)
{
    return VDMSet.setComp(new Expression() // the expression
                {
                        public Object action(final Object elementIn)
```

```
                        {
                            Robot rob = (Robot) elementIn;

                            return rob.name;

                        }
                    },
                    robots.rng(), // the set from which the elements are drawn
                    new Testable() // the test
                        {
                            public boolean test(final Object elementIn)
                            {
                                Robot rob = (Robot) elementIn;

                                return sectorIn.equals(rob.sector);
                            }
                        } );

    }
```

You will recall that the set comprehension method of VDMSet has been overloaded to allow for a number of different possibilities. The version used here involves the use of three parameters – an Expression object, a VDMSet and a Testable object. The expression picks out the *name* field of the robot (*r.name*) by defining the action method of an anonymous class. The required set is the range of the set of robots (implemented as robots.rng()). Finally the Testable object ensures that the name used as the key is the same as the name field of the associated robot with the line:

```
    return sectorIn.equals(rob.sector);
```

There is something here that we have to be very careful about. You will recall from the specification that it is possible that the *sector* field of a robot could be equal to **nil**. As we have seen, this is implemented in Java by using the **null** value. If the sector itself were **null**, then calling its equals method would cause an exception to be thrown. Thus we could not have implemented the above method as:

```
    return rob.sector.equals(rob.sectorIn);
```

The other method that uses set comprehension is *numberToRepair*. Here is its specification again:

---

numberToRepair() *number* : $\mathbb{N}$

ext rd   *robots* : *String* $\xrightarrow{\ m\ }$ *Robot*

pre   TRUE

post   *number* = **card** $\{r \mid r \in \textbf{rng}\ robots \bullet r.mode = \text{BROKEN}\}$

This time, however, we need only two parameters as there is no need for an `Expression` object. Thus the method is implemented as:

```
public int numberToRepair()

{

    VDMSet set = VDMSet.setComp(robots.rng(), // the set from which the elements are drawn

                    new Testable() // the test

                    {

                        public boolean test(final Object elementIn)

                        {

                            Robot rob = (Robot) elementIn;

                            return rob.mode.equals(Mode.BROKEN);

                        }

                    } );

    return set.card();

}
```

Notice that this time it is the cardinality of the set that is required, hence the use of the `card` method in the last line.

This completes our discussion of the `RobotMonitor` class – once again you will have the opportunity to test this class in the exercises at the end of this chapter.

We have now completed our coverage of VDM-SL, and the way in which we can implement VDM specifications in Java. Our final two chapters deal with a case study in which you will see the specification and implementation of a more complex software system that make use of many of the concepts that we have dealt with in this text.

1. In exercise 1 of the previous chapter you were given two maps to consider:

$$m1 = \{a \mapsto x, b \mapsto y, c \mapsto x\} \qquad m2 = \{b \mapsto y, c \mapsto y, d \mapsto y\}$$

   Write a tester program to implement these maps and evaluate all the expressions from the same question.

2. Write a program that tests out the RobotMonitor class. As with previous examples, you might wish to use menu-driven program such as the following:

   ```
   Robot Tester
   1. Add a robot
   2. Remove a robot
   3. Set to work
   4. Finish work
   5. Needs repair
   6. Fixed
   7. In sector
   8. Number to repair
   9. Show all
   ```

   As with previous examples, each menu option can test a method of the RobotMonitor class – again, the 'Show all' option can simply make use of the toString method of RobotMonitor.

3. Implement the specification of the *High Security Building* software developed in the previous chapter.

4. Test the HighSecurityBuilding class by developing an appropriate tester program.

5. Implement the Space Station software that you specified in exercise 2 of the last chapter.

6. Test the SpaceStation class by developing an appropriate tester program.

Case Study Part 1: Specification

13.1 Introduction

In this chapter and the next, we bring together all the concepts covered in previous chapters to specify formally and to implement a piece of software that records and monitors customer account transactions. Such software is clearly business critical, and is ideally suited for formal development. We begin by describing the requirements.

13.2 The Requirements Definition

The software is required to record account details and transactions for a number of account holders. A transaction will either involve a deposit or a withdrawal of money from an account. As well as having a unique account number, each account holder will have recorded for them their history of transactions, their personal details, their current money balance and an overdraft limit. The software is expected to be able to do the following:

- Create a new account.
- Remove an existing account.
- Record a deposit transaction.
- Record a withdrawal transaction.
- Update the personal details of a customer's account.
- Change the overdraft limit associated with an account.
- Produce a statement of transactions associated with an account.
- Display the balance of an account.
- Display the personal details of an account.

From these requirements a list of operations and attributes needs to be identified and recorded in the specification stage. First the informal specification.

13.3 The Informal Specification

We will call the software required to monitor and record account transactions the *AccountSys* class. A single attribute is required for the *AccountSys* class, a collection of account records. The operations of the *AccountSys* class should allow the user requirements identified in the earlier section to be met. The methods we have identified are listed in the UML specification of the *AccountSys* class presented in Figure 13.1. They should be fairly self-explanatory from their names and interfaces.

Several user-defined types are identified in Figure 13.1. The internal details of the *AccNum* type and the *Details* type play no role in the specification and so do not need to be analysed further at this stage. There is no requirement for the transactions to be kept in date order, nor are there any operations that require the value of a date to be interrogated. For these reasons we can also abstract away from the details of a date and need not analyse it any further. The internal details of the *Account* and *Transaction* types are important here, however, so do require further analysis.

An account record needs to consist of an account number, some customer details, a balance, an agreed overdraft limit and a history of transactions. Figure 13.2 gives the UML specification for this *Account* type.

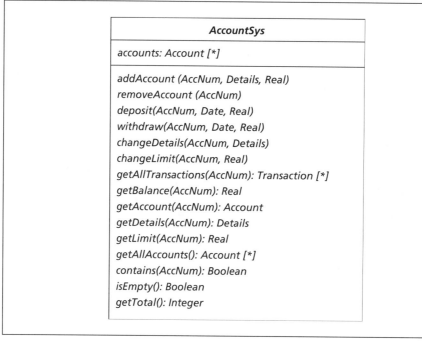

Figure 13.1 The UML specification of the *AccountSys* class

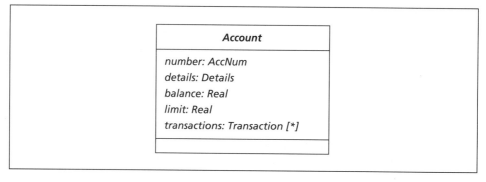

Figure 13.2 The UML specification of the *Account* type

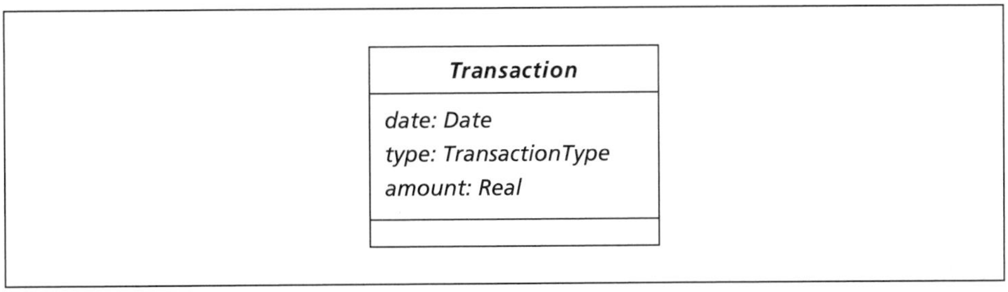

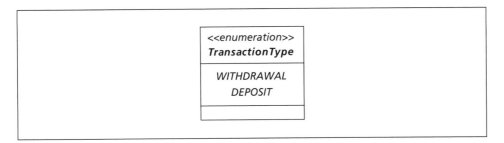

Figure 13.3   The UML specification of the *Transaction* type

<<enumeration>>
TransactionType

WITHDRAWAL
DEPOSIT

Figure 13.4   The UML specification of the *TransactionType* type

When a transaction takes place the date of the transaction should be recorded, the type of transaction (withdrawal or deposit) and the amount of the transaction. Figure 13.3 gives the UML specification for the *Transaction* type.

Figure 13.3 introduces yet another type, *TransactionType*. This is an enumerated type that can either have a value of WITHDRAWAL or DEPOSIT (see Figure 13.4).

Now that the informal specification is complete, we turn to the formal specification of the *AccountSys* class.

13.4   The Formal Specification

As always, before the operation specifications, we consider the state specification.

13.4.1 THE *ACCOUNTSYS* STATE SPECIFICATION

It was noted earlier that the types *AccNum*, *Date* and *Details* do not require further analysis. We will record this formally by declaring them to be TOKEN types:

types

$AccNum$ = TOKEN

$Date$ = TOKEN

$Details$ = TOKEN

The *TransactionType* type was analysed to be an enumerated type. We record this as the following union of two quote types in VDM-SL:

$$TransactionType = \; < \text{WITHDRAWAL} > | < \text{DEPOSIT} >$$

Both the types *Transaction* and *Account* can be specified as composite objects in VDM-SL. First *Transaction*:

Transaction :: *date* : *Date*

  amount : $\mathbb{R}$

  transactionType : *TransactionType*

The field names and types follow directly from the UML diagram of Figure 13.3. Specifying this type formally allows us to consider a data type invariant. A transaction amount must always be greater than zero. The following data type invariant is therefore defined:

inv mk-*Transaction*(-,a,-) $\underline{\Delta}$ $a > 0$

Now the *Account* type. One of the fields is specified in the UML diagram of Figure 13.2 to be a collection of transactions. A sequence is the appropriate VDM-SL type to use here as two or more identical transactions may need to be recorded, and it will be useful to preserve the ordering of transactions for later inspection:

Account :: *number* : *AccNum*

  details : *Details*

  balance : $\mathbb{R}$

  limit : $\mathbb{R}$

  transactions : *Transaction**

Again, a data type invariant can be considered here. There are three restrictions we need to place on *Account* objects:

- The overdraft limit is always non-negative.
- Any negative balance should not exceed the overdraft limit.
- The balance of an account should be consistent with the transactions that have taken place.

To simplify this data type invariant, we will assume the existence of a *balanceOf* function (which we will formally specify later) that returns the balance implied by a sequence of transactions:

inv mk-*Account*(-,-,*b*,*l*,*t*) $\underline{\Delta}$ $l \geq 0 \wedge b \geq -l \wedge balanceOf(t) = b$

That completes the specification of the user-defined types. Now we consider the state attributes. The UML diagram in Figure 13.1 makes clear that there is only one attribute, a collection of accounts:

accounts : Account [*]

Ordering of accounts is not important here, and each account is unique due to the unique account numbers. We could use a set to model this collection but, as account numbers are unique, account look-up and modification will be made easier if a map is used, with account numbers being used as domain elements:

state *AccountSys* **of**

accounts : AccNum $\xrightarrow{\ m\ }$ *Account*

A state invariant is needed to ensure that account numbers in the domain match the corresponding account numbers of account records in the range:

inv mk-*AccountSys*(*a*) $\underline{\Delta}$ $\forall$ *num* $\in$ **dom** *a* • *num* = *a*(*num*).*number*

Finally, we note that initially the record of accounts should be empty:

init mk-*AccountSys*(*a*) $\underline{\Delta}$ *a* = {$\mapsto$}

13.4.2 AUXILIARY FUNCTIONS

A *balanceOf* function is required that receives a sequence of transactions and returns the balance implied by the history of deposits and withdrawals. One way to specify this function would be to specify two sequences, one consisting of all the deposited amounts, the other all the withdrawal amounts. The sum of the withdrawal amounts can then be subtracted from the sum of the deposit amounts. Here is a specification that assumes the existence of a suitable *sum* function (which we specify later):

balanceOf(*transIn* : *Transactions**) *total* : $\mathbb{R}$

pre TRUE

post let   *dep* = [*transIn*(*i*).*amount* | *i* $\in$ **inds** *transIn* • *transIn*(*i*).*transactionType* = <DEPOSIT>]

  in   **let** *withd* = [*transIn*(*i*).*amount* | *i* $\in$ **inds** *transIn* • *transIn*(*i*).*transactionType* = <WITHDRAWAL>]

    in *total* = *sum*(*dep*) - *sum*(*withd*)

Here a **let ... in** clause has been employed to define a sequence, *dep*, through sequence comprehension. The comprehension filters the original sequence for deposit amounts. Another **let ... in** clause is used to define a sequence, *withd*, which filters the original sequence for withdrawal amounts. A further auxiliary function, *sum*, is then called to calculate the respective balances of these two sequences in order to arrive at a final balance. We can give a very concise explicit specification of this function with the use of recursion as follows:

$sum : \mathbb{R}^* \rightarrow \mathbb{R}$

$sum(seqIn) \underline{\Delta}$ **if** $seqIn = [\,]$

               then 0

               else hd $seqIn + sum(\textbf{tl}\ seqIn)$

You can see that this recursion stops when the sequence sent to the function is empty. If the sequence is non-empty the *sum* of the sequence is equal to the value of the **hd** of the sequence plus the *sum* of the remaining elements (the **tl** of the sequence). Constantly calling the *sum* function with the **tl** of the parameter will eventually result in an empty sequence being sent to the function and the recursion will terminate.

13.4.3 OPERATION SPECIFICATIONS

We begin by looking at the *addAccount* operation. Here, as a quick reminder, is the UML interface:

    addAccount (AccNum, Details, Real)

An account record should be created with the customer's account number, details and overdraft limit. Here is the operation specification:

$addAccount(numberIn : AccNum, detailsIn : Details, limitIn : \mathbb{R})$

ext wr $accounts : AccNum \xrightarrow{\ m\ } Account$

pre $numberIn \notin \textbf{dom}\ accounts \wedge limitIn \geq 0$

post $accounts = \overline{accounts} \cup \{numberIn \mapsto \textbf{mk-}Account(numberIn, detailsIn, 0, limitIn, [\,]\}$

An account record consists of the three parameters to this operation as well as a balance and a history of transactions. The postcondition makes clear that a new customer should have a zero balance and no transaction history. As you can see, the account number is used as the domain element for the given composite account object. The precondition records the restriction that the account number should not be one currently in use. The precondition also records the fact that the overdraft limit on an account should be non-negative (as noted in the *Account* invariant).

The *removeAccount* operation needs to remove the account record with the given account number. Since we have used a map to model this collection of account records, the map deletion operator succinctly captures the requirements of this operation:

---

removeAccount(numberIn : AccNum)

ext wr   *accounts* : *AccNum* $\xrightarrow{m}$ *Account*

pre   *numberIn* $\in$ **dom** *accounts*

post   *accounts* = {*numberIn*} $\vartriangleleft$ $\overline{accounts}$

The precondition records the requirement that the given account number should originally be amongst the collection of recorded account numbers.

The *deposit* operation takes the account number of the account in which to deposit money, the date of the deposit and the amount to deposit and updates the appropriate account record accordingly. Here is the operation specification:

---

deposit(numberIn : AccNum, dateIn : Date, amountIn : $\mathbb{R}$)

ext wr   *accounts* : *AccNum* $\xrightarrow{m}$ *Account*

pre   *numberIn* $\in$ **dom** *accounts* $\wedge$ *amountIn* > 0

post let *bal* = $(\overline{accounts}\ (numberIn)).balance$

    in let *trans* = $(\overline{accounts}\ (numberIn)).transactions$

       in   let *newTrans* = **mk**-*Transaction*(*dateIn*, *amountIn*,< DEPOSIT>)

          in *accounts* = $\overline{accounts}$ † {*numberIn* $\mapsto$ $\mu(\overline{accounts}\ (numberIn),$

                           balance $\mapsto$ *bal* + *amountIn*,

                           transactions $\mapsto$ *trans* $^\frown$ [*newTrans*])}

The precondition records the requirement that the account number should be one currently recorded, and the amount being deposited should be greater than zero.

The postcondition makes use of several **let ... in** clauses. The first gives a name, *bal*, to the balance of the old account record:

let *bal* = $(\overline{accounts}\ (numberIn)).balance$

The second **let ... in** gives a name, *trans*, for the transaction history of the old account record:

let *trans* = $(\overline{accounts}\ (numberIn)).transactions$

The final **let ... in** clause gives a name, *newTrans*, for the new transaction consisting of the given date and amount, plus the appropriate transaction type – DEPOSIT:

let *newTrans* = **mk-***Transaction*(*dateIn, amountIn*,< DEPOSIT>)

These three values are then used in the final expression:

$$accounts = \overline{accounts} \dagger \{numberIn \mapsto \mu(\overline{accounts} \ (numberIn),$$
$$balance \mapsto bal + amountIn,$$
$$transactions \mapsto trans \ \hat{} \ [newTrans])\}$$

A *mu* function is used to indicate that the new account record is identical to the old account record but with a few fields (*balance* and *transactions*) modified.

The *withdraw* operation is similar to the *deposit* operation except the amount is reduced from the account rather than added.

withdraw(*numberIn* : *AccNum, dateIn* : *Date, amountIn* : $\mathbb{R}$)

ext wr *accounts* : *AccNum* $\xrightarrow{m}$ *Account*

pre *numberIn* $\in$ **dom** *accounts* $\wedge$ *amountIn* > 0

$\wedge \ (\overline{accounts}(numberIn)).balance\text{-}amountIn \geq \text{-} (accounts(numberIn)).limit$

post let *bal* = ($\overline{accounts}$ (*numberIn*)).*balance*

    in let *trans* = (*accounts* (*numberIn*)).*transactions*

        in let *newTrans* = **mk-***Transaction*(*dateIn, amountIn*,< WITHDRAWAL>)

        in *accounts* = $\overline{accounts}$ $\dagger$

        {*numberIn* $\mapsto$ $\mu(\overline{accounts}(numberIn)$, *balance* $\mapsto$ *bal - amountIn,*

        transactions $\mapsto$ *trans* $\hat{}$ [*newTrans*])}

Notice the additional restriction on the precondition, that the overdraft limit is not exceeded by the amount of the requested withdrawal:

$(accounts(numberIn)).balance\text{-}amountIn \geq \text{-} (accounts(numberIn)).limit$

The *changeDetails* operation should change a single field of the account record. That field is the *details* field:

---

changeDetails(*numberIn* : *AccNum, detailsIn* : *Details*)

ext wr *accounts* : *AccNum* $\xrightarrow{m}$ *Account*

pre *numberIn* $\in$ **dom** *accounts*

post *accounts* = $\overline{accounts}$ † {*numberIn* $\mapsto$ μ($\overline{accounts}$ (*numberIn*), *details* $\mapsto$ *detailsIn*)}

The *changeLimit* operation also changes a single field of the account record. That field is the *limit* field. Care needs to be taken here though. The overdraft limit should not be changed if the given customer is already beyond the new proposed limit. The precondition can record this restriction:

---

changeLimit(*numberIn* : *AccNum, limitIn* : $\mathbb{R}$)

ext wr *accounts* : *AccNum* $\xrightarrow{m}$ *Account*

pre *numberIn* $\in$ **dom** *accounts* $\land$ *limitIn* $\geq$ 0 $\land$ *accounts*(*numberIn*).*balance* $\geq$ - *limitIn*

post *accounts* = $\overline{accounts}$ † {*numberIn* $\mapsto$ μ($\overline{accounts}$ (*numberIn*), *limit* $\mapsto$ *limitIn*)}

Notice that the precondition also records the familiar restriction of a valid account number being required and the fact that the new limit must always be non-negative.

The operations *getDetails, getBalance, getLimit* and *getAllTransactions* all return an appropriate field from the given customer's account record:

---

getDetails(*numberIn* : *AccNum*) *detailsOut* : *Details*

ext rd   *accounts* : *AccNum* $\xrightarrow{m}$ *Account*

pre *numberIn* $\in$ **dom** *accounts*

post *detailsOut* = (*accounts*(*numberIn*)).*details*

getBalance(*numberIn* : *AccNum*) *balanceOut* : $\mathbb{R}$

ext rd   *accounts* : *AccNum* $\xrightarrow{m}$ *Account*

pre *numberIn* $\in$ **dom** *accounts*

post *balanceOut* = (*accounts*(*numberIn*)).*balance*

getLimit(numberIn : AccNum) limitOut : $\mathbb{R}$

ext rd   *accounts : AccNum* $\xrightarrow{m}$ *Account*

pre *numberIn* $\in$ **dom** *accounts*

post *limitOut = (accounts(numberIn)).limit*

getAllTransactions(numberIn : AccNum) transactionsOut : Transaction*

ext rd   *accounts : AccNum* $\xrightarrow{m}$ *Account*

pre *numberIn* $\in$ **dom** *accounts*

post *transactionsOut = (accounts(numberIn)).transactions*

Two query operations are required: *contains*, which reports on whether or not a given account number is amongst the recorded account numbers, and *isEmpty*, which reports on whether or not the account collection is empty:

contains(numberIn : AccNum) query : $\mathbb{B}$

ext rd   *accounts : AccNum* $\xrightarrow{m}$ *Account*

pre   TRUE

post *query $\Leftrightarrow$ numberIn* $\in$ **dom** *accounts*

isEmpty() query : $\mathbb{B}$

ext rd *accounts : AccNum* $\xrightarrow{m}$ *Account*

pre TRUE

post *query $\Leftrightarrow$ accounts = { $\mapsto$ }*

Finally, the *getTotal* operation returns the number of account holders currently recorded:

getTotal() totalOut : $\mathbb{N}$

ext rd   *accounts : AccNum* $\xrightarrow{m}$ *Account*

pre   TRUE

post   *totalOut =* **card dom** *accounts*

The complete formal specification of the *AccountSys* class is now presented below:

---

types

AccNum = TOKEN

Date = TOKEN

Details = TOKEN

TransactionType = < WITHDRAWAL > | < DEPOSIT >

Transaction :: *date* : *Date*

             amount : $\mathbb{R}$

             transactionType : *TransactionType*

inv mk-*Transaction*(-,a,-) $\underline{\Delta}$ $a > 0$

Account :: *number* : *AccNum*

             details : *Details*

             balance : $\mathbb{R}$

             limit : $\mathbb{R}$

             transactions : *Transaction**

inv mk-*Account*(-,-,b,l,t) $\underline{\Delta}$ $l \geq 0 \wedge b \geq -l \wedge$ *balanceOf*(t) = b

state *AccountSys* **of**

       accounts : *AccNum* $\xrightarrow{\ m\ }$ *Account*

       inv mk-*AccountSys*(a) $\underline{\Delta}$ $\forall$ *num* $\in$ **dom** *a* $\bullet$ *num* = a(num).*number*

       init mk-*AccountSys*(a) $\underline{\Delta}$ $a = \{ \mapsto \}$

end *AccountSys*

functions

balanceOf(transIn : Transactions*) *total* : $\mathbb{R}$

pre TRUE

post let $dep = [transIn(i).amount \mid i \in \textbf{inds } transIn \bullet transIn(i).transactionType = <\text{DEPOSIT}>]$

in let $withd = [transIn(i).amount \mid i \in \textbf{inds } transIn \bullet$

$transIn(i).transactionType = <\text{WITHDRAWAL}>]$

in $total = sum(dep) - sum(withd)$

$sum : \mathbb{R}^* \to \mathbb{R}$

$sum(seqIn) \underline{\Delta} \quad$ **if** $seqIn = [\ ]$

then 0

else hd $seqIn + sum(\textbf{tl } seqIn)$

operations

$addAccount(numberIn : AccNum, detailsIn : Details, limitIn : \mathbb{R})$

ext wr $accounts : AccNum \xrightarrow{m} Account$

pre $\overline{numberIn \in \textbf{dom } accounts} \wedge limitIn \geq 0$

post $accounts = accounts \cup \{numberIn \mapsto \textbf{mk-}Account(numberIn, detailsIn, 0, limitIn, [\ ]\}$

$removeAccount(numberIn : AccNum)$

ext   wr $accounts : AccNum \xrightarrow{m} Account$

pre $numberIn \in \textbf{dom } accounts$

post $accounts = \{numberIn\} \triangleleft accounts$

$deposit(numberIn : AccNum, dateIn : Date, amountIn : \mathbb{R})$

ext wr $accounts : AccNum \xrightarrow{m} Account$

pre $numberIn \in \textbf{dom } accounts \wedge amountIn > 0$

post let $bal = (\overline{accounts} \, (numberIn)).balance$

in let $trans = (\overline{accounts} \, (numberIn)).transactions$

in let $newTrans = \textbf{mk-}Transaction(dateIn, amountIn, <\text{DEPOSIT}>)$

in $accounts = \overline{accounts} \dagger \{numberIn \mapsto \mu(\overline{accounts}(numberIn),$

$balance \mapsto bal + amountIn,$

$transactions \mapsto trans \frown [newTrans])\}$

withdraw(numberIn : AccNum, dateIn : Date, amountIn : $\mathbb{R}$)

ext wr *accounts : AccNum* $\xrightarrow{\ m\ }$ *Account*

pre *numberIn* $\in$ **dom** *accounts* $\land$ *amountIn* > 0

$\land$ *(accounts(numberIn)).balance - amountIn* $\geq$- *(accounts(numberIn)).limit*

post let *bal* = *($\overline{accounts}$ (numberIn)).balance*

in let *trans* = *$\overline{accounts}$ (numberIn)).transactions*

in let *newTrans* = **mk**-*Transaction(dateIn, amountIn,$<$ WITHDRAWAL$>$)*

in *accounts* = *$\overline{accounts}$* †

{numberIn $\mapsto$ *μ($\overline{accounts}$ (numberIn), balance* $\mapsto$ *bal-amountIn,*

transactions $\mapsto$ *trans* $^\frown$ *[newTrans])}*

changeDetails(numberIn : AccNum, detailsIn : Details)

ext   wr *accounts : AccNum* $\xrightarrow{\ m\ }$ *Account*

pre   *numberIn* $\in$ **dom** *accounts*

post *accounts* = *$\overline{accounts}$* † *{numberIn* $\mapsto$ *μ($\overline{accounts}$(numberIn), details* $\mapsto$ *detailsIn)}*

changeLimit(numberIn : AccNum, limitIn : $\mathbb{R}$)

ext wr *accounts : AccNum* $\xrightarrow{\ m\ }$ *Account*

pre   *numberIn* $\in$ **dom** *$\overline{accounts}$* $\land$ *limitIn* $\geq 0 \land$ *$\overline{accounts}$(numberIn). balance* $\geq$ - *limitIn*

post *accounts* = *accounts* † *{numberIn* $\mapsto$ *μ(accounts(numberIn), limit* $\mapsto$ *limitIn)}*

getDetails(numberIn : AccNum) detailsOut : Details

ext rd   *accounts : AccNum* $\xrightarrow{\ m\ }$ *Account*

pre *numberIn* $\in$ **dom** *accounts*

post *detailsOut* = *(accounts(numberIn)).details*

getBalance(numberIn : AccNum) balanceOut : $\mathbb{R}$

ext rd   *accounts : AccNum* $\xrightarrow{\ m\ }$ *Account*

pre *numberIn* $\in$ **dom** *accounts*

post *balanceOut* = *(accounts(numberIn)).balance*

getLimit(numberIn : AccNum) limitOut : $\mathbb{R}$

ext rd   *accounts : AccNum* $\xrightarrow{m}$ *Account*

pre *numberIn* $\in$ **dom** *accounts*

post *limitOut = (accounts(numberIn)).limit*

getAllTransactions(numberIn : AccNum) transactionsOut : Transaction*

ext rd   *accounts : AccNum* $\xrightarrow{m}$ *Account*

pre *numberIn* $\in$ **dom** *accounts*

post *transactionsOut = (accounts(numberIn)).transactions*

contains(numberIn : AccNum) query : $\mathbb{B}$

ext rd   *accounts : AccNum* $\xrightarrow{m}$ *Account*

pre   TRUE

post *query* $\Leftrightarrow$ *numberIn* $\in$ **dom** *accounts*

isEmpty() query : $\mathbb{B}$

ext rd   *accounts : AccNum* $\xrightarrow{m}$ *Account*

pre TRUE

post *query* $\Leftrightarrow$ *accounts* $= \{ \mapsto \}$

getTotal() totalOut : $\mathbb{N}$

ext rd   *accounts : AccNum* $\xrightarrow{m}$ *Account*

pre   TRUE

post *totalOut =* **card dom** *accounts*

EXERCISES

1. The formal specification of operations *deposit* and *withdrawal* are very similar. Simplify them by specifying an auxiliary function, *update*Transactions, which accepts a sequence of transactions, the account number associated with the transaction, the date of the transaction, the amount of the transaction and the transaction type (deposit or

withdrawal). The function should return a new sequence of transactions, identical to the sequence sent to the function but with the given transaction recorded for the given customer.

2. Specify an additional operation, *getLastTransactions*, which accepts an integer, *n*, and an account number, *accln*, and returns the last *n* transactions for account number *accln*.

3. The current specification puts no limit on the number of transactions that can be kept for each customer. In reality, there would probably be a fixed limit to this number. If this were to be the case, the specification would have to be modified to allow deletions to take place – adjustments would then need to be made to maintain the integrity of the total balance.

Make any modifications necessary to the VDM specification to limit the number of transactions recorded for a customer to, say, 100.

Case Study
Part 2: Implementation

14.1 Introduction

In this final chapter we implement the *AccountSys* class that we specified in Chapter 13. We then create an application that uses this class. We have designed this as a simple graphical interface with a basic file-handling system that reads and writes the records to permanent storage. The work covered in this chapter illustrates clearly how formal development improves the operational and testing phases of the development process by greatly increasing the prospect of producing correct code first time round, and then by easily trapping errors and consequently reducing the overall time spent on testing a system.

14.2 Developing the *AccountSys* Class

Inspection of the *AccountSys* specification indicates that three items, *AccNum, Details* and *Date*, have been declared as TOKEN types. When we first introduced the idea of a TOKEN we explained that this meant that the detail could be left until implementation time. Until now we have simply implemented this type by extending the 'bare bones' VDMToken class that we provided. Now that we are developing what could be a real system, however, we need to consider what is required by this application. First we consider the *AccNum* type, which represents the account number. In practice, most financial institutions would require that the account numbers conform to a particular format. Here we will impose the restriction that the account number must consist of a string containing precisely eight characters. This is achieved by providing an invariant on the type. Thus we can specify *AccNum* by making an enhancement to the original VDM-SL specification as follows:

....
values
$LENGTH : \mathbb{N} = 8$
....

types
$String = Char*$
$AccNum :: value : String$
inv mk-$AccNum(v) \underline{\Delta}$ **len** $v = LENGTH$
....

In the implementation, as well as overriding the `equals` method and the `toString` method, in this case we must also override the `hashCode` method, as we told you in Chapter 12; this is because objects of `AccNum` will be used as keys in a hash table (as defined by the `VDMMap` class). A `hashCode` method needs to return an identical value for two identical objects – in this example, this can be achieved simply by returning the value generated by the predefined `hashCode` method of the single `String` attribute. This leads to the following implementation of the *AccNum* class.

The *AccNum* class

```
// implementation of a token type
class AccNum implements InvariantCheck
{
   // the account number must be a string of exactly eight characters
   private final int LENGTH = 8;
   private String value;
   public AccNum(String valueIn)
   {
      value = valueIn;
      VDM.invTest(this);
   }
   public boolean inv()
   {
      return value.length() == LENGTH;
   }
   public boolean equals(Object accNumIn)
   {
      AccNum num = (AccNum) accNumIn;
      return value.equals(num.value);
   }
   public String toString()
   {
      return value;
   }
   /* objects of this class will be used as keys in a hashtable; it is there-
      fore necessary to override the hashCode method of Object */
   public int hashCode()
   {
      return value.hashCode();
   }
}
```

Next we consider the *Details* type. In practice, an account-holder's details would normally consist of such items as the name, address, telephone, number, date of birth and so on. Here, for, simplicity, we will simply consider two fields, *name* and *address*.

The specification would therefore require a final enhancement as follows:

....

types

....

Details :: *name : String*

address : String

....

This gives rise to the following class definition:

The *Details* class

```
// implementation of a token type
class Details
{
   // the details will comprise a name and an address
   public String name;
   public String address;
   public Details (String nameIn, String addressIn)
   {
       name = nameIn;
       address = addressIn;
   }
   public boolean equals(Object detailsIn)
   {
       Details details = (Details) detailsIn;
       return name.equals(details.name) && address.equals(details.address);
   }
   public String toString()
   {
       return name + '\n' + address;
   }
}
```

The other type that has been specified as a TOKEN is the *Date* type. We will implement this by making use of the Java Date class that is part of the java.util package.

Now that we have implementations for our TOKEN types, we can turn our attention to the quote types that need to be implemented. Here the *TransactionType* is a union of quote types. The two possible values in this case are <DEPOSIT> and <WITHDRAWAL>; we have seen how to implement a union of quote types before. The code for *TransactionType* is as shown below.

The *TransactionType* class

```
// implementation of a quote type
class TransactionType
{
private int value;

public final static TransactionType DEPOSIT = new TransactionType(0);
public final static TransactionType WITHDRAWAL = new TransactionType(1);

private TransactionType(int x)
{
   value = x;
}
public boolean equals(Object typeIn)
{
   TransactionType t = (TransactionType) typeIn; // type cast
   return t.value == value;
}
public String toString()
{
   switch(value)
   {
     case 0 : return "DEPOSIT";
     default : return "WITHDRAWAL";
   }
 }
}
```

Having implemented the token types and the quote types, we can now consider the composite objects, the first of which is *Transaction*. There is nothing new in this class, and the implementation below requires no further explanation.

The *Transaction* class

```
// implementation of composite object
import java.util.*; // for the Date class
class Transaction implements InvariantCheck
{
  public final Date date;
  public final double amount;
  public final TransactionType transactionType;

  public Transaction(Date dateIn, double amountIn, TransactionType typeIn)
  {
      date = dateIn;
      amount = amountIn;
      transactionType = typeIn;
```

```
      VDM.invTest(this);
   }
   public boolean inv()
   {
      return amount > 0;
   }
   public boolean equals(Object transactionIn)
   {
       Transaction transaction = (Transaction) transactionIn;
       return date.equals(transaction.date)
           && amount == transaction.amount
           && transactionType.equals(transaction.transactionType);
   }
   public String toString()
   {
      return "mk-Transaction(" + date + "," + amount + "," + transactionType + ")";
   }
}
```

The other composite object that we must implement is *Account*. Its implementation appears below:

The *Account* class

```
// implementation of composite object
class Account implements InvariantCheck
{
   public AccNum number;
   public Details details;
   public double balance;
   public double limit;
   public VDMSequence transactions;
   public boolean inv()
   {
     return limit >= 0 && balance >= -limit && balanceOf(transactions) == balance;
   }
   public Account(AccNum numberIn, Details detailsIn,
                     double balanceIn, double limitIn, VDMSequence transIn)
   {
           number = numberIn;
           details = detailsIn;
           balance = balanceIn;
           limit = limitIn;
           transactions = transIn;
           VDMinvTat(this);
   }
```

```
// implemention of the functions
private double sum(VDMSequence seqIn)
{
    double total = 0;
    for(int i = 1; i <= seqIn.len(); i++)
    {
        Double seq = (Double) seqIn.index(i);
        total = total + seq.doubleValue();
    }
    return total;
}
private double balanceOf(final VDMSequence transIn)
{
    final VDMSequence dep,withd;
    // sequence comprehension
    dep = VDMSequence.sequenceComp(
    new ExpressionInt() // the expression
    {
        public Object action(int i)
        {
            return transIn.index(i);
        }
    },
    transIn.inds(), // the set
    new TestableInt()
    {
        public boolean test(int i) // the test
        {
            Transaction trans = (Transaction) transIn.index(i);
            return trans.transactionType.equals(TransactionType.DEPOSIT);
        }
    });
    // sequence comprehension
    withd = VDMSequence.sequenceComp(
            new ExpressionInt()// the expression
            {
                public Object action(int i)
                {
                return transIn.index(i);
                }
            },
            transIn.inds(), // the set
            new TestableInt()
            {
                public boolean test(int i) // the test
                {
                    Transaction trans = (Transaction) transIn.index(i);
```

```
                return trans.transactionType.equals(TransactionType.WITHDRAWAL);
            }
        });
            return sum(dep) - sum(withd);
    }
    public boolean equals(Object accountIn)
    {
            Account account = (Account) accountIn;
            return number.equals(account.number)
                    && details.equals(account.details)
                    && balance == account.balance
                    && limit == account.limit
                    && transactions.equals(account.transactions);
    }
    public String toString()
    {
        return "mk-Account("+ number +","
                            + details +","
                            + balance +","
                            + limit +","
                            + transactions +")";
    }
}
```

Here, some explanation is required, mainly in regard to the implementation of the functions *sum* and *balanceOf*. Because these functions are required only by the Transaction class we have implemented them as part of this class. In Chapter 13 the *sum* function was specified explicitly as follows:

$$sum : \mathbb{R}^* \to \mathbb{R}$$
$$sum(seqIn) \; \underline{\Delta} \quad \textbf{if } seqIn = [\,]$$
$$\textbf{then } 0$$
$$\textbf{else hd } seqIn + sum(\textbf{tl } seqIn)$$

Although we might sometimes specify a function recursively, we should avoid this technique when it comes to implementation, since it is very easy for a recursive function to lead to stack overflow with possibly disastrous results – not what we want for a supposedly critical system!

Inspection of the Accounts class reveals that we have implemented the *sum* function by means of a for loop, which iterates through the sequence. If we were developing the implementation completely formally, we would have to offer a formal proof that showed that this particular implementation meets the specification. However, since we are taking a 'VDM-lite' approach here, we will instead argue this rigourously.

Bearing in mind the axiomatic nature of the assignment statement, we can assert that because the total was initialized to zero, and because each iteration of the loop comprises an assignment statement that adds the next item to the total, then when the loop terminates, the total will be equal to the sum of all items in the sequence.

The sum function is in turn used by the balanceOf function. Here again is its specification:

---

balanceOf(transit : Transactions*) total : $\mathbb{R}$

pre   TRUE

post   **let** *dep = [transIn(i).amount | i ∈* **inds** *transIn ● transIn(i).transactionType = <DEPOSIT>]*
        in let *withd = [transIn(i).amount | i ∈* **inds** *transIn ● transIn(i).transactionType = <WITHDRAWAL>]*
           in *total = sum(dep) − sum(withd)*

This function is implemented by making use of the sequenceComp method of the VDM class. You have come across this before and it does not therefore require further explanation.

At last we are in a position to implement the AccountSys class itself. Interestingly this is now a fairly straightforward business as we simply make use of the techniques that we have used in previous chapters. The comments included in the code below should provide all the necessary explanation.

The *AccountSys* class

```java
import java.util.*; // for the Date class
class AccountSys implements InvariantCheck
{
        // the state
        private VDMMap accounts;
        public AccountSys()
        {
           accounts = new VDMMap();
           VDM.invTest(this); // ensure that the initialization process preserves the invariant
        }
        // the state invariant
        public boolean inv()
        {
           return VDM.forall(accounts.dom(), // the set over which the forall statment is bound
           new Testable()
           {
               public boolean test(Object objectIn) // the test
               {
                    AccNum num = (AccNum) objectIn;
                    Account acc = (Account) accounts.applyTo(num);
                    return num.equals(acc.number);
               }
           });
        }
// the operation
public void addAccount(AccNum numberIn, Details detailsIn, double limitIn)
{
        // ensure that the precondition is met
        VDM.preTest(accounts.dom().doesNotContain(numberIn) && limitIn >= 0);
        Account acc = new Account(numberIn, detailsIn, 0, limitIn, new VDMSequence());
```

```
        accounts = accounts.union(new VDMMap(new Maplet(numberIn, acc)));
        VDM.invTest(this); // ensure that the invariant is preserved
}
public void removeAccount(AccNum numberIn)
{

    // ensure that the precondition is met
    VDM.preTest(accounts.dom().contains(numberIn));
    accounts = accounts.domDelete(new VDMSet(numberIn));
    VDM.invTest(this); // ensure that the invariant is preserved
}
public void deposit(AccNum numberIn, Date dateIn, double amountIn)
{
    Account acc = (Account) accounts.applyTo(numberIn);
    double bal = acc.balance;

    // ensure that the precondition is met
    VDM.preTest(accounts.dom().contains(numberIn) && amountIn > 0);
    VDMSequence trans = acc.transactions;
    Transaction newTrans = new Transaction(dateIn, amountIn, TransactionType.DEPOSIT);

    Account newAcc = new Account(numberIn, acc.details, bal + amountIn, acc.limit,
                            acc.transactions.concat(new VDMSequence(newTrans)));
    accounts = accounts.override(new VDMMap(new Maplet(numberIn, newAcc)));
    VDM.invTest(this); // ensure that the invariant is preserved
}
public Account getAccount(AccNum numberIn)
{

    // ensure that the precondition is met
    VDM.preTest(accounts.dom().contains(numberIn));
    return (Account) accounts.applyTo(numberIn);
}
public void withdraw(AccNum numberIn, Date dateIn, double amountIn)
{
    Account acc = (Account) accounts.applyTo(numberIn);
    double bal = acc.balance;
    double lim = acc.limit;

    // ensure that the precondition is met
    VDM.preTest(accounts.dom().contains(numberIn)
                    && amountIn > 0
                    && bal - amountIn >= -lim);
    VDMSequence trans = acc.transactions;
    Transaction newTrans = new Transaction(dateIn, amountIn, TransactionType.WITHDRAWAL);

    Account newAcc = new Account(numberIn, acc.details, bal - amountIn, acc.limit,
                            acc.transactions.concat(new VDMSequence(newTrans)));
    accounts = accounts.override(new VDMMap(new Maplet(numberIn, newAcc)));
    VDM.invTest(this); // ensure that the invariant is preserved
}
public void changeDetails(AccNum numberIn, Details detailsIn)
{
    double bal = ((Account) accounts.applyTo(numberIn)).balance;
    double lim = ((Account) accounts.applyTo(numberIn)).limit;
    VDMSequence trans = ((Account) accounts.applyTo(numberIn)).transactions;

    // ensure that the precondition is met
    VDM.preTest(accounts.dom().contains(numberIn));

    // the μ-function is implemeneted by calling the constructor
    Account newAcc = new Account(numberIn, detailsIn, bal, lim, trans);
    accounts = accounts.override(new VDMMap(new Maplet(numberIn, newAcc)));
    VDM.invTest(this); // ensure that the invariant is preserved
}
public void changeLimit(AccNum numberIn, double limitIn)
{
    double bal = ((Account) accounts.applyTo(numberIn)).balance;
    Details det = ((Account) accounts.applyTo(numberIn)).details;
```

```
        VDMSequence trans = ((Account) accounts.applyTo(numberIn)).transactions;
        // ensure that the precondition is met
        VDM.preTest(accounts.dom().contains(numberIn) && limitIn >= 0 && bal >= -limitIn);
        // the μ-function is implemeneted by calling the constructor
        Account newAcc = new Account(numberIn, det, bal, limitIn, trans);
        accounts = accounts.override(new VDMMap(new Maplet(numberIn, newAcc)));
        VDM.invTest(this); // ensure that the invariant is preserved
    }
    public Details getDetails(AccNum numberIn)
    {
        // ensure that the precondition is met
        VDM.preTest(accounts.dom().contains(numberIn));
        return ((Account) accounts.applyTo(numberIn)).details;
    }
    public double getBalance(AccNum numberIn)
    {
        // ensure that the precondition is met
        VDM.preTest(accounts.dom().contains(numberIn));
        return ((Account) accounts.applyTo(numberIn)).balance;
    }
    public double getLimit(AccNum numberIn)
    {
        // ensure that the precondition is met
        VDM.preTest(accounts.dom().contains(numberIn));
        return ((Account) accounts.applyTo(numberIn)).limit;
    }
    public VDMMap getAllAccounts()
    {
        return accounts;
    }
    public VDMSequence getAllTransactions(AccNum numberIn)
    {
        // ensure that the precondition is met
        VDM.preTest(accounts.dom().contains(numberIn));
        return ((Account)accounts.applyTo(numberIn)).transactions;
    }
    public boolean contains(AccNum numberIn)
    {
        return accounts.dom().contains(numberIn);
    }
    public boolean isEmpty()
    {
        return accounts.isEmpty();
    }
    public int getTotal()
    {
        return accounts.dom().card();
    }
}
```

14.3   Using the *AccountSys* Class in an Application

Having developed the AccountSys class we are in a position to use it in an application. Here we have developed a graphical application as shown in Figure 14.1.

This has been achieved by implementing a class that we have called Bank, which extends the JPanel class of the Java Swing package. A Bank object can then be added to a JFrame in a short program such as the one below:

The *BankApplication* class

```java
import java.awt.*;
import java.awt.event.*;
import java.io.*;
import javax.swing.*;
public class BankApplication
{
        public static void main(String[] args)
        {
            JFrame frame = new JFrame();
            frame.setDefaultCloseOperation(1);
            frame.setTitle("Accounts System");
            Bank bank = new Bank();
            frame.setBackground(Color.lightGray);
            frame.getContentPane().add(bank);
            frame.setSize(800,640);
            frame.setVisible(true);
            class ExitingFrame extends WindowAdapter
            {
                    public void windowClosing(WindowEvent e)
                    {
                            System.exit(0);
                    }
            }
            frame.addWindowListener(new ExitingFrame());
        }
}
```

The Bank class itself is not shown in full here, but can be downloaded from the website. We should point out that pressing the 'Save and quit' button invokes a method called saveRecords that writes the records to a file in the current directory; a method called readRecords reads this file when the class is first instantiated. One further point is worth noting. You have already seen that we are making use of the java Date class. You will see from Figure 14.1 that we do not ask the user to enter the date of a transaction – instead we make use of the fact that the Date class has an empty constructor that picks up the current date, and, as you will see we use this in the event-handler for the 'Make transaction' button.

Here we look at one of the event-handlers, and show how the testing process was greatly facilitated by the fact that we used a formal approach in developing the AccountSys class. The other event-handlers are similar and do not require further explanation.

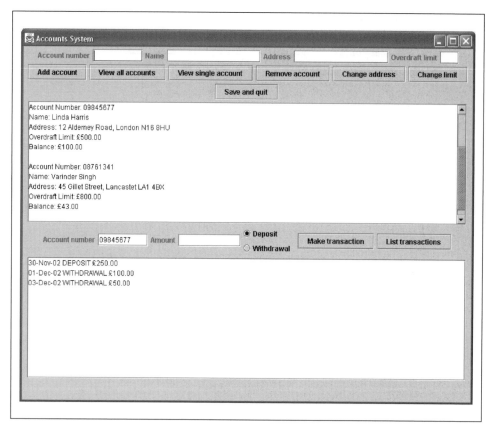

Figure 14.1 The graphical user interface for the *AccountSys* class

Below is the event-handler for the `addButton`:

```
if(e.getSource() == addButton)
{
    String numberEntered = numberField.getText();
    String nameEntered = nameField.getText();
    String addressEntered = addressField.getText();
    String limitEntered = limitField.getText();
    // if a field is left blank
    if(numberEntered.length() == 0 || nameEntered.length() == 0
                || addressEntered.length() == 0 || limitEntered.length() == 0)
    {
      JOptionPane.showMessageDialog(this,"All fields must be entered",
                                        null,JOptionPane.ERROR_MESSAGE);
    }
    else
    {
      try
      {
        // if the account number entered is not precisely 8 characters in length
```

```
    if(numberEntered.length() != 8)
    {
       JOptionPane.showMessageDialog(this,"Account number must be exactly 8 characters",
                                          null,JOptionPane.ERROR_MESSAGE);
    }
    // if the account number entered isalready exists
    else if(list.contains(new AccNum(numberEntered)))
    {
        JOptionPane.showMessageDialog(this,"Account number already exists",
                                          null,JOptionPane.ERROR_MESSAGE);
    }
    // if the overdraft limit entered is negative
    else if(Double.parseDouble(limitEntered) < 0)
    {
        JOptionPane.showMessageDialog(this,"Overdraft limit cannot be negative",
                                          null,JOptionPane.ERROR_MESSAGE);
    }
    else
    {
        displayArea.setText("");
        // add the new account
        list.addAccount(new AccNum(numberEntered),
                             new Details(nameEntered, addressEntered),
                                    Double.parseDouble(limitEntered));
        numberField.setText("");
        nameField.setText("");
        addressField.setText("");
        limitField.setText("");
        JOptionPane.showMessageDialog(this,"Account successfully added",
                                       null,JOptionPane.INFORMATION_MESSAGE);
    }
}
catch(VDMException ex)
{
    /* if a VDMException is thrown, print the stack trace and signal a system error -
       ideally, this will occur only during testing */
    ex.printStackTrace();
    JOptionPane.showMessageDialog(this,"System error",null,JOptionPane.ERROR_MESSAGE);
}
    catch(NumberFormatException ex)
    {
        JOptionPane.showMessageDialog(this,"Invalid amount",null,JOptionPane.ERROR_MESSAGE);
    }
  }
}
```

This implementation brings out some important issues. You will see that after checking that all relevant fields have been entered, a **try ... catch** block is introduced to trap any VDMExceptions. Here a number of checks are made. The first of these ensures that the account number is precisely eight characters long. If this were not the case, then the invariant of AccNum would be violated. If the user enters an invalid number, a pop-up message appears as shown in Figure 14.2.

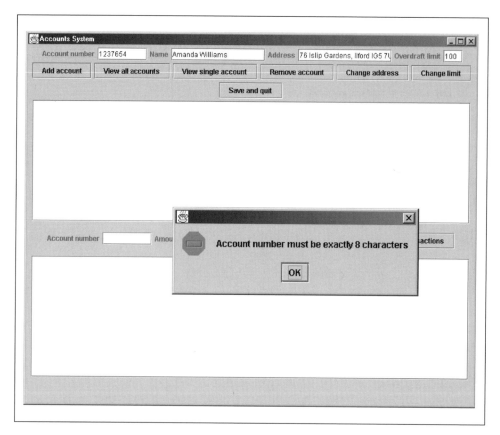

Figure 14.2 An invalid account number has been entered

What is interesting here, however, is the way in which the formal development helps us. What might have happened if we had neglected to validate the account number in this way? You can see from the code that the throwing of any VDMException will result in a pop-up menu telling us that there has been a system error; clearly this is something we do not wish to happen when the application is eventually delivered to the user – but it is extremely helpful to us when we are implementing and testing our application. We can demonstrate this by taking out the lines of code that check the number of characters entered. The result is shown in Figure 14.3.

You can see from the code that we have also arranged for the stack trace to be printed when an exception is thrown in this way. As you can see from Figure 14.4, the stack trace shows that there has been an invariant violation, and allows us to follow the error to its source.

A similar situation occurs if a precondition is not met. Figure 14.5 shows the stack trace produced as a result of removing the lines of code that check that an account number does not already exist.

You will recall that it is the responsibility of a calling operation to ensure that it meets the precondition of the operation that is being called. This is illustrated nicely by the above example – if the operation is coded correctly, then any attempt to call the operation with an invalid account number will result in a pop-up message advising of

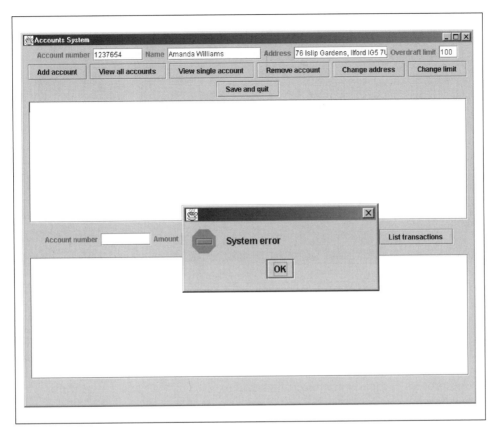

Figure 14.3 A coding error has caused a VDMException to be thrown

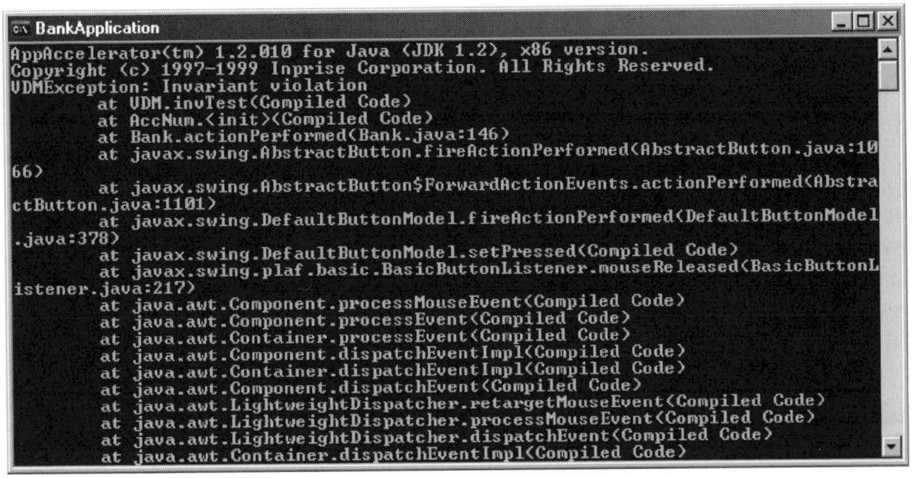

Figure 14.4 The stack trace produced as a result of throwing a VDMException – in this case an invariant has been violated

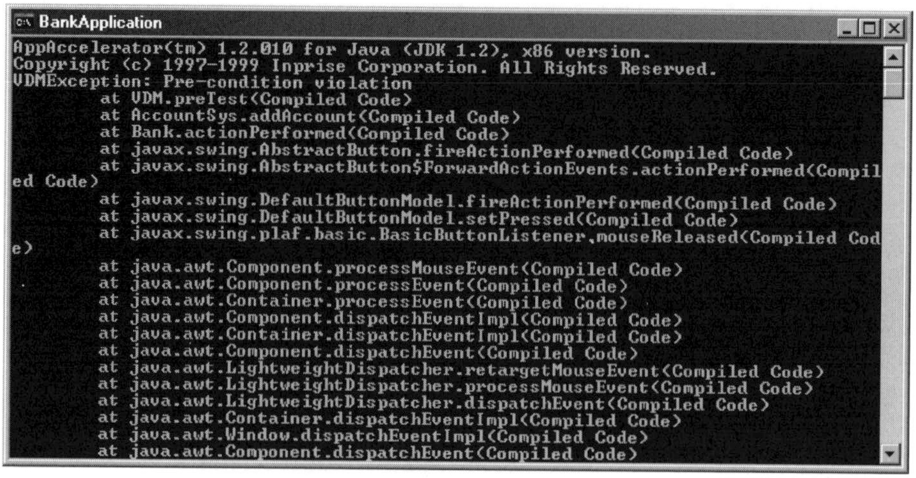

Figure 14.5   The stack trace produced as a result of throwing a VDMException – in this case the precondition of an operation has not been met

the problem. If the implementer had forgotten to do this, however, and the precondition is not met then an exception is raised. It should be apparent from this that the testing process is greatly enhanced by having such built-in checks that result from formal development.

14.4   Concluding Remarks

The case study demonstrates many of the benefits that can be gained from a formal approach to software development. It illustrates the way in which a formal specification allows a greater degree of precision when recording software requirements than does an informal specification. It shows how ambiguity is removed by recording pre- and postcondition assertions, and how important integrity checks can be recorded in state and type invariants. Often, it is the rigour required in the production of a formal specification that uncovers potential ambiguities and resolves them.

The lightweight formal method for program development that we have propounded in this book, allows these integrity checks to be monitored during runtime and enhances the integrity of the final system. The utility classes that we have provided, along with the accompanying guidelines for program implementation, also make implementation a much more straightforward task. The extra time spent in producing a formal specification is therefore amply rewarded by a shorter development time.

EXERCISES

1. Download and implement the classes that make up the bank application.
2. Implement the changes that you made to the specification in the exercises from the previous chapter.

Index